Law and Revelation

Raymond Chapman is Emeritus Professor of English in the University of London and a Vice-President of the Prayer Book Society. He is a non-stipendiary priest in the Diocese of Southwark and is the author of numerous literary and religious books, including *Leading Intercessions*, *Stations of the Nativity*, *Stations of the Resurrection* and *Godly and Righteous, Peevish and Perverse: Clergy and Religious in Literature and Letters*. In the *Canterbury Studies in Spiritual Theology* series, he has also edited volumes on Lancelot Andrewes and the Oxford Movement.

CANTERBURY STUDIES IN SPIRITUAL THEOLOGY

Law and Revelation

Richard Hooker and His Writings

Edited by

Raymond Chapman

CANTERBURY
PRESS
Norwich

© In this compilation Raymond Chapman 2009

First published in 2009 by the Canterbury Press Norwich
Editorial office
13–17 Long Lane,
London, EC1A 9PN, UK

Canterbury Press is an imprint of Hymns Ancient and Modern Ltd
(a registered charity)
St Mary's Works, St Mary's Plain,
Norwich, NR3 3BH, UK

www.scm-canterburypress.co.uk

British Library Cataloguing in Publication data

A catalogue record for this book is available
from the British Library

978-1-85311-991-0

Printed and bound in Great Britain by
CPI Antony Rowe Chippenham SN14 6LH

Contents

Editorial Note

Hooker's *Laws of Ecclesiastical Polity* is a huge work. The selections made from it here are intended to give a fair view of its contents and development, of Hooker's method and style, and particularly of its continuing relevance for the ecclesiastical leviathan which has come to be known as Anglicanism.

By the late sixteenth century, written English was settling into an accepted convention which would not radically change and is not opaque today. Some words have become obsolete or changed their meaning, and a glossary of these is provided. It can fairly be assumed that readers having some acquaintance with Shakespeare, the Book of Common Prayer and the King James Version of the Bible will have no difficulty with forms like 'saith' and 'teacheth' or the singular second person pronouns. Capital letters have been kept for words which are given a special significance in their context. Italics are used for direct quotations from the Bible or other sources, and from the works of opponents to which he was replying. The question of original or modernized spelling is always a difficult one in dealing with early texts. Here the spelling has generally been modernized, but some words current then but not now have been retained, and glossed at the end of the book. The aim has been to make his work accessible to the modern reader without unnecessary impediments but without losing its distinctive qualities

The word 'Anglican' is used to avoid continual repetition of 'Belonging or pertaining to the Church of England', although it does not seem to have been current in Hooker's lifetime. 'Puritan' similarly avoids attempts to differentiate the various aspects and degrees of opposition to the Established Church, and is generally adopted by modern historians of the period. As this is not a detailed exercise in ecclesiastical history, one name must cover those who were dissatisfied with the extent and direction of changes following the Reformation, disliked episcopacy in the form it had taken, and found the Book of Common Prayer not sufficiently reformed. It includes those who wanted changes within the Church, and those who set up separate religious organizations.

[   ] denotes editorial additions or comments within extracts.
[. . .] denotes editorial omissions from the original text.
< > denotes expansion of initials or abbreviations in the text.

Sources

The Works of Richard Hooker, The Folger Library Edition, ed. W. Speed Hill, Cambridge Mass. and London: The Bellknap Press of Harvard University Press, 1977

The Works of that Learned and Judicious Divine Mr Richard Hooker, ed. John Keble, Oxford: Clarendon Press (1836), seventh edition 1888

Isaac Walton, *The Lives of John Donne, Sir Henry Wotton, Richard Hooker etc.*, London: Oxford University Press, 1962

The text is taken from Keble's edition, as revised by R. W. Church and F. Paget. This is probably the edition most readily accessible in libraries and has the advantage of clear reference numbering. Following the method and style of the seventh edition, references are by book, chapter, paragraph and page. Thus V xx 7–10, 76–9 leads to Book Five, chapter 20, paragraphs seven to ten, with pages 76 to 79 as additional guidance. The Folger edition is undoubtedly the most scholarly but it is still not so easily accessed and is expensive to buy. It keeps the original spelling, valuable for the serious researcher but less easy for continuous reading to follow Hooker's thought. Readers who use it will find the same book and chapter numbering. The introductory and informative matter in the Folger volumes should be consulted by any who wish to learn more about the complex and sometimes obscure story of the publication of the *Laws*, particularly of the later books, and of Hooker's other writings.

I

Introduction

The Elizabethan Church

When Elizabeth I came to the throne in 1558, the Church of England
had not yet established its identity. In little more than two decades,
centuries of papal supremacy had been broken and the King declared
Supreme Head of the Church in his realm. The religious houses had
been dissolved, while traditional catholic doctrines were affirmed. In
1547 the accession of Edward VI, a boy strongly in sympathy with reform and swayed by two successive protestant Protectors, began a reign
which saw a radical move away from Rome not only in authority but
in doctrine and practice. The First Book of Common Prayer in 1549
created a vernacular liturgy which still was in many ways close to tradition; the Second in 1552 took the Church much further in the ways
of the Reformation. After a reign of six years, Edward was succeeded
by his half-sister Mary, who restored the country to Roman obedience,
with the Mass in Latin and the persecution even to death of clergy and
laity alike who openly defied the royal will. After another six years,
the people of England were bruised by continual change, some hoping
for a return to stronger Reformation principles, some for continuation
of papal authority, the majority bewildered and longing for peace and
assurance.

This was the inheritance of Elizabeth, a young woman of 25, herself newly released from suspicion and danger in the previous reign.
By the end of the century, the Church of England would have found
its identity, still to be led in a more catholic direction, suppressed for
a time, then restored to stability and a new confidence tainted by au-
thoritarian pride. In 1558 the questions were many and urgent. Under
whose authority would the Church of England be governed? Would its
structure still be episcopal? In what form, and in what language, would

public worship be conducted? The Queen, who would lead the way to resolving these and other questions, was intelligent, well informed and, importantly, without the intransigence of her late brother and sister. She was personally devout, distrustful of the extremes which had been tearing the country apart, tolerant by nature but aware of the need for firm central control. In worship her preference was for a moderate catholic practice. There were lights and a crucifix on the altar in her private chapel but she forbade Elevation of the Host and rebuffed the monks of Westminster who greeted her with candles and incense, saying 'Away with those torches, for we see very well'. Here was a ruler who many hoped could bring stability and a peaceful settlement for the religion of the nation.

The immediate need was for a decision about how people were to worship. The Book of Common Prayer, splendid in language and precise in formulation, was ready for renewed authority: but which book – conservative 1549 or radical 1552? In January 1559 Elizabeth's first Parliament passed two Acts which set the course for the restored Church. The Act of Supremacy affirmed that neither the Pope nor any foreign power had jurisdiction in England, and declared that the Queen was 'Supreme Governor' in all matters both of Church and State. It was a small but subtle difference from the title of Supreme Head taken by Henry VIII. The Act of Uniformity required the use in all public worship of the Book of Common Prayer. It was effectively the 1552 version; Elizabeth, and many others favoured the 1549 book, but there was enough pressure for the opinion of some of the more extreme reformers, particularly in London, to prevail. The 1559 book contained a few changes, notably the omission of the petition in the Litany to be delivered from 'the Bishop of Rome and all his detestable enormities' already removed under Mary, and of the 'Black Rubric' which enjoined kneeling to receive communion, but denied any intention of adoration. The two sentences for administration of communion were combined, the 1549 form speaking of the Body and the Blood of Christ, the 1552 ordering 'remembrance' of the Atonement. The 'Ornaments Rubric', restoring the use of church ornaments and vestments to those used in the second year of Edward VI, was destined to cause much controversy, then and to the end of the nineteenth century.

The Act of Uniformity was supported by a list of Royal Injunctions, setting out rules for clerical dress, bowing and kneeling at appropriate times, ordering the clergy to be more attentive to preaching and catechizing, and prohibiting any man in holy orders from marrying without the approval of his bishop. There was enough in the Prayer Book and the Injunctions to rouse objections among those who had hoped for a more strongly Reformed settlement, and the seeds of decades of controversy were sown. In the summer of the same year, royal commissioners were sent around the country to see that the law was being obeyed.

In spite of the controversies and acts of disobedience, the Elizabethan Settlement was carried through peacefully as compared with wars of religion elsewhere in Europe. Elizabeth and her advisers wanted a Church which would meet the spiritual needs of the English people and would help to maintain stability in the realm. It was in fact to be an essentially English Church, not influenced either by Roman claims or by Continental Reformers. However, both these sources of opposition were present and would make their presence felt. Although the country as a whole was glad to see the end of Mary I with her persecutions and foreign marriage, there were still many who clung to the 'old religion'; throughout the rest of the century there were many Roman Catholic sympathizers who made no open avowal of their faith. Again, there were many who wanted to return to the reformed spirit which was leading change at the end of the reign of Edward VI.

The governing powers in both Church and State were working to establish the Church order which would later be called Anglican. The apostolic succession was affirmed to be maintained in the Church of England. The forty-two articles of Religion drawn up in 1553 were revised, reduced to thirty-nine, and all clergy were required to assent to them. Public services other than those in the Prayer Book were illegal, but generally there was not any close enquiry into details of usage, unless complaint was made or there was extreme deviation. There was no compromise on the assumption that Church and State were linked together. There was no place for a theocracy or any independent authority; disobedience to the Acts of Supremacy and Uniformity were offences against the law of the land and could even be treasonable.

In the earlier part of the reign the threat of a forced return to papal obedience seemed to be strong and serious. At first reasonable latitude was allowed to 'Church papists' who fulfilled the law by attending worship in their parish churches irrespective of their private beliefs, and even to the 'recusants' who in conscience absented themselves on payment of a fine. This tolerance gradually turned to suspicion and hostility; English people who held to the Roman Catholic faith were seen as enemies to the Crown, potential traitors and allies of foreign enemies. Pope Pius IV went no further than sending envoys in the hope of converting Elizabeth, and Philip of Spain did not intend to add to the problems of his own realm by becoming embroiled again in the affairs of England. Pius V, who became Pope in 1566, was of different metal, encouraged by the reaffirmations made at the Council of Trent. Opposition to Elizabeth was given a new hope in Mary Stuart, Queen of Scots, who in 1568 left the Scotland of John Knox and sought refuge in England. She became the focus of aggressive Romanists, and the hope of more than one plot to depose Elizabeth and place her on the throne. In 1570 Pius V excommunicated Elizabeth and declared her subjects free from their allegiance to her.

There followed a hard time for those who desired a return to the Roman obedience, however loyal hey might be as subjects of the Queen. Penalties for recusancy were drastically increased and there was legislation against bringing into the country any objects which might seem to support traditional devotions. English Colleges were opened in Douai and in Rome to train men who would come as missionaries for the conversion of England. Most of them were genuinely concerned only with preaching their faith, but they suffered heavy pressure from Rome to stir up political opposition. Some were detected and suffered the terrible death imposed for treason. Mary Queen of Scots was deemed too dangerous to be left alive and was executed in 1587, with the reluctant consent of Elizabeth. In 1588 the great Armada, sent to win England by military force, was routed by a combination of English seamanship and adverse weather. Further restraints were imposed on recusants and some were executed for their constancy. It was a troubled start for the Church settlement, marred by cruelty which by the reckoning of that time was thought to be justified. Distrust and fear of Rome did not go away, but by the last decade of the century it no longer seemed a serious danger to national security.

Opposition from the protestant side was in all ways different. It did not threaten internal violence or foreign aggression. It did not question the lawful position of the Queen, although her title of Supreme Governor was less acceptable. As the Roman peril receded, the demands of the other wing became stronger and more vocal, and it was these demands which brought Richard Hooker to write his great work. The name of Puritan is most convenient for the several groups who believed that the Reformation in England had not gone far enough and that the Church was still tainted with Romish doctrines and practices. The word has come to be associated with the enemies of Charles I, the Roundheads of the next century, but it was used well before then. It was generally a scornful term for those who preferred to refer to themselves as 'the Godly'. It included those who wanted to remain in a Church of

England much further reformed, and those who would have none of it, went their own way and became known as Separatists.

While the Roman opposition was receiving support from abroad, the Puritan wing drew strength from men who had gone into exile in Reformed parts of Europe to escape the Marian persecution and were now returned filled with new enthusiasm for the ideals of Luther, Zwingli, and particularly of Calvin. The wanted to accomplish in England what John Knox had done in Scotland: to establish presbyterial government of the Church by assemblies instead of bishops, with more power given to the devout laity. Liturgies, ceremonies and vestments which had any link with the Roman past were to be abolished. The Book of Common Prayer, even in its 1559 revision, still savoured of popery. Ceremonies like the sign of the cross in Baptism, giving the ring in marriage, laying on episcopal hands at Confirmation, had no place among the godly. Nor did any veneration of the saints, music in services or antiphonal singing of the Psalms.

At first the complaints of those dissatisfied with the Elizabethan Settlement were little more than an irritation to the authorities. Many leading clergy and laity who supported the Establishment had some sympathy with Calvinist ideas but were committed to conformity for the sake of national peace and security. Gradually the opposition became more radical, attacking the whole structure of the Church of England and, more seriously, its doctrine. Calvinism stood firmly on the doctrine of predestination, interpreted by different groups with greater or less severity, but basically holding that the free grace of God had chosen certain people to be saved. The elect were sure of their calling and final perseverance, did not trust their own virtues but strove to live a good life in token and gratitude of the gift they had been given. The corollary was that the human race was divided between the elect and the rest, with the conclusion that the rest were doomed to damnation. It was a doctrine born of humility before the power of God and rejection of any thought that fallible human beings could win salvation by their own merits: it too often led to spiritual pride and condemnation of the outsiders.

The Puritans found support for their doctrine in the Bible, now more easily available in the vernacular for a population in which literacy, though still low, had increased. It is a calumny to say that the medieval church had paid little attention to Scripture, a truism to say that printing and translation had made it easier for the Churches of the Reformation to make much more use of it in their services and to encourage laypeople to read it for themselves. The principle of *sola scriptura*, Scripture alone, undergirded the faith of Christians in England who supported the Settlement and of those who attacked it. The difference was that the conformists accepted other sources of authority, the traditions of the Church and the rulings of godly governments, while the Puritans would have nothing that their reading of the Bible did not support. Their convictions ranged from believing that nothing was permissible that seemed unsupported in the Scripture, to refusing anything which was not specifically enjoined in it. Rather than the Bishops' Bible authorized to be read in churches, they favoured the Geneva Bible, a translation with a more reformed slant in some of its choice of words, and the first English Bible to have verse numbering.

With such convictions and such authority, the objectors were not to be for ever satisfied with individual mutterings and local protests. A vocal and courageous leader emerged. Thomas Cartwright was Lady Margaret Professor of Divinity at Cambridge, a formidable biblical scholar who was dismissed from his university post after openly recommending a Presbyterian system of government for the Church, and then spent a short time in Geneva. In 1572 *An Admonition to Parliament* was published, containing many and detailed objections to the doctrine, organization and practice of the Church of England as by law established. It was ascribed to two Puritan clergymen, John Field and Richard Wilcox, who were committed to prison in Newgate. The objections of the Bishops to the work were answered by a second *Admonition*, almost certainly by Cartwright, who in 1574 published an English translation of the *Disciplina Eccelsiastica Anglicanae* by Walter Travers, later to become the principal opponent of Richard Hooker and at this time acting as minister to the English congregation in Antwerp. There were many in the House of Commons who sympathized with the *Admonitions*. Peter Wentworth was one of the most vocal in raising questions about Church government and order, defying the command of the Queen that the Commons should not concern themselves with ecclesiastical matters.

These were challenges more difficult to counter than the perceived dangers of Romanism. There was no obvious disloyalty to the Crown, no hint of foreign political interference, though there was strong doctrinal influence from abroad. Things were going too far for the governing powers of the Church to tolerate. Some clergy were trying to create systems of presbyteries in their areas. There was little open evasion of the requirement to attend Anglican worship, but many were supplementing desultory celebrations of Prayer Book services with meetings for prayer and study known as 'prophesyings'. These were in themselves harmless, often valuable as giving opportunity for serious study and exchange of views. Some of the bishops, including Grindal the Archbishop of

Canterbury, even approved of them, but the Queen was strongly opposed to them as being subversive, and in 1577 tried without much success to get the bishops to suppress them. More disturbing to the Church hierarchy were the 'classes' in which laypeople were encouraged to take part and to express their views. If the prophesyings were cautiously acceptable to some, the classes were inadmissible. These and other open defiance of the Acts of Supremacy and Uniformity could not be tolerated. What had been minor irritations were developing into a serious threat, and the situation was exacerbated still further by the *Marprelate Tracts*, powerful and scurrilous attacks on episcopacy published under the pseudonym 'Martin Marprelate' in 1588 and 1589. Clergy who failed to conform began to suffer legal penalties, and the leaders were dealt with severely. Cartwright had to go into exile abroad until 1585 and in 1590 was arrested and imprisoned for two years.

While the authorities skirmished with Puritans who demanded internal reform of the Church, they were more severe with those who became 'Separatists' and created independent congregations and clergy. Robert Browne was one of the first to do so, in Norwich, and Henry Barrow in London. Browne was briefly imprisoned, on release took his congregation with him to Holland and after a career of wandering and controversy was ordained in the Church of England. The legacy of the 'Brownists' was powerful in the later Congregational Church. Barrow was charged with sedition and eventually hanged. In 1593 an 'Act Against Seditious Sectaries' imposed severe penalties, even to death, for attending Separatist conventicles.

This was the turbulent history which Richard Hooker inherited, and the tense situation within which he wrote his great work. The Church of England had achieved a longer continuous period of establishment than at any time since the break with Rome. Her official authority was firmly established and equally firmly enforced. Active supporters of the Roman obedience were now a persecuted minority. If an Anglican identity was to develop and claim general acceptance, the war to be fought was a war of words, and there was a man who could lead the defence by a brilliant attack.

Life of Richard Hooker

Richard Hooker was born in 1554, early in the reign of Mary I, when it seemed as if the nascent Church of England which he was one day to defend was lost in a return to the Roman obedience. His home was the village of Heavitree near Exeter. The family had their origin in Wales, and changed their name of Vowell to Hooker after moving into England. Richard's father, Roger, was often absent from the family, employed as a steward to important families in England and later in Ireland. Nothing is known of his mother. His parents were able to send him to a grammar school in Exeter, where the master was so highly impressed by his ability and behaviour that he decided that the boy must go on to a university. Richard's uncle John Hooker was Chamberlain of Exeter, a high civic office in the prosperous county town of Devonshire, the county that produced Walter Raleigh and Francis Drake, to become famous in the later Elizabethan years. More importantly for young Richard, it was the native county of John Jewel, a clergyman exiled in the Marian years and now returned from abroad and made one of the commissioners sent around the country in 1559 to enforce obedience to the Acts of Supremacy and Uniformity. Devonshire was part of Jewel's assignment, and when in Exeter he became friendly with John Hooker. In 1560 he was consecrated Bishop of Salisbury, and there John Hooker called upon him to seek support for the promising young Richard.

Jewel may be said to have laid a foundation for Hooker's work, with the publication in 1562 of a robust defence of the Anglican settlement. His *Apologia Ecclesiae Anglicanae* claimed that reform of the Church had been essential, that the newly formed Council of Trent could not serve the purpose, and that national churches had the right to pass their own legislation through provincial synods. Like Hooker and Lancelot Andrewes after him, and many Anglican apologists down to the Tractarians in the nineteenth century, he appealed to the writings of the early Fathers to justify a continuing catholic tradition that was not dependent on Roman developments. Hooker would differ from him in some respects, less hostile to Rome and having to confront more vigorous and articulate Puritan opposition, but he owed much to this first extended defence of the Elizabethan Settlement. He also received more immediate help from Jewel, who was so impressed by the petition of the uncle and the report of the schoolmaster that he arranged for Richard to go up to Corpus Christi College, Oxford in 1567 and provided money for his time at the university. Despite an illness early in his time there, Richard predictably did well, took his degree, was elected to a Fellowship at his college in 1577, was ordained, and became deputy Professor of Hebrew two years later.

Jewel had died in 1571, but his patronage outlived him. He had commended Richard to Edwin Sandys, Bishop of London and later

Archbishop of York. Jewel's opinion impressed Sandys so much that he decided to send his son, also Edwin, to Hooker for guidance and tuition. This was earlier in Hooker's time at Corpus Christi; there were not many years in age between the two young men, and they formed a close friendship which would endure. Another pupil who became a valued and influential friend was George Cranmer, a grand-nephew of the martyred archbishop Thomas Cranmer.

Oxford was by no means a quiet haven at that time. It was a city not of dreaming spires but of vigorous and sometimes vicious debate in which religious differences could make or destroy a career. But it was partly sheltered from the perilous affairs of London, a shelter from which Hooker was temporarily removed in 1584 when he was required, in accordance with one of the College statutes, to preach a sermon at St Peter's Oxford, or at St Paul's Cross in London. The latter fell to him, and he set off for London where he arrived weary and unwell after a difficult journey. The St Paul's preacher was given lodging in a house owned by John Churchman, a merchant draper. It was known as the Shunamite House, with reference to the woman of Shunam who gave lodging to the prophet Elisha. John Churchman's wife Joan took charge of Hooker, gave him advice and remedies for his condition, and got him back into good shape to preach his sermon, in which he disputed Calvin's teaching on freewill and predestination. To preach at St Paul's Cross was a distinguished and also an exacting commission. Many eminent divines occupied that open-air pulpit, heard by a large crowd of divided religious sympathies, subject to interruption and even to later retribution if anything was said which could be regarded as seditious. Hooker apparently acquitted himself well, but his personal life was now taking a new turn. He was offered and accepted the living of Drayton Beauchamp in Buckinghamshire, and left Oxford to become a parish priest.

For subsequent events successive biographers have worked from the life of Hooker by Isaac Walton, published in 1665. Although Walton admits that he did not know Hooker and was dependent on the reports of others, he has been quoted as the principal source of information, until a number of his assertions were discredited by recent biographers. According to Walton, Joan Churchman took advantage of her brief ministration to Hooker on his arrival in London to persuade him that he needed a wife to take care of him, and that her daughter Joan was the ideal choice. He married the young woman who, Walton says, 'brought him neither beauty nor portion'. He tells the story of how Edwin Sandys and George Cranmer went to visit Hooker in his parish and found him looking after his small flock of sheep. He told them that he had to be in the field because his servant had gone home to help his wife. When they went to his parsonage, he was soon called by his wife to rock the baby's cradle, a duty considered more demeaning for a man in the sixteenth century than in the twenty-first. If there is any truth at all in the story, it may be that Hooker was henpecked, or that he was in advance of his time in humility and consideration. However, as he was not married until 1588, by which time he had left Drayton Beauchamp, where he may not have resided regularly or at all, the whole legend is rather more than flawed. Walton's obvious bias, shared by many then and later, was that a great man was not likely to find a woman worthy of him. We shall never know much about Joan Hooker, but she has probably been the victim of prejudice and oral report.

A more reliable account is that Sandys asked his father, then Bishop of London, to do something for Hooker. In 1585 the position of Master of the Temple became vacant, was offered to Hooker and accepted by him. He now had the incumbency of the Temple Church, a medieval foundation associated with the Knights Templar, which served the Inner and Middle Temple Inns of Court. It was a prestigious position, giving him a pulpit from which to preach to budding and established lawyers in that litigious period, and to many others who came to hear sermons in that ancient church situated close to the London centres of commerce and politics. It gave him freedom from routine parish duties, and with opportunity for study and writing as well as preaching, but it did not offer him a peaceful life. The apparently idyllic situation was clouded by the presence of a rival candidate. Walter Travers, a distant cousin of Hooker by marriage, was a former Fellow of Trinity College, Cambridge, a man of Puritan principles who had gone off to Geneva and then to Antwerp, where he was ordained as a minister by Cartwright and served the congregation there before returning to London. He had been Reader or lecturer at the Temple since 1581, and would almost certainly have succeeded to the Mastership had he not refused to receive Anglican orders. He was favoured by the influential Burleigh, the Lord Treasurer with strong Reformed sympathies, but regarded as dangerous by John Whitgift, Archbishop of Canterbury, not least because of his authorship of the *Disciplina Ecclesiae Anglicanae* previously mentioned. After much correspondence and the mention of a third candidate approved by Whitgift, Hooker was appointed.

Travers continued as Reader, with the result of competitive preaching between himself and Hooker. It was not a unique situation in the Elizabethan Church: lecturers were appointed in some parishes, funded by corporations or individuals, as regular preachers. They were an effective way for the Puritans to promulgate their views. According to the seventeenth-century historian Thomas Fuller, at the Temple 'the pulpit spake pure Canterbury in the morning and Geneva in the afternoon'. To the credit of both men, there seems to have been little personal antagonism between them. Hooker later wrote to Whitgift, 'My particular contests here with Mr Travers have proved the more unpleasant to me because I believe him to be a good man'. Years later, Travers is reported to have said, 'I take Mr Hooker to be a holy man'. Like Joan Hooker, Travers has suffered from unsympathetic treatment by Hooker's admirers. He was a scholar, and seemingly an honest man with a generous disposition. However, the opinions which he preached became more extreme, while the Puritan party in the Church became more aggressive, and eventually Whitgift inhibited him from preaching. In 1594 he left London to become the first Provost of Trinity College, Dublin, recently founded and long maintained exclusively for Irish Anglicans, but now a distinguished and open university.

According to Walton, the incitement to write his great work came to Hooker first from the complaints of the Benchers of the Temple about the removal of Travers. They respected Hooker, but he 'nevertheless met with many neglects and oppositions by those of Mr Travers's judgment'. He decided that the best way of defence was to write 'a deliberate and sober treatise', setting out at length his opinions on Church order and government. The Temple could no longer offer him the peace and leisure to undertake such a work, and he asked Whitgift for a new appointment. In 1591 he was made incumbent of the parish of Boscombe near Salisbury, and also a minor prebend of the cathedral, 'which prebend was of no great value, but intended chiefly to make him capable of a better preferment in the Church'. No better preferment came his way, and he now had time to write the first four books of the *Laws*. It is likely that the Boscombe living was a sinecure and that he did not reside or do regular duties in the parish. His new task was supported by his friends Sandys and Cranmer, and encouraged by Whitgift, who was anxious to have a strong refutation of the Puritans' demands. In 1595 Hooker was presented by the Queen to the parish of Bishopsbourne near Canterbury, where he wrote the fifth book of the *Laws*, which he dedicated to Whitgift.

The years of controversy, study and writing were having their effect, and although he was far from being an old man even by the expectations of the time, his health was beginning to fail. His eyesight was weak, his body was thin and his posture stooping. But his spiritual strength did

not diminish, and he taxed his frail body further by fasting and morti-
fication. He observed the rules of the Book of Common Prayer which
he had defended so loyally in writing, exhorting his parishioners to
observe seasons of fasting and to be earnest in prayer, especially to pray
on the Ember Days for a learned and pious clergy. In 1600, according
to Walton, he made one of his occasional visits to London and returned
with a chill from which he never recovered. Whether or not this story
is true, he died on 2 November after months of increasing weakness,
having received absolution and communion from Hadrian Saravia, a
native of Flanders who had been ordained in the Church of England
and became a close friend and confidant of Hooker.

His widow remarried soon after his death and died within a few
months. They had four daughters, of two of whom nothing more is
known. The other two became involved in dispute and litigation about
the printing of the *Laws*. For those who wish to read about them, the
events are examined in detail by C. J. Sisson in *The Judicious Marriage of Mr Hooker*. It is an unedifying story, best left to lie in its legal
record, but for those interested it tells much about publishing, intellectual property and litigation in the early seventeenth century. Many
people attested to Richard Hooker's humility and holiness in his life.
The *Laws* are his lasting memorial.

Of the Laws of Ecclesiastical Polity

The great events of history can often be traced to a series of causes which
come to a head on a particular occasion. Puritan opposition to the
Elizabethan Church settlement had been growing in many places, from
the minor disobediences of parish clergy to the more powerful arguments of men like Travers and Cartwright. Hooker had been defending
the establishment in his sermons, and in March 1586 Travers preached
at the Temple on three successive Sundays against the assertion that any
who denied the doctrine of justification by faith alone, notably Roman
Catholics, could not hope for salvation. Hooker equally strongly as-
serted that the mercy of God could extend to those who failed through
ignorance, if their faith was strong and sincere in other ways. It was
this piece of defiance by Travers, the climax of controversy and division in the Temple, that made Hooker consider the need for a reasoned
reply to the whole Puritan position. So Hooker moved from being a
weekly preacher to writing *A Treatise of the Laws of Ecclesiastical*

Polity. At a time when works on every opinion about religion and the Church were being published, it did not seem likely to be the one which would outlive the rest.

John Whitgift had become Archbishop of Canterbury in 1583, in succession to Edmund Grindal, who had been sympathetic to the Puritan position and even been suspended from his judicial function for refusing to ban the 'prophesyings'. Whitgift was not totally opposed to Calvinism, but he had a strong regard for the discipline of the Church and a feud with Cartwright which went back to Cambridge days. He would look favourably on Hooker as a man who would reply in detail to Cartwright's *Admonition*, and generally make the case for the Church of England as it now stood. But the *Laws* was not commissioned as an official reply on behalf of the Established Church: Whitgift was sympathetic to the project but had already asked the Bishops of London and of Winchester to produce something. The great work seems to have been engendered by Hooker's own desire to state more fully and systematically the issues which he had addressed in his sermons at the Temple and in various arguments against Puritan objections. The first four books were published in 1594, with financial support from his old friend Edwin Sandys. These books may be seen as an extended prologue to the fifth, published in 1597, which is as long as the first four put together and contains his detailed defence of the Church. The remaining three books had a more obscure and doubtful history. Book Six certainly suffered some interference and shortening. It did not appear in print until 1648, together with Book Eight, which deals largely with the relationship between Church and State and the question of lawful authority. Book Seven came out in 1662. It is therefore the first five Books, especially the fifth, which are the most important and of lasting interest, and from which most of the passages in this selection have been taken.

Hooker did not set out to make a watertight and complete case for the Church of England as the sole and perfect Church. His intention was to defend it against Puritan objections, to give support to what was now established by law but had suffered changes, attacks and suppression in earlier reigns and was still not pleasing to some influential sections of the population. His patron John Jewel had written the first extended defence in 1562 with his *Apologia Ecclesiae Anglicanae*. At that time the Roman Catholic claims seemed to form the biggest threat, though the more extreme Reformers were already making their case. By the last decade of the century fears of Rome were more political than doctrinal, and it was the Puritan attacks which needed attention. The success of Calvinism had led from doctrinal to structural changes. In places where it was dominant, government was by ministerial power, in a hierarchy of function rather than ordination, with regard for lay influence which was stronger in theory than in practice.

Hooker's case is basically that the Church of England is a true Church, faithful in doctrine and practice to the Will of God and the unbroken orthodox tradition. He points to her faithfulness to what would later be known as the Lambeth Quadrilateral: Scripture as the Word of God; the tradition handed down by the Apostles to the early Church; the historic episcopate; the Gospel sacraments of Baptism and Eucharist. His declared concern is with practice and discipline rather than doctrine, but he knew that they cannot be separated: then as always, orthodoxy and orthopraxis go together. The fifth book of the *Laws* is a robust and detailed defence of the Book of Common Prayer, the authority for Anglican worship in its liturgy, and for the realization of that liturgy in its rubrics and the adjoined Articles of Religion.

Something more needs to be said about his allegiance to the fourfold principles. No theologian has been more committed to Scripture as the source of divine revelation, teaching and commandment. He found biblical warrant for his arguments and quoted copiously from both Testaments. Yet here was the chief problem with the Puritans, who held to the Reformation principle of *sola scriptura*. For them, everything had to be justified by reference to Scripture, which contained not only doctrine and moral guidance but was the source for all that was right in the structure and government of the Church. The more extreme would allow nothing that was not specifically enjoined in Scripture; all agreed that it was the only criterion for the Church of their own time. Hooker held that in addition human reason was a divine gift which should properly be exercised in faith, and that there was a natural and universal law, fulfilled in revealed truth and guiding us towards it. Reformed theologians gave much attention to the will and to personal feelings of assurance and revelation; Hooker did not deny these things but argued for understanding Reason as a gift from God.

For Hooker, as for many authorities in the Church of England including Thomas Cranmer, Scripture worked along with tradition, the *paradosis*, the handing down of divinely warranted truth. He was as familiar with the patristic writings as with the Bible. In a way which partly anticipates Newman's detailed work on *The Development of Christian Doctrine*, he looks to the Fathers to find guidance for the continuing Church, growing through many centuries and in many lands but still true to the deposit of faith, and there finds warrant for

practice, discipline, and government. Tradition can never rival or con-
tradict Scripture, or be given the same reverence. It can express the
mind of the Church in matters indifferent or not otherwise provided
for, and in that way should command obedience. It must be understood
that the Puritan divines did not dismiss tradition or neglect patristics.
Cartwright quoted copiously from the Fathers, but his references were
selective, with particular regard for Tertullian who would not generally
be regarded as a leading authority. Hooker ranges much more widely,
not looking for proof-texts to support his own assertions, but seeking a
consensus of authorities, expounding and applying rather than simply
quoting.

The maintenance of a separate and superior order of bishops was
one of the main grievances of the Puritans. They regarded differences
among ordained ministers as relating to function, not to status or special sacramental powers. Hooker held to the statement in the Preface
to the Ordinal that the existence of bishops, priests and deacons in
the Apostolic age was 'evident' to all. He defended the sacerdotal and
judicial power of bishops, and the office of archbishop, particularly in
his seventh Book. He sometimes seems inclined to regard episcopacy
as being of the *bene esse* rather than the *esse* of the Church, and to accept the full status of churches which did not possess it, but he was not
prepared to make any concession in the matter to Puritan objections to
Anglican orders.

He takes a high view of the sacraments as divinely ordained, obliga-
tory for every Christian and to be celebrated and received with reverence. The Puritan tendency to marginalize them in favour of preaching,
he regarded as part of their denial, even fear, of the material world
and bodily responses which were sanctified by the Incarnation. He
sometimes tends towards a receptionist view of Holy Communion, as
if favouring the second rather than the first of the two sentences of
administration brought together in the 1559 Book of Common Prayer.
In the Church of England there was still the fear of the Mass as an act
of adoration in which the consecrated elements would be reverenced:
something excluded by the rather abrupt ending of the Prayer of Consecration in the 1552 Prayer Book which was retained in 1559, and in
1662. This caution does not lead him into regarding the sacraments
as simply signs and confirmation of grace already received. He writes:
'Sacraments are the powerful instruments of God to eternal life'.

He has no sympathy with the idea of restricting the sacrament to
those who show themselves to be worthy through full belief and godly
living, with infrequent celebrations or requiring the whole congregation

to receive. Hooker may be accepted as making no firm philosophical statement about the sacraments which he valued so highly. There has never been any official Anglican definition of exactly *what* happens in the Eucharist. Members of the Church have held, and continue to hold, opinions ranging from Zwinglian receptionism to transubstantiation.

His sacramental theology is rooted in his continual assurance of the ongoing reality of the Incarnation. The Puritans were certainly Christocentric in their assurance of the redeeming grace given in Christ, but they tended to underplay the patristic sense of all human life as participation in the eternal being of God. Hooker comes near to the early Fathers like Irenaeus and Athanasius in claiming *theosis*, a deification of our human nature: 'He became Man that we might become God'. In his own words, God hath deified our nature, though not by turning it into himself, yet by making it his own inseparable habitation' (V. liv 5 235). He is sure that through the Incarnation we are continually drawn towards God and are incomplete until we come to union with him. As St Augustine wrote, 'Thou hast made us for thyself, and our hearts are restless until they find their rest in thee'.

One of the reasons for his dispute with the Puritans, which frequently appears in his arguments, was their extreme individualism in matters of religion. The right of private judgment and personal choice were hallmarks of the Reformation, though they were not always honoured in nations and communities under Protestant government. Hooker never denies the supreme importance of the individual soul and the need for individual response to God, but his vision of the Church was wider than that of divines who saw churches as gatherings of souls who were saved and could make their own decisions about government and worship. Hooker made his reputation as a preacher before he wrote the *Laws*, in an age when sermons were long and expository, and regarded by the established Church as so important that not all clergy were licensed to preach, but might be required to read one of the official Homilies instead. Hooker's objection to Puritan worship was that the sermon would become the centre of the whole service, so that listening to a preacher and sharing his response to Scripture would push other aspects of worship to the margin. The Eucharist, through which the universal Church may be said to be praying together, became less important than 'sharing the Word' in a small group.

So although the words 'Laws' and 'Polity' are fundamental to what he wrote, his thought is not confined to matters of structure and discipline. The theme of each Book will be considered in relation to the extracts which follow, but a brief overview may be helpful. The Preface justifies his work by a robust general attack on Puritan demands and polemical writings. Book One then presents the basic principle of his argument, concerning the general nature of law which comes from God and should govern human action. He is near to Thomas Aquinas in his emphasis on Natural Law, to be obeyed through Reason and not arbitrarily, not opposed to the law of divine revelation but concomitant with it. It lays a foundation which makes it the most important of the first four Books. Book Two takes up the Puritan claim that Scripture alone is the source of divine law. Book Three takes the matter further by challenging the belief that Scripture is the only authority for what is to be done in the Church government and discipline. Book Four begins his defence of the order, liturgy and ceremonies to be used in the Christian Church; particularly that what is shared with the Roman Catholic Church is not automatically tainted by it. Then the long and detailed Book Five examines what is being done in the Church of England and justifies the authorized practice with biblical and patristic references. It is the greatest defence made until that time, and seldom equalled since, of the Book of Common Prayer. The remaining books are less well developed, having suffered from passing through different hands and being partly altered before their late publication, but they still contain some valuable matter. Book Six, which seems to have been intended as a discussion of Church Elders, is addressed mainly to a discussion of repentance. Book Seven takes up the disputed question of episcopacy. Book Eight contains his arguments about Church and State, particularly the position of the monarch as Supreme Governor of the Church. The complex history of these texts is examined in detail by the Folger editors. In 1599 an anonymous *Christian Letter* was published, attacking the *Laws* as damaging to the Church which Hooker claimed to be defending. His incomplete *Answer*, left unfinished at his death, was preserved in manuscript at Trinity College, Dublin, and known as the Dublin Fragments. It can be found, with some of his sermons, in Keble's edition, and with commentary in the Folger edition. It is in the *Laws* that his beliefs and arguments are sequentially worked out, with the exercise of Reason which he valued so highly.

This brief analysis of his main themes in the books should not leave the impression that each one is exclusive in its concerns. In his own words, 'I have endeavoured throughout the body of this whole Discourse, that every former part might give strength unto all that follow, and every latter bring some light unto all before' [23]. The whole work is directed by questions which were hotly disputed when it was written, and which have never ceased to be important. Deeply respectful of

Scripture, he claims divine authority also for tradition and reason. He examines the extent of human reason and will: how far are we free in our decisions and actions? How does the grace of God work to justify us in our sinful state? Can there be any merit in the deeds which we perform in accordance with the Will of God? All that he writes about Church order and worship is undergirded by great theological issues.

Style

Hooker wrote at a time when English prose style was gaining strength. Most early Tudor prose is not very elegant or easy to read, although it is too often assumed that the splendid language of the Book of Common Prayer is typical of an age of fine writing. Cranmer had a mastery of prose unusual for his time, aided by the power of the Latin which lay behind much of the new liturgy. Hooker was a contemporary of some of our greatest poets and dramatists, but the quality of great English prose would not emerge until well into the next century. Although we may not read him for the sheer pleasure of his style, he has the confidence and the fluency which was developing as prose became a powerful medium for polemic, in religion, politics and aesthetics – the last found notably in the work of Sidney and Puttenham. His writing has an elegance and grace which are lacking in most of the adversarial religious publications of the sixteenth century, and in a strong contrast to such extreme treatises as the Marprelate tracts. He sometimes wanders into complex sentences and discursive arguments, but he has the great merit of never leading the reader far away from the point at issue. He handles the periodic sentence with the confident skill of a man steeped in Latin but not forced into a falsely Latinate style of English. He usually begins a section with a sentence which may be long but which introduces the theme, and ends it with a triumphant air of having made his point. Even when the presentation of the argument is in danger of becoming heavy, he restores our attention by a brief epigrammatic and memorable statement.

He can equally produce the short, pithy and memorable sentence. It is presumptuous to deny that the long tradition of the Church, ratified by public acceptance, is not valid: 'They which have stood up yesterday to challenge it as of defect, must prove their challenge'. In a sentence resembling the words attributed to Elizabeth I that she did not wish to open a window into men's souls, he warns against too much severity in judging who is worthy to receive the sacraments, 'For neither doth God thus bind us to dive into men's consciences, nor can their fraud and deceit hurt any man but themselves'. He sums up in a single sentence an aspect of the darker side of Puritanism, still found today and as much among secular as religious extremists. 'There is crept into the minds of men, at this day, a secret pernicious and pestilent conceit, that the greatest perfection of a Christian man doth consist in discovery of other men's faults, and in wit to discourse of our own profession.'

Like all educated people of his time, he was trained in the art of rhetoric, of marshalling his argument and presenting it persuasively with the help of recognized linguistic devices. Although he seldom becomes irascible, and never vicious, he is a master of irony. He can deflate the opposing claims by seeming to press them in a way which reduces them to absurdity. Puritan leaders seem to believe that Scripture was written to justify them: 'They are taught to apply all things spoken of repairing the walls and decayed parts of the City, and Temple of God, by Esdras, Nehemias, and the rest; as if purposely the Holy Ghost had therein meant to fore-signify what the authors of admonitions to the Parliament, of supplications to the Council, of petitions to her Majesty, and of such other-like writs, should either do or suffer in behalf of this their cause.' To suggest that set prayers often repeated are not acceptable to God is as if 'it be right to judge him by our own bellies, and to imagine that he doth loathe to have the self-same supplications often iterated, even as we do to be every day fed without alteration or change of diet'. Fear of anything taken from Roman practice is absurd. 'We are also persuaded, that it is but conceit in them to think that those Romish Ceremonies, whereof we have hitherto spoken, are like leprous clothes, infectious to the Church, or like soft and gentle poisons the venom whereof being insensibly pernicious, worketh death, and yet is never felt working.'

He has his favourite words to introduce and strengthen the argument. 'Forasmuch' presents a point as being generally accepted by all reasonable people and therefore giving credibility to what follows from it. It is much used in the Book of Common Prayer which Hooker loved; it begins the Exhortation at the end of the Baptism Service, introduces the order for Communion of the Sick and begins the Prayer of Committal in the Burial service. When he wants to argue against a point just noticed, 'notwithstanding' comes in with a great sweep of demolition. 'Albeit' serves him well when something must be partly acknowledged before the contrary argument begins.

When, as often, his own contentions are to be supported by scriptural or patristic authority, he cites his sources with an unselfconscious ease which links their authority with his own. He moves confidently from past to present, like a man calling on a trusted friend for support in a discussion. There is no virtue in a minister of religion, 'if he praise not God with all his might; if he pour not out his soul in prayer; if he take not their causes to heart, and speak not as Moses, Daniel, and Ezra did for their people'.

His learning is prodigious and authorities are cited with due weight, but he can also support his thesis by homely analogies. Elizabethan writing in all genres shows this regard for the realities of daily life, the world going on outside the study or the playhouse. Puritan leaders may seem to offer free election of ministers but do not always honour the popular voice. 'What is this else but to deal with the people as those nurses do with infants, whose mouths they besmear with the backside of the spoon, as though they had fed them, when they themselves do devour the food?' [127] To suppose that the giving of the Law made sinful things which were not so before is absurd, 'even as in darkness candle-light may serve to guide men's steps, which to use in the day were madness.'

He brings us close to the social life of the later sixteenth century, but makes little reference to political events. His contemporary Lancelot Andrewes could refer in his sermons to the Spanish Armada and other memorable happenings of his earlier years, but Andrewes lived much longer, narrowly escaped death from the Gunpowder Plot, and as Court Preacher had to commemorate it annually. Hooker's concern is rather with the symbiotic relationship between Church and State, the power of civil government over ecclesiastical discipline and the deeply respected but not unlimited power of the Monarch. He was a man of his time in believing that all God's Creation was a structured and hierarchical universe, ranked from God himself to inanimate things, and with each rank owing obedience to what was above and consideration for what was below. To fall out of the shape of things decreed from the beginning was to veer towards anarchy and threatened a return to primal chaos. As Shakespeare's Ulysses says,

Take but degree away, untune that string,
And hark what discord follows.

(*Troilus and Cressida* I. iii)

His manner of writing is generally courteous and tolerant, in contrast to that of many of his contemporaries writing about matters of religion. He can occasionally indulge that Elizabethan power of invective which today is distasteful but yet arouses a certain admiration for its power of language. Thus he writes, not of Christian opponents but of atheists:

> [T]he fury of this wicked brood hath the reins much at liberty, their tongues walk at large, the spit venom of their poisoned hearts breaketh out to the annoyance of others, what their untamed lust suggesteth the same their licentious mouths do everywhere set abroach.

Much more typical is his response to Puritan objections to set places and positions in church services:

> We are still persuaded that a bare denial is answer sufficient to things which mere fancy objecteth; and that the best apology to words of scorn and petulancy, is Isaac's apology to his brother Ishmael, the apology which patience and silence maketh. Our answer therefore to their reasons is, No; to their scoffs, nothing.

Later reputation

Hooker's reputation has been firm over the four centuries since his death, but there have been various opinions of his doctrinal position. It is no longer possible, if indeed it ever was, to regard him as simply a learned churchman hired by Whitgift to defend the Establishment. Nor was he a proto-Tractarian, promoting an Anglican *via media*. He was a man of the Reformation, committed to acceptance of national churches, a vernacular liturgy and a denial of religious observances as in themselves efficacious towards salvation. Most of the English Christians of his time who had not held fast to the Roman obedience were in the Calvinist tradition. Some, like Hooker's Puritan antagonists, wanted nothing less than a replica of the Genevan pattern in doctrine and government. Others were more moderate and found no difficulty in accepting many of the Calvinist principles in the rule of bishops, episcopally ordained clergy, and a formal set liturgy. Hooker was far apart from men like Cartwright and Travers in holding firmly to these principles, and refusing the extreme and harsher aspects of Calvinism. He did not condemn Roman Catholics as reprobate and outside salvation. Although he could be forceful, he would not dismiss those who disagreed with him as unworthy of consideration. Above all, he maintained that the Church to which he belonged was neither a new creation nor the rebirth of a primitive church which had fallen from purity, but one which taught and practised nothing which could not be held as consistent with the unbroken tradition of the One, Holy, Catholic and Apostolic Church.

His reputation as a founding father of Anglicanism developed in the seventeenth century, when his taking on of the Puritans was manna to the Laudian church. After the Restoration, an even stronger reaction against the Puritans enhanced his reputation further, and Isaac Walton's *Life* enthroned him as an Anglican icon. The forced abdication of James II and the Glorious Revolution which brought William III to the throne raised him to new favour as an embryonic Whig. His idea of a fundamental political contract was congenial to the generation of John Locke, controverting any idea of ecclesiastical power overriding the secular. This period is covered in detail by Michael Brydon. The Whig presentation of Hooker survived into the next century; he was cited and praised in the Whig bishop William Warburton's *The Alliance Between Church and State* (1736). The Oxford Movement brought a return to the Laudian estimation, elevating him to an even higher position in the maintenance of true Catholicism in the Church of England. Keble, who brought out a new edition of his writings in 1836, hoped that they would 'appear in their true light, as a kind of warning voice from antiquity, a treasure of primitive, catholic, maxims and sentiments, seasonably provided for this Church, at a time when she was, humanly speaking, in a fair way to fall as low towards rationalism, as the lowest of the protestant congregations are now fallen'.

More recent scholarship has tended to emphasize his position as a Reformed theologian, though not without argument. He has been seen as more radical, creating a model different from that of Whitgift and the other Church authorities of his time and creating what was to become distinctively Anglican. This is the view of Peter Lake, somewhat revised in his later work. Others, like Nigel Atkinson, have found a closer affinity to Calvinism, especially in his sacramental theology, and claimed him as closer to true Reformation principles than his opponents. Nigel Voak studies him in the context of some of the major themes in the theology of the Reformation. Egil Grislis largely agrees, but is inclined towards the view that Hooker did in fact help to create an Anglican *via media*. No serious scholar has tried to elevate Hooker again to the height of Tractarian veneration, though his thought is still congenial to traditional Anglo-Catholics. Peter Munz finds scholastic method and the influence of Aquinas in the *Laws*. For Arthur Middleton, an important and essentially Anglican quality is his knowledge and use of patristic sources.

*These writers are cited here only by name. Their books are fully refer-
enced in the suggestions for further reading.*

The eight Books of the *Laws* do not constitute a systematic work of
theology like the *Summa* of Aquinas or the *Institutes* of Calvin. They
are not a foundation document for Anglicanism like the Westminster
Confession for Presbyterianism. It is impossible to think of the Anglican communion as 'Hookerite' on the analogy of Lutheran or Calvinist. Hooker was addressing a particular situation at a critical time for
the Church of England, answering attacks not by the scurrilous Marprelate tracts but by the most intelligent and fluent Puritan apologists
like Travers and Cartwright. He provided a reasoned and vigorous defence of a Church which did not and does not claim perfection, which
is willing to discuss and justify its structure and usage, resting firmly
on the Bible but respecting also tradition and the wisdom of the past.
He shows it to be tolerant of differences, but prepared when necessary
to invoke a clear discipline. Much of what he wrote remains valid for
that Church today, not because he directly influenced it, but because he
could discern and expound the distinctive qualities which it was developing. For that he is still to be honoured, studied and heeded as one of
our greatest divines.

2

Preface

Concerning the present state of the Church of God

The Preface to the whole work is addressed to the objectors, explaining why he is making this defence. He has some good words for Calvin but deplores the divisions which have resulted from his influence. He begins in an irenical and conciliatory tone, though with a quiet irony which seems to flatter the Puritans before contradicting their argument.

Though for no other cause, yet for this; that posterity may know we have not loosely through silence permitted things to pass away, as in a dream, there shall be for men's information extant thus much concerning the present state of the Church of God, what established amongst us, and their careful endeavours which would have upheld the same. At your hands, beloved in our Lord and Saviour Jesus Christ, (for in him the love which we bear unto all that would but seem to be born of him, it is not the sea of your gall and bitterness that shall ever drown) I have no great cause to look for other, than the self-same portion and lot, which your manner hath been hitherto to lay on them that concur not in opinion and sentence with you. But our hope is, that the God of peace shall (notwithstanding man's nature, too impatient of contumelious malediction) enable us quietly, and even gladly, to suffer all things for that work sake, which we covet to perform. The wonderful zeal and fervour wherewith ye have withstood the received orders of this Church, was the first thing which caused me to enter into consideration, whether (as all your published books and writings peremptorily maintain) every Christian man fearing God stand bound to join with you for the furtherance of that which ye term *the Lord's Discipline*. Wherein I must plainly confess unto you, that before I examined your sundry declarations in that behalf, it could not settle in my head to think, but that undoubtedly such tempers of otherwise right well-affected and most religiously inclined minds, had some marvellous reasonable inducements which led them with so great earnestness that way. But when once, as near as my slender ability would serve, I had with travail and care performed that part of the Apostle's advice and counsel in such cases whereby he willeth to *try all things*, and was come at the length so far, that there remained only the other clause to be satisfied, wherein he concludeth that what good, is, must be held; there was in my poor understanding no remedy, but to set down this as my final resolute persuasion. Surely the present form of Church government, which the laws of this land have established, is such, as no law of God, nor reason of Man, hath hitherto been alleged of force sufficient to prove they do ill, who to the uttermost of their power withstand the alteration thereof. Contrariwise, the other, which instead of it we are required to accept, is only by error and misconduct named the ordinance of Jesus Christ, no one proof as yet brought forth whereby it may clearly appear to be so in very deed. The explication of which two things I have here thought good to offer into your own hands; heartily beseeching you even by the meekness of Jesus Christ whom I trust ye love, that, as ye tender the peace and quietness of this Church, if there be in you that gracious humility which hath ever been the crown and glory of a christianly disposed mind; if your own souls, hearts and consciences (the sound integrity whereof can but hardly stand with the refusal of truth in personal respects) be, as I doubt not but they are, things most dear and precious unto you; *Let not the faith which ye have in our Lord Jesus Christ be blemished with partialities*, regard not who it is which speaketh, but weigh only what is spoken. Think not that ye read the words of one who bendeth himself as an adversary against the truth, which ye have already embraced, but the words of one who desireth even to embrace together with you the self-same truth, if it be the truth; and for that cause (for no other, God he knoweth) hath undertaken the burthensome labour of this painful kind of conference. For the plainer access whereunto, let it be lawful for me to rip up the very bottom, how, and by whom your Discipline was planted, at such time as this age we live in began to make first trial thereof.

Preface i 1–3, 125–7

One of the main points of contention was the Puritans' way of inter-
preting Scripture to their own purpose and wanting to organize Church
order and discipline accordingly, instituting their own idea about the
orders of ministry. He introduces the test of Reason which he expounds
at more length in the main work.

Assuredly, the very cause which maketh the simple and ignorant to think
they even see how the Word of God runneth currently on your side, is
that their minds are forestalled, and their conceits perverted beforehand,
by being taught, that an Elder doth signify a Layman, admitted only to
the office or rule of government in the Church; a Doctor, one which may
only teach, and neither preach nor administer the Sacraments; a Deacon,
one which hath the charge of the alms-box, and of nothing else: that
the Sceptre, the Rod, the Throne and Kingdom of Christ, are a form of
regiment, only by Pastors, Elders, Doctors, and Deacons; that by mystical resemblance, Mount Sion and Jerusalem are the Churches which
admit; Samaria and Babylon, the Churches which oppugn the said form
of regiment. And in like sort, they are taught to apply all things spoken
of repairing the walls and decayed parts of the City, and Temple of God,
by Esdras, Nehemias, and the rest; as if purposely the Holy Ghost had
therein meant to fore-signify what the authors of admonitions to the
Parliament, of supplications to the Council, of petitions to her Majesty,
and of such other-like writs, should either do or suffer in behalf of this
their cause. From hence they proceed to a higher point, which is the persuading of men credulous and over-capable of such pleasing errors that
it is the special illumination of the Holy Ghost, whereby they discern
those things in the Word, which others reading, yet discern them not.
Dearly beloved, saith St John, *give not credit unto every spirit.* There
are but two ways whereby the Spirit leadeth men into all truth; the one
extraordinary, the other common; the one belonging but unto some few,
the other extending itself unto all that are of God; the one, that which we
call by a special divine excellency, Revelation; the other, Reason. If the
Spirit by such Revelation have discovered unto them the secrets of that
Discipline out of Scripture, they must profess themselves to be all (even
men, women, and children) prophets: or if reason be the hand which
the Spirit hath led them by, forasmuch as persuasions grounded upon
reason are either weaker or stronger, according to the force of those reasons, whereupon the same are grounded, they must every of them, from
the greatest to the least, be able for every several article to show some
special reason, as strong as their persuasion therein is earnest: otherwise
how can it be, but that some other sinews there are, from which that

overplus of strength in persuasion doth arise? Most sure it is that when men's affections do frame their opinions, they are in defence of error more earnest a great deal, than (for the most part) sound believers in the maintenance of truth, apprehended according to the nature of that evidence which Scripture yieldeth: which being in some things plain, as in the principles of Christian Doctrine; in some things, as in these matters of Discipline, more dark and doubtful, frameth correspondently that inward assent, which God's most gracious Spirit worketh by it, as by his effectual instrument. It is not therefore the fervent earnestness of their persuasion, but the soundness of those reasons, whereupon the same is built, which must declare their opinions in these things to have been wrought by the Holy Ghost, and not by the fraud of that evil spirit, which is even in his illusions strong. After that the fancy of the common sort hath once thoroughly apprehended the Spirit to be the author of their persuasions concerning Discipline, then is instilled into their hearts, that the same Spirit, leading men into this opinion, doth thereby seal them to be God's children; and that, as the state of the times now standeth, the most special token to know them that are God's own from others, is an earnest affection that way. This hath bred high terms of separation between such, and the rest of the world; whereby the one sort are named the Brethren, the Godly, and so forth; the other worldlings, time-servers, pleasers of men, not of God, with such like. From hence they are easily drawn on to think it exceeding necessary, for fear of quenching that good Spirit, to use all means whereby, the same may be both strengthened in themselves, and made manifest unto others. This maketh them diligent hearers of such as are known that way to incline: this maketh them eager to take and seek all occasions of secret conference with such: this maketh them glad to use such as counsellors and directors in all their dealings, which are of weight, as contracts, testaments, and the like: this maketh them through an unweariable desire of receiving instruction from the masters of that company, to cast off the care of those very affairs which do most concern their estate, and to think that they are like unto Mary, commendable for making choice of the better part.

Preface iii 9–12, 148–52

Warning against the danger of individual interpretation and of following a few leaders in defiance of the consensus of the Church.

It fareth many times with men's opinions, as with rumours and reports. That which a credible person telleth, is easily thought probable by such as are well persuaded of him: but if two, or three, or four, agree all in the same tale, they judge it then to be out of controversy, and so are many times overtaken for want of due consideration; either some common cause leading them all into error, or one man's oversight deceiving many through their too much credulity and easiness of belief. Though ten persons be brought to give testimony in any cause, yet if the knowledge they have of the thing whereunto they come as witnesses, appear to have grown from some one amongst them, and, to have spread itself from hand to hand, they all are in force but as one testimony. Nor is it otherwise here where the daughter Churches do speak their mother's dialect; here, where so many sing one song, by reason that he is the guide of the quire, concerning whose deserved authority amongst even the gravest divines, we have already spoken at large. Will ye ask what should move those many learned to be followers of one man's judgment, no necessity of argument forcing them thereunto? Your demand is answered by yourselves. Loth ye are to think that they whom ye judge to have attained as sound knowledge in all points of doctrine as any since the Apostles' time, should mistake in Discipline. Such is naturally our affection, that whom in great things we mightily admire, in them we are not persuaded willingly that any thing should be amiss. The reason, whereof is, *For that as dead flies putrefy the ointment of the apothecary, so a little folly him that is in estimation for wisdom.* This in every profession hath too much authorized the judgment of a few. This with Germans hath caused Luther, and with many other Churches Calvin, to prevail in all things. Yet are we not able to define, whether the wisdom of that God (who setteth before us in Holy Scripture so many admirable patterns of virtue, and no one of them without somewhat noted wherein they were culpable; to the end that to him alone it might always be acknowledged, *Thou only art holy, thou only art just*) might not permit those worthy vessels of his glory to be in some things blemished with the stain of human frailty, even for this cause, lest we should esteem of any man above that which behoveth.

Preface iv 8, 162–3

Introduction to the intention and plan of the work.

Nor is mine own intent any other in these several books of discourse, than to make it appear unto you, that for the Ecclesiastical Laws of this land we are led by great reason to observe them, and ye by no necessity bound to impugn them. It is no part of my secret meaning, to draw you hereby into hatred, or to set upon the face of this cause any fairer gloss than the naked truth doth afford; but my whole endeavour is to resolve the conscience, and to show, as near as I can, what in this controversy the heart is to think, if it will follow the light of sound and sincere judgment, without either cloud of prejudice or mist of passionate affection. Wherefore, seeing that Laws and Ordinances in particular, whether such as we observe, or such as yourselves would have established; when the mind doth sift and examine them, it must needs have often recourse to a number of doubts and questions, about the nature, kinds, and qualities of Laws in general; whereof, unless it be thoroughly informed, there will appear no certainty to stay our persuasion upon; I have for that cause set down in the first place, an Introduction on both sides needful to be considered; declaring therein what Law is, how different kinds of Laws there are, and what force they are of, according unto each kind. This done, because ye suppose the Laws for which ye strive are found in Scripture; but those not, against which ye strive; and, upon this surmise, are drawn to hold it, as the very main pillar of your whole cause, *That Scripture ought to be the only rule of all your actions*; and consequently, that the Church-orders which we observe, being not commanded in Scripture, are offensive and unpleasant unto God; I have spent the second book in sifting of this point, which standeth with you for the first and chiefest principle whereon ye build. Whereunto the next in degree is, That as God will have always a Church upon earth, while the world doth continue, and that Church stand in need of government; of which government it behoveth himself to be both the author and teacher; so it cannot stand with duty, that man should ever presume in any wise to change and alter the same; and therefore that in Scripture there must of necessity be found some particular form of Ecclesiastical Polity, the Laws whereof admit not any kind of alteration. The first three books being thus ended, the fourth proceedeth from the general grounds and foundations of your cause, unto your general accusations against us; as having in the orders of our Church (for so you pretend) corrupted the right form of Church-polity with manifold Popish Rites and Ceremonies, which certain reformed Churches have banished from amongst them, and have thereby given us such example as (you think) we ought to follow. This your assertion hath herein drawn us to make search, whether these be just exceptions against the customs of our Church, when ye plead, that they are the same which the Church of Rome hath, or that they are not the same which some other reformed Churches have devised. Of those four books which remain, and are bestowed about the specialties of that cause which lieth in controversy, the first examineth the causes by you alleged, wherefore the public duties of Christian

Religion, as our Prayers, our Sacraments and the rest, should not be ordered in such sort as with us they are; nor that power whereby the persons of men are consecrated unto the Ministry, be disposed of in such manner as the Laws of this Church do allow. The second and third are concerning the power of Jurisdiction; the one, whether Laymen, such as your governing Elders are, ought in all congregations for ever to be invested with that power? The other, whether Bishops may have that power over other Pastors, and therewithal that honour which with us they have? And because besides the power of Order, which all consecrated persons have, and the power of Jurisdiction, which neither they all, nor they only have, there is a third power, a power of Ecclesiastical Dominion, communicable, as we think, unto persons not Ecclesiastical, and most fit to be restrained unto the Prince, our sovereign commander over the whole body politic; the eighth book we have allotted unto this question, and have sifted therein your objections against those preeminences royal which thereunto appertain. Thus have I laid before you the brief of these my travels, and presented under your view the limbs of that cause litigious between us, the whole entire body whereof being thus compact, it shall be no troublesome thing for any man to find each particular controversy's resting place, and the coherence it hath with those things, either on which it dependeth, or which depend on it.

Preface vii 1–7, 171–3

He ends the Preface with an irenical appeal to his opponents to reconsider and to live in unity.

The best and safest way for you therefore, my dear Brethren, is to call your deeds past to a new reckoning, to re-examine the cause ye have taken in hand, and to try it even point by point, argument by argument, with all the diligent exactness ye can, to lay aside the gall of that bitterness wherein your minds have hitherto over-abounded, and with meekness to search the truth. Think ye are men; deem it not impossible for you to err; sift impartially your own hearts, whether it be force of reason, or vehemency of affection which hath bred, and still doth feed these opinions in you. If truth do anywhere manifest itself, seek not to smother it with glozing delusion, acknowledge the greatness thereof, and think it your best victory, when the same doth prevail over you.

That ye have been earnest in speaking or writing again and again the contrary way, should be no blemish or discredit at all unto you. Amongst so many, so huge volumes, as the infinite pains of St Augustine have brought forth, what one hath gotten him greater love, commendation, and honour, than the book wherein he carefully collecteth his own oversights, and sincerely condemneth them? Many speeches there are of Job's, whereby his wisdom and other virtues may appear; but the glory of an ingenious mind he hath purchased by these words only, *Behold, I will lay mine hand on my mouth. I have spoken once; yet will I not therefore maintain argument: yea, twice; howbeit for that cause further I will not proceed.* Far more comfort it were for us (so small is the joy we take in these strifes) to labour under the same yoke, as men that look for the same eternal reward of their labours, to be enjoined with you in bands of indissoluble love and amity, to love as if our persons being many, our souls were but one, rather than in such dismembered sort, to spend our few and wretched days in a tedious prosecuting of wearisome contentions: the end whereof, if they have not some speedy end will be heavy even on both sides.

Preface ix 1–3, 194–5

3

BOOK ONE

Concerning Laws and their several kinds in general

Having stated his overall position in the Preface, he sets out 'The cause of writing this general discourse concerning Laws'. He describes the Natural Law which comes from God and should govern all human action.

He that goeth about to persuade a multitude, that they are not so well governed as they ought to be, shall never want attentive and favourable hearers; because they know the manifold defects whereunto every kind of regiment is subject; but the secret lets and difficulties, which in public proceedings are innumerable and inevitable, they have not ordinarily the judgment to consider. And because such as openly reprove supposed disorders of State, are taken for principal friends to the common benefit of all, and for men that carry singular freedom of mind; under this fair and plausible colour, whatsoever they utter passeth for good and current. That which wanteth in the weight of their speech, is supplied by the aptness of men's minds to accept and believe it. Whereas on the other side, if we maintain things that are established, we have not only to strive with a number of heavy prejudices, deeply rooted in the hearts of men, who think that herein we serve the time, and speak in favour of the present State, because thereby we either hold or seek preferment; but also to bear such exceptions as minds, so averted beforehand, usually take against that which they are loth should be poured into them. Albeit therefore much of that we are to speak in this present cause may seem to a number perhaps tedious, perhaps obscure, dark, and intricate; (for many talk of the truth, which never sounded the depth from whence it springeth: and therefore when they are led thereunto, they are soon weary, as men drawn from those beaten paths wherewith they have been inured); yet this may not so far prevail, as to cut off that which the matter itself requireth, howsoever the nice humour of some be therewith pleased or no. They unto whom we shall seem tedious, are in no wise injured by us, because it is in their own hands to spare that labour which they are not willing to endure. And if any complain of obscurity, they must consider that in these matters it cometh no otherwise to pass, than in sundry the works both of art and also of nature, where that which hath greatest force in the very things we see, is notwithstanding itself oftentimes not seen. The stateliness of houses, the goodliness of trees when we behold them, delighteth the eye; but that foundation which beareth up the one, that root which ministereth unto the other nourishment and life, is in the bosom of the earth concealed; and if there be occasion at any time to search into it, such labour is then more necessary than pleasant, both to them which undertake it, and for the lookers-on. In like manner, the use and benefit of good Laws, all that live under them may enjoy with delight and comfort, albeit the grounds and first original causes from whence they have sprung be unknown, as to the greatest part of men they are. But when they who withdraw their obedience pretend that the Laws which they should obey are corrupt and vicious; for better examination of their quality, it behoveth the very foundation and root, the highest wellspring and fountain of them to be discovered. Which because we are not oftentimes accustomed to do, when we do it the pains we take are more needful a great deal than acceptable, and the matters which we handle seem, by reason of newness, (till the mind grow better acquainted with them) dark, intricate, and unfamiliar. For as much help whereof, as may be in this case, I have endeavoured throughout the body of this whole Discourse, that every former part might give strength unto all that follow, and every latter bring some light unto all before. So that if the judgments of men do but hold themselves in suspense, as touching these first more general meditations, till in order they have perused the rest that ensue; what may seem dark at the first will afterwards be found more plain, even as the latter particular decisions will appear, I doubt not, more strong when the other have been read before. The Laws of the Church, whereby for so many ages together we have been guided in the exercise of Christian Religion, and the service of the true God, our Rites, Customs, and Orders of Ecclesiastical Government are called in question. We are accused as men that will not have Christ Jesus to rule over them; but have wilfully cast his statutes behind their backs, hating to be reformed and made subject unto the sceptre of his discipline. Behold therefore, we offer the Laws whereby we live unto the general trial and judgment of the whole world; heartily beseeching Almighty God, whom we desire to serve according to his own will, that both we and others (all kind of partial affection being clean laid aside) may have eyes to see and hearts to embrace the things that in his sight are most acceptable. And because the point about which we strive is the quality of our Laws, our first entrance hereinto cannot better be made, than with consideration of the nature of Law in general, and of that Law which giveth life unto all the rest which are commendable, just, and good, namely, the Law whereby the Eternal himself doth work. Proceeding from hence to the Law, first of Nature, then of Scripture, we shall have the easier access unto those things which come after to be debated, concerning the particular cause and question which we have in hand.

I I 1–3, 198–200

A rather difficult philosophical argument, but important as stating that Law is inherent in the very Being of God, demonstrated in the Trinity, and therefore not open to human questioning.

All things that are, have some operation not violent or casual: neither doth any thing ever begin to exercise the same, without some fore-conceived end for which it worketh. And the end which it worketh for is not obtained, until the work be also fit to obtain it by; for unto every end every operation will not serve. That which doth assign unto each thing the kind, that which doth moderate the force and power, that which doth appoint the form and measure of working, the same we term a Law. So that no certain end could ever be attained, unless the actions whereby it is attained were regular that is to say, made suitable, fit, and correspondent unto their end, by some canon, rule, or Law. Which thing doth first take place in the works even of God Himself. All things therefore do work after a sort according to Law; all other things according to a Law, whereof some superior, unto whom they are subject, is author; only the works and operations of God have him both for their worker, and for the Law whereby they are wrought. The Being of God is a kind of Law to his working; for that perfection which God is, giveth perfection to that he doth. Those natural, necessary, and internal operations of God, the generation of the Son, the Proceeding of the Spirit are without the compass, of my present intent; which is to touch only such operations as have their beginning and being by a voluntary purpose, wherewith God hath eternally decreed when and how they should be; which eternal decree is that we term an eternal Law. Dangerous it were for the feeble brain of man to wade far into the doings of the most High; whom although to know be life, and joy to make mention of his name; yet our soundest knowledge is, to know that we know him not as indeed he is, neither can know him: and our safest eloquence concerning him, is our silence, when we confess without confession, that his glory is inexplicable, his greatness above our capacity and reach. He is above, and we upon earth; therefore it behoveth our words to be wary and few. Our God is one, or rather very oneness, and mere unity, having nothing but Itself in Itself, and not consisting (as all things do besides God) of many things. In which essential Unity of God, a Trinity personal nevertheless subsisteth, after a manner far exceeding the possibility of man's conceit. The works which outwardly are of God, they are in such sort of him being one, that each person hath in them somewhat peculiar and proper. For being Three, and they all subsisting in the essence of one Deity, from the Father, by the Son, through the Spirit, all things are. That which the Son doth hear of the Father, and which the Spirit doth receive of the Father and the Son, the same we have at the hands of the Spirit, as being the last; and therefore the nearest unto us in order, although in power the same with the second and the first. The wise and learned amongst the very Heathens themselves have all acknowledged some First Cause, whereupon originally the being of all things dependeth. Neither have they otherwise spoke of that cause than as an agent, which knowing what and why it worketh, observeth in working a most exact order or Law.

I ii 1–3, 200–1, 58–60

Natural Law as ordained by God controls all Creation. The idea of Natural Law is itself scriptural: St Paul writes of the Gentiles having a law written in their hearts, although they are ignorant of the Jewish Mosaic law (Romans 2.14f.). It was generally favoured by the medieval Scholastic theologians but rejected by many of the Reformers. This passage introduces Hooker's case against the claim that Scripture is the sole guide for life in this world and that nothing outside it conveys the will of God. It also shows a typically sixteenth-century regard for the ordered universe and the great chain of being.

I am not ignorant, that by Law eternal, the learned for the most part do understand the order, not which God hath eternally purposed himself in all his works to observe, but rather that, which with himself he hath set down as expedient to be kept by all his creatures, according to the several conditions wherewith he hath endued them. They who thus are accustomed to speak, apply the name of Law unto that only rule of working, which superior authority imposeth; whereas we somewhat more enlarging the sense thereof, term any kind of rule or canon, whereby actions are framed, a Law. Now that Law which, as it is laid up in the bosom of God, they call eternal, receiveth, according unto the different kind of things which are subject unto it, different and sundry kinds of names. That part of it which ordereth natural agents, we call usually Nature's Law; that which Angels do clearly behold, and without any swerving observe, is a law celestial and heavenly; the Law of Reason, that which bindeth creatures reasonable in this world, and with which by reason they most plainly perceive themselves bound; that which bindeth them, and is not known but by special revelation from God, divine Law. Human Law, that which out of the Law, either of reason or of God, men probably gathering to be expedient, they make it a Law. All things therefore, which are as they ought to be, are conformed unto this second Law eternal; and even those things, which to this eternal Law are not conformable, are notwithstanding in some sort ordered by the first eternal Law. For what good or evil is there under the sun; what action correspondent or repugnant unto to the Law which God hath imposed upon his creatures, but in, or upon it, God doth work according to the Law which himself hath eternally purposed to keep; that is to say, the first eternal Law? So that a twofold Law eternal being thus made, it is not hard to conceive how they both take place in all things. Wherefore to come to the Law of Nature albeit thereby we sometimes mean that manner of working which God hath set for each created thing to keep; yet forasmuch as those things are termed most properly natural agents, which keep the Law of their kind unwittingly, as the heavens and elements of the world, which can do no otherwise than they do: and forasmuch as we give unto our intellectual natures the name of voluntary agents, that so we may distinguish them from the other, expedient it will be that we sever the Law of Nature observed by the one from that which the other is tied unto. Touching the former, their strict keeping of one tenure, statute, and Law is spoken of by all, but hath in it more than men have as yet attained to know, or perhaps ever shall attain, seeing the travel of wading herein is given of God to the sons of men; that perceiving how much the least thing in the world hath in it; in more than the wisest are able to reach unto, they may by this means learn humility. Moses, in describing the work of creation, attributeth speech unto God: *God said, Let there be light: let there be a firmament: let the waters under the heavens be gathered together into one place: let the earth bring forth, let there be lights in the firmament of heaven.* Was this only the intent of Moses, to signify the infinite greatness of God's power, by the easiness of his accomplishing such effects, without travel, pain, or labour? Surely, it seemeth that Moses had herein, besides this, a further purpose, namely, first to teach that God did not work as a necessary, but a voluntary agent, intending beforehand, and decreeing with himself that which did outwardly proceed from him. Secondly, to show that God did then institute a Law natural to be observed by creatures; and therefore according to the manner of Laws; the institution thereof is described, as being established by solemn injunction. His commanding those things to be which are, and to be in such sort as they are, to keep that tenure and course which they do, importeth the establishment of Nature's Law. The world's first creation, and the preservation since of things created, what is it, but only so far forth a manifestation by execution, what the eternal Law of God is concerning things natural? And as it cometh to pass in a kingdom rightly ordered that after a Law is once published, it presently takes effect far and wide, all states framing themselves thereunto; even so let us think it fareth in the natural course of the world: since the time that God did first proclaim the edicts of his Law upon it, heaven and earth have hearkened unto his voice, and their labour hath been to do his will: *he made a Law for the rain*; he gave his *decree unto the sea, that the waters should not pass his commandment.* Now, if Nature should intermit her course, and leave altogether, though it were but for a while, the observation of her own Laws; if those principal and mother-elements of the world, whereof all things in this lower world are made, should lose the qualities which now they have; if the frame of that heavenly arch erected over our heads should loosen and dissolve itself; if celestial spheres should forget their wonted motions, and by irregular volubility turn themselves any way as it might happen; if the prince of the lights of heaven, which now as a giant doth run his unwearied course, should, as it were, through a languishing faintness, begin to stand, and to rest himself; if the moon should wander from her beaten way, the times and seasons of the year blend themselves by disordered and confused mixture, the winds breathe out their last gasp, the clouds yield no rain, the earth be defeated of heavenly influence, the fruits of the earth pine away, as children at the breasts of their mother, no longer able to yield them relief; what would become of man himself, whom these things do now all serve? See we not plainly, that obedience of creatures unto the Law of Nature is the stay of the whole world?

I iii 1–2, 204–8

Human beings, directed towards imitation of God, must grow into knowledge of this Law which he has made. The contemporary sense

of degree and hierarchy in nature is developed further: even inanimate
things have their own special qualities. We are born without knowledge,
like a blank page on which the understanding of the Law of God must
gradually be written.

Sith there can be no goodness desired, which proceedeth not from God
himself, as from the supreme cause of all things; and every effect doth
after a sort contain, at leastwise resemble, the cause from which it proceedeth; all things in the world are said in some sort to seek the highest,
and to covet more or less the participation of God himself; yet this doth
nowhere so much appear, as it doth in Man, because there are so many
kinds of perfection which Man seeketh. The first degree of goodness is
that general perfection which all things do seek, in desiring the continuance of their being; all things therefore coveting, as much as may be,
to be like unto God in being ever, that which cannot hereunto attain
personally doth seek to continue itself another way; that is by offspring
and propagation. The next degree of goodness is that which each thing
coveteth, by affecting resemblance with God, in the constancy and excellency of those operations which belong unto their kind. The immuta-
bility of God they strive unto, by working either always, or for the most
part, after one and the same manner; his absolute exactness they imitate,
by tending unto that which is most exquisite in every particular. Hence
have risen a number of Axioms in Philosophy, showing how the works
of Nature do always aim at that which cannot be bettered. These two
kinds of goodness rehearsed, are so nearly united to the things themselves which desire them, that we scarcely perceive the appetite to stir
in reaching forth her hand towards them. But the desire of those which
grow externally is more apparent, especially of such as are not expressly
desired, unless they be first known, or such as are not for any other cause
than for knowledge itself desired. Concerning perfections in this kind,
that by proceeding in the knowledge of truth, and by growing in the
exercise of virtue, Man, amongst the creatures of this inferior world, aspireth to the greatest conformity with God. This is not only known unto
us, whom he himself hath so instructed, but even they do acknowledge,
who amongst men are not judged the nearest unto him. With Plato,
what one thing more usual, than to excite men unto a love of wisdom by showing how much wise men are thereby exalted above men;
how knowledge doth raise them up into heaven; how it maketh them,
though not Gods, yet as Gods, high, admirable, and divine? [. . .]
   In the matter of knowledge, there is between the Angels of God and the
children of Men this difference: Angels already have full and complete

knowledge in the highest degree that can be imparted unto them: Men, if we view them in their spring, are at the first without understanding or knowledge at all. Nevertheless, from this utter vacuity they grow by degrees, till they come at length to be even as the Angels themselves are. That which agreeth to the one now, the other shall attain unto in the end; they are not so far disjoined and severed, but that they come at length to meet. The soul of Man being therefore at the first as a book, wherein nothing is, and yet all things may be imprinted; we are to search by what steps and degrees it riseth unto perfection of knowledge. Unto that which hath been already set down concerning natural agents, this we must add, that albeit therein we have comprised, as well creatures living, as void of life, if they be in degree of nature beneath men; nevertheless, a difference we must observe between those natural agents that work altogether un-wittingly; and those which have, though weak, yet some understanding what they do, as fishes, fowls, and beasts have. Beasts are in sensible ca-pacity as ripe even as men themselves, perhaps more ripe. For as stones, though in dignity of nature inferior to plants, yet exceed them in firmness of strength, or durability of being; and plants, though beneath the excel-lency of creatures endued with sense, yet exceed them in the faculty of vegetation, and of fertility; so beasts, though otherwise behind men, may notwithstanding in actions of sense and fancy go beyond them; because their endeavours of Nature, when it hath an higher perfection to seek, are in lower the more remiss, not esteeming thereof so much as those do, which have no better proposed unto them. The Soul of Man therefore, being capable of a more divine perfection, hath (besides the faculty of growing unto sensible knowledge, which is common unto us with beasts) a further capability, whereof in them there is no show at all, the abil-ity of reaching higher than unto sensible things. Till we grow to some ripeness of years, the Soul of Man doth only store itself with conceits of things of inferior and more open quality, which afterwards do serve as instruments unto that which is greater; in the meanwhile, above the reach of meaner creatures it ascendeth not. When once it comprehendeth anything above this, as the differences of time, affirmations, negations, and contradiction in speech, we then count it to have some use of natural reason. Whereunto, if afterwards there might be added the right helps of true art and learning (which helps, I must plainly confess, this age of the world, carrying the name of a learned age, doth neither much know, nor greatly regard) there would undoubtedly be almost as great difference in maturity of judgment between men therewith inured, and that which now men are, as between men that are now, and innocents.

I v 2, vi 3, 215–8

Reason moves humans towards choosing the good; appetite may work against reason and lead in the wrong way. Puritans were generally not enthusiastic about affirming the strength of the individual to choose by exercise of the Will.

By reason Man attaineth unto the knowledge of things that are, and are not sensible; it resteth, therefore, that we search how Man attaineth unto the knowledge of such things unsensible, as are to be known that they may be done. Seeing then that nothing can move unless there be some end, the desire whereof provoketh unto motion; how should that divine power of our Soul, that *spirit of our mind*, as the Apostle termeth it, ever stir itself unto action unless it have also the like spur? The end for which we are moved to work, is sometimes the goodness which we conceive of the very working itself, without any further respect at all; and the cause that procureth action is the mere desire of action, no other good besides being thereby intended. Of certain turbulent wits it is said, 'They thought the very disturbance of things established an hire sufficient to set them on work'. Sometimes that which we do is referred to a further end, without the desire whereof we would leave the same undone; as in their actions that gave alms to purchase thereby the praise of men. [. . .] Man in perfection being made according to the likeness of his Maker, resembleth him also in the manner of working; so that whatsoever we work as men, the same we do wittingly work and freely: neither are we according to the manner of natural agents any way so tied, but that it is in our power to leave the things we do undone. The good which either is gotten by doing, or which consisteth in the very doing itself, causeth not action, unless apprehending it as good we so like and desire it. That we do unto any such end, the same we choose and prefer before the leaving of it undone. Choice there is not, unless the thing which we take to be so in our power, that have refused and left it. If fire consumeth the stubble, it chooseth not so to do, because the nature thereof is such that it can do no other. To choose, is to will one thing before another; and to will is to bend our souls to the having or doing of that which they see to be good. Goodness is seen with the eye of the understanding, and the light of that eye is reason. So that two principal fountains there are of human action, Knowledge and Will; which Will, in things tending towards any end, is termed *choice*. Concerning Knowledge; 'Behold', saith Moses, 'I have set before you this day good and evil, life and death'. Concerning Will, he addeth immediately, 'Choose life'; that is to say, the things that tend unto life, them choose. But of one thing we must have special care, as being a matter of no small moment, and that is, how the Will, properly and strictly taken, as it is of things which are referred: unto the end that man desireth, differeth greatly from that inferior natural desire which we call Appetite. The object of Appetite is whatsoever sensible good may be wished for; the object of Will is that good which Reason doth lead us to seek. Affections as joy, and grief, and fear, and anger, with such like, being as it were the sundry fashions and forms of Appetite, can neither rise at the conceit of a thing indifferent, nor yet choose but rise at the sight of some things. Wherefore it is not altogether in our power, whether we will be stirred with affections or no. Whereas actions which issue from the disposition of the Will, are in the power thereof to be performed or stayed. Finally, Appetite is the Will's solicitor, and the Will is Appetite's controller; what we covet according to the one, by the other we often reject. Neither is any other desire termed properly Will, but that where Reason and, understanding, or the show of Reason, prescribeth the thing desired. It may be therefore a question, whether those operations of men are to be counted voluntary, wherein that good which is sensible provoketh Appetite, and Appetite causeth action, Reason being never called to counsel; as when we eat or drink, and betake ourselves unto rest, and such like. The truth is, that such actions in men, having attained to the use of Reason, are voluntary: for as the authority of higher powers hath force even in those things which are done without their privity, and are of so mean reckoning, that to acquaint them therewith it needeth not: in like sort, voluntarily we are said to do that also, which the Will, if it listed, might hinder from being done, although about the doing thereof we do not expressly use our Reason or understanding, and so immediately apply our Wills thereunto. In cases therefore of such facility, the Will doth yield her assent, with a kind of silence, by not dissenting; in which respect her force is not so apparent as in express mandates or prohibition, especially upon advice and, consultation going before. Where understanding therefore needeth, in those things, Reason is the director of man's Will, by discovering in action what is good. For Laws of well-doing are the dictates of right Reason. Children which are not as yet come unto those years whereat they may have; again, innocents which are excluded by natural defect from ever having; thirdly, madmen, which for the present cannot possibly have the use of right Reason to guide themselves, have for their guide the Reason that guideth other men, which are tutors over them to seek and procure their good for them. In the rest there is that light of Reason, whereby good may be known from evil; and which discovering the same rightly is termed right. The Will, notwithstanding, doth not incline to have or do that which Reason teacheth to be good, unless same do also teach it to be possible. For albeit the Appetite, being more general, may wish any seemeth good, be it never so impossible; yet for such things the reasonable Will of man doth never seek. Let Reason teach impossibility in anything, and the Will of man doth let it go; a thing impossible it doth not affect, the impossibility thereof being manifest. There is in the Will of man naturally that freedom, whereby it is apt to take or refuse any particular object whatsoever being presented unto it. Whereupon it followeth, that there is no particular object so good but it may have the show of some difficulty or unpleasant quality annexed to it, in respect whereof the Will may shrink and decline it; contrariwise (for so things are blended) there is no particular evil which hath not some appearance of goodness whereby to insinuate itself. For evil, as evil, cannot be desired; if that be desired which is evil, the cause is the goodness which is or seemeth to be joined with it. Goodness doth not move by being, but by being apparent; and therefore many things are neglected which are most precious, only because the value of them lieth hid. Sensible Goodness is most apparent, near, and present which causeth the Appetite to be therewith strongly provoked. Now pursuit and refusal in the Will do follow, the one the affirmation, the other the negation of goodness; which the understanding apprehendeth, grounding itself upon sense, unless some higher Reason do chance to teach the contrary. And if Reason have taught it rightly to be good, yet not so apparently that the mind receiveth it with utter impossibility of being otherwise, still there is place left for the Will to take or leave.

I vii 1–6, 219–23

Reason leads people to form societies and to make and keep laws for their maintenance. This is the sort of argument which in the late seventeenth century gave Hooker a reputation as a political thinker.

That which hitherto we have set down, is (I hope) sufficient to show their brutishness, which imagine that Religion and Virtue are only as men will account of them; that we might make as much account, if we would, of the contrary, without any harm unto ourselves, and that in nature they are as indifferent one as the other. [. . .] We see then how Nature itself teacheth Laws and Statutes to live by. The Laws, which have been hitherto mentioned, do bind men absolutely, even as they are men, although they have never any settled fellowship, never any solemn agreement amongst themselves what to do, or not to do. But forasmuch as we are not by ourselves sufficient to furnish ourselves with competent store of things needful for such a life as our nature doth desire, a life fit for the dignity of man; therefore to supply those defects and imperfections which are in us living single and solely by ourselves, we are naturally induced to seek communion and fellowship with others. This was the cause of men's uniting themselves at the first in politic societies, which societies could not be without government, nor government without a distinct kind of Law from that which hath been already declared. Two foundations there are which bear up public societies; the one, a natural inclination whereby all men desire sociable life and fellowship; the other, an order expressly or secretly agreed upon touching the manner of their union in living together. The latter is that which we call the Law of a Commonweal, the very soul of a politic body, the parts whereof are by Law animated, held together; and set on work in such actions as the common good requireth. Laws politic, ordained for external order and regiment amongst men, are never framed as they should be, unless presuming the will of man to be inwardly obstinate, rebellious, and averse from all obedience unto the sacred Laws of his Nature: in a word, unless presuming man to be in regard of his depraved mind little better than a wild beast, they do accordingly provide notwithstanding so to frame his outward actions, that they be no hindrance unto the common good for which societies are instituted; unless they do this, they are not perfect. It resteth therefore that we consider how Nature findeth out such Laws of government as serve to direct even Nature depraved to a right end. All men desire to lead in this world an happy life: that life is led most happily, wherein all virtue is exercised without impediment or let.

I x 1–2, 239–40

After stating the need for agreement between nations about Natural Law he considers its application to Christian unity. The appeal to the early Councils of the Church is typical of Anglican apologetics and not so acceptable to the Puritans. Article 21 of the Articles of Religion is more cautious and says that General Councils 'may err, and sometimes have erred' and have no authority except what can be proved from Scripture: a caution which Hooker heeds in his argument.

As there is great cause of communion, and consequently of Laws, for the maintenance of communion amongst nations; so amongst nations Christian, the like in regard even of Christianity hath been always judged needful. And in this kind of correspondence amongst nations the force of general Councils doth stand. For as one and the same Law divine, whereof in the next place we are to speak, is unto all Christian churches a rule for the chiefest things; by means whereof they all in that respect make one Church, as having all but *One Lord, one Faith, one Baptism*; so the urgent necessity of mutual communion for preservation of our unity in these things, as also for Order in some other things convenient to be everywhere uniformly kept, maketh it requisite that the Church of God here on earth have her Laws of spiritual commerce between Christian nations; Laws, by virtue whereof all Churches may enjoy freely the use of those reverend religious, and sacred consultations, which are termed Councils general. A thing whereof God's own blessed Spirit was the author; a thing practised by the holy Apostles themselves; a thing always afterwards kept and observed throughout the world; a thing never otherwise than most highly esteemed of, till pride, ambition, and tyranny began by factious and vain endeavours to abuse that divine intention unto the furtherance of wicked purposes. But as the just authority of civil Courts and Parliaments is not therefore to be abolished, because sometimes there is cunning used to frame them according to the private intents of men over-potent in the commonwealth; so the grievous abuse which hath been of Councils, should rather cause men to study how so gracious a thing may again be reduced to that first perfection, than in regard of stains and blemishes, sitthence growing, be held for ever in extreme disgrace. To speak of this matter as the cause requireth would require very long discourse. All I will presently say is this, whether it be for the finding out of any thing whereunto divine Law bindeth us, but yet in such sort, that men are not thereof on all sides resolved; or for the setting down of some uniform judgment to stand touching such things, as being neither way matters of necessity, are notwithstanding offensive and scandalous, when there is open opposition about them; be it for the ending of strifes, touching matters of Christian belief, wherein the one part may seem to have probable cause of dissenting from the other; or be it concerning matters of polity, order, and regiment in the Church. I nothing doubt but that Christian men should much better frame themselves to those heavenly Precepts which our Lord and Saviour with so great instancy gave, as concerning peace and unity, if we did all concur in desire to have the use of ancient Councils again renewed, rather than these proceedings continued, which either make all contentions endless, or bring them to one only determination, and that of all other the worst, which is by sword. It followeth therefore, that a new foundation being laid, we now adjoin hereunto that which cometh in the next place to be spoken of; namely, wherefore God hath himself by Scripture made known such Laws as serve for direction of men.

I x 14–15, 252–3

Natural Law is not contrary to Scripture; many aspects of it are to be found in the sacred writings. It guides us to the Will of God, who because of our fallen nature has given us also divine revelation. Little is known of Gratian except that in the twelfth century he wrote a treatise which collected and harmonized many judgments on ecclesiastical discipline and became the foundation of canon law in the Roman Catholic Church.

When supernatural duties are necessarily exacted, natural are not rejected as needless. The law of God therefore is though principally delivered for instruction in the one, yet fraught with precepts of the other also. The Scripture is fraught even with Laws of Nature. In so much that Gratian defining natural right (whereby is meant the right which exacteth those general duties, that concern men naturally even as they are men) termeth natural right that which the books of the Law and the Gospel do contain. Neither is it vain that the Scripture aboundeth with so great store of Laws in this kind. For they are either such as we of ourselves could not find out, and then the benefit is not small to have them readily set down to our hands, or if they be so cleared and manifest that no man endued with Reason can lightly be ignorant of them; yet the Spirit as it were borrowing them from the school of Nature as serving to prove things less manifest, and to induce a persuasion of somewhat which were in itself more hard and dark, unless it should in such sort be cleared, the very applying of them unto cases particular is not without most singular use and profit many ways for men's instruction. Besides, be they plain of themselves or obscure, the evidence of God's own testimonies added unto the natural assent of Reason concerning the certainty of them doth not a little comfort and confirm the same. Wherefore inasmuch as our actions are conversant about things beset with many circumstances, which cause men of sundry wits to be also of sundry judgments concerning that which ought to be done: requisite it cannot seem the rule of divine Law should herein help our imbecility that we might the more infallibly understand what is good. The first principles of the Law of Nature are easy, hard it were to find men ignorant of them: but concerning the duty which Nature's Law doth require at the hands of men in a number of things particular, so far hath the natural understanding even of sundry whole nations been darkened, that they have not discerned, no, not gross iniquity to be sin. Again, being so prone as we are to fawn upon ourselves, and to be ignorant as much as may be of our own deformities, without the feeling sense whereof we are most wretched, even so much the more, because not knowing them we cannot as much as desire to have them taken away: how should our festered sores be cured, but that God hath delivered a Law as sharp as the two edged sword, piercing the very closest and most unsearchable corners of the heart which the Law of Nature can hardly, human Laws by no means possible, reach unto? Hereby we know even secret concupiscence to be sin, and are made fearful to offend though it be but in a wandering cogitation. Finally of those things which are for the direction of all the parts of our life needful, and not impossible to be discerned by the light of Nature itself, are there not many which few men's natural capacity, and some which no man's have been able to find out? They are, saith Saint Augustine, but a few, and they indued with great ripeness of wit and judgment, free from all such affairs as might trouble their meditations, instructed in the sharpest and the subtlest points of learning, who have, and that very hardly, been able to find out but only the Immortality of the Soul. The Resurrection of the Flesh what man did ever at any time dream of having not heard it otherwise than from the school of Nature? Whereby it appeareth how much we are bound to yield unto our Creator the Father of all mercy eternal thanks, for that he hath delivered his Law unto the world, a Law wherein so many things are laid open clear and manifest; as a light which otherwise should have been buried in darkness, not without the hazard, or rather not with the hazard, but with the certain loss of infinite thousands of souls undoubtedly now saved. We see therefore that our sovereign good is desired naturally; that God the author of that natural desire had appointed natural means whereby to fulfil it; that man having utterly disabled his nature unto those means hath other revealed from God, and hath received from heaven a Law to teach him how that which is desired naturally must now be attained; finally we see that because those latter exclude not the former quite and clean as unnecessary, therefore together with such supernatural duties as could not possibly have been otherwise known to the world, the same Law that teacheth them, teacheth also with them such natural duties as could not by light of Nature easily have been known.

I xii 1–3, 262–4

Exposition of the place of Scripture, as giving all that is needed but also allowing development of belief; a first examination of the issue which occupies much of Book Three. Both Testaments are necessary, the Old as foreshadowing, and the New as proclaiming, the coming of Christ. Scripture contains all necessary for salvation, but God has given other guides as well. Unwritten traditions derived from the Apostles, but not those brought into the Church later by human authority, are to be followed. This would become a basic Anglican approach.

Albeit Scripture do profess to contain in it all things that are necessary unto salvation; yet the meaning cannot be simply of all things which are necessary, but all things that are necessary in some certain kind or form; as all things which are necessary, and either could not at all or could not easily be known by the light of natural discourse; all things which are necessary to be known that we may be saved; but known with presupposal of knowledge concerning certain principles whereof it receiveth us already persuaded, and then instructeth us in all the residue that are necessary. In the number of these principles, one is the sacred authority of Scripture. Being therefore persuaded by other means that these Scriptures are the Oracles of God, themselves do then teach us the rest, and lay before us all the duties which God requireth at our hands as necessary unto salvation. Further there hath been some doubt likewise, whether *containing in Scripture* do import express setting down in plain terms; or else comprehending, in such sort that by Reason, we may from thence conclude all things which are necessary. Against the former of these two constructions, instances have sundry ways been given. For our belief in the Trinity, the Co-eternity of the Son of God with his Father, the proceeding of the Spirit from the Father and the Son, the duty of baptizing infants: these with such other principal points, the necessity whereof is by none denied, are notwithstanding in Scripture nowhere to be found by express mention, only deduced they are out of Scripture by collection. This kind of comprehension in Scripture being therefore received, still there is no doubt how far we are to proceed by collection before the full and complete measure of things necessary be made up. For let us not think, that as long as the world doth endure, the wit of man shall be able to sound the bottom of that which may be concluded out of the Scripture; especially, if things contained by collection do so far extend, as to draw in whatsoever may be at any time out of Scripture but probably and conjecturally surmised. But let necessary collection be made requisite, and we may boldly deny, that of all those things which at this day are with so great necessity urged upon this Church under the name of reformed Church-discipline, there is any one which their books hitherto have made manifest to be contained in the Scripture. Let them, if they can, allege but one properly belonging to their cause, and not common to them and us, and show the deduction thereof out of Scripture to be necessary. It hath been already showed, how all things necessary unto salvation, in such sort as before we have maintained, must needs be possible for men to know; and that many things are in such sort necessary, the knowledge whereof is by the light of Nature impossible to be attained. Whereupon it followeth, that either all flesh is excluded from the possibility of salvation, which to think were most barbarous; or else, that God hath by supernatural means revealed the way of Life so far as doth suffice. For this cause, God hath so many times and ways spoken to the sons of men: neither hath he by speech only, but by writing also instructed and taught his Church. The cause of writing hath been, to the end that things by him revealed unto the world might have the longer continuance, and the greater certainty of assurance; by how much that which standeth on record hath in both those respects preeminence above that which passeth from hand to hand, and hath no pens but the tongues, no books but the ears of men to record it. The several books of Scripture having had each some several occasional and particular purpose which caused them to be written, the contents thereof are according to the exigence of that special end whereunto they are intended. Hereupon it groweth that every book of Holy Scripture doth take out of all kinds of truth, natural, historical, foreign, supernatural, so much as the matter handled requireth. Now forasmuch as there have been reasons alleged sufficient to conclude that all things necessary unto salvation must be made known, and that God himself hath therefore revealed his will, because otherwise men could not have known so much as is necessary; his surceasing to speak to the world, since the publishing of the Gospel of Jesus Christ, and the delivery of the same in writing, is unto us a manifest token that the way of salvation is now sufficiently opened, and that we need no other means for our full instruction than God hath already furnished us withal. The main drift of the whole New Testament is that which St John setteth down as the purpose of his own history, *These things are written, that ye might believe, that Jesus is Christ the Son of God, and that in believing ye might have life through his name*. The drift of the Old, that which the Apostle mentioneth to Timothy, *The Holy Scriptures are able to make thee wise unto salvation*. So that the general end both of Old and New is one; the difference between them consisting in this, that the Old did make wise by teaching salvation through Christ that should come; the New, by teaching that Christ the Saviour is come;

and that Jesus whom the Jews did crucify, and whom God did raise again from the dead, is he. When the Apostle therefore affirmeth unto Timothy, that the Old was able to make him wise to salvation, it was not his meaning, that the Old alone can do this unto us which live sithence the publication of the New. For he speaketh with presupposal of the doctrine of Christ, known also unto Timothy; and therefore first it is said, *Continue thou in those things which thou hast learned and art persuaded, knowing of whom thou hast been taught them.* Again, those Scriptures he granteth were able to make him wise to salvation; but he addeth, *through the faith which is in Christ.* Wherefore without the doctrine of the New Testament, teaching that Christ hath wrought the redemption of the world; which redemption the Old did foreshow he should work; it is not the former alone which can on our behalf perform so much as the Apostle doth avouch, who presupposeth this, when he magnifieth that so highly. And as his words concerning the books of ancient Scripture do not take place but with presupposal of the Gospel of Christ embraced; so our own words also, when we extol the complete sufficiency of the whole entire body of the Scripture, must in like sort be understood with this caution, that the benefit of Nature's light be not thought excluded as unnecessary, because the necessity of a diviner light is magnified. There is in Scripture therefore no defect, but that any man, what place or calling soever he hold in the Church or God, may have thereby the light of his natural understanding so perfected, that the one being relieved by the other, there can want no part of needful instruction unto any good work which God himself requireth, be it natural or supernatural, belonging simply unto men, as men; or unto men, as they are united in whatsoever kind of society. It sufficeth therefore that Nature and Scripture do serve in such full sort, that they both jointly, and not severally either of them, be so complete, that unto everlasting felicity, we need not the knowledge of anything more than these two may easily furnish our minds with on all sides. And therefore they which add Traditions as a part of supernatural necessary truth, have not the truth, but are in error. For they only plead, that whatsoever God revealeth as necessary for all Christian men to do or believe, the same we ought to embrace, whether we have received it by writing or otherwise, which no man denieth; when that which they should confirm, who claim so great reverence unto Traditions, is that the same Traditions are necessary to be acknowledged divine and holy. For we do not reject them only because they are not in the Scripture, but because they are neither in Scripture, nor can otherwise sufficiently by any reason be proved to be of God. That which is of God, and may be evidently proved to be so, we deny not but it hath in his kind, although unwritten, yet the self-same force and authority with the written Laws of God. It is by ours acknowledged, *That the Apostles did in every Church institute and ordain some rites and customs, serving for the seemliness of Church-regiment: which rites and customs they have not committed unto writing.* Those rites and customs being known to be Apostolical, and having the nature of things changeable, were no less to be accounted of in the Church, than other things of the like degree; that is to say, capable of like sort of alteration, although set down in the Apostles' writings. For both being known to be Apostolical, it is not the manner of delivering them unto the Church, but the author from whom they proceed, which doth give them their force and credit.

I xiv 1–5, 268–72

The argument is developed further. Natural Law and Reason are necessary as well as Divine Law; his opponents are wrong to maintain that the Divine Law is found only in Scripture. The present divisions in the Church are proof of their error.

As they rightly maintain, that God must be glorified in all things, and that the actions of men cannot tend unto his glory unless they be framed after this Law; so it is their error to think that the only Law which God hath appointed unto men in that behalf is the sacred Scripture. By that which we work naturally, as when we breathe, sleep, move, we set forth the glory of God as natural agents do, albeit we have no express purpose to make that our end, nor any advised determination therein to follow a Law, but do that we do (for the most part) not as much as thinking thereon. In reasonable and moral actions another Law taketh place; a Law, by the observation whereof we glorify God in such sort, as no creature else under man is able to do; because other creatures have not judgment to examine the quality of that which is done by them, and therefore in that they do they neither can accuse or approve themselves. Men do both, as the Apostle teacheth; yea, those men which have no written Law of God to show what is good or evil, carry written in their hearts the universal Law of mankind, the Law of Reason, whereby they judge as by a rule which God has given unto all men for that purpose. The Law of Reason doth somewhat direct men how to honour God as their Creator; but how to glorify God in such sort as is required, to the end that he may be an everlasting Saviour, this we are taught by divine Law, which Law both ascertaineth the truth, and supplieth unto us the want of that other Law. So that in moral actions, divine Law helpeth exceedingly the Law of Reason to guide man's life; but in supernatural it alone guideth. Proceed we further; let us place man in some public society with others, whether civil or spiritual; and in this case there is no remedy, but we must add yet a further Law. For although, even here likewise, the Laws of Nature and Reason be of necessary use; yet somewhat over and besides them is necessary, namely, human and positive Law, together with that Law which is commerce between grand societies, the Law of Nations, and of nations Christian. For which cause, the Law of God hath likewise said, *Let every soul be subject to the higher powers.* The public power in all societies is above every soul contained in the societies. And the principal use of that power is to give Laws unto all that are under it; which in such case we must obey, unless there be reason showed which may necessarily enforce that Law of Reason or of God doth enjoin the contrary; because, except our own private and but probable resolutions be by the Law of public determinations overruled, we take away all possibility of sociable life in the world. A plainer example whereof than ourselves we cannot have. How cometh it to pass, that we are at this present day so rent with mutual contentions, and that the Church is so much troubled about the polity of the Church? No doubt, if men had been willing to learn how many Laws their actions in this life are subject unto, and what the true force of each Law is, all these controversies might have died the very day they were first brought forth. It is both commonly said, and truly, that the best men otherwise are not always the best in regard of society. The reason whereof is, that the Law of men's actions is one, if they be respected only as men; and another, when they are considered as parts of a politic body. Many men there are, than whom nothing is more commendable when they are singled; and yet in society with others, less fit to answer the duties which are looked for at their hands. Yea, I am persuaded, that of them with whom in this cause we strive, there are whose betters among men would be hardly found, if they did not live amongst men, but in some wilderness by themselves. The cause of which their disposition so unframable unto societies wherein they live is, for that they discern not aright what place and force these several kinds of Laws ought to have in all their actions. Is their question either concerning the regiment of the Church in general, or about conformity between one Church and another, or of ceremonies, offices, powers, jurisdictions, in our own Church? Of all these things they judge by that rule which they frame to themselves with some little show of probability; and what seemeth

in that sort convenient, the same they think themselves bound to practise; the same by all means they labour mightily to uphold; whatsoever
any Law of man to the contrary hath determined, they weigh it not.
Thus by following the Law of private Reason, where the Law of public
should take place, they breed disturbance.

I xvi 5–6, 280–2

4

BOOK TWO

Concerning Sufficiency of
Holy Scripture

'Concerning their first position who urge Reformation in the Church of England: namely That Scripture is the only rule of all things, which in this life may be done by men.'

This Book takes up the chief point of disagreement between Hooker and the Puritans. He reverences the word of Scripture as much as they do, but is sure that it is not the sole sanction for human belief, conduct and government.

Not all of God's will is proved directly from Scripture. He has granted us also the gift of Wisdom.

In all parts of knowledge, rightly so termed, things most general are most strong. Thus it must be inasmuch as the certainty of our persuasion touching particulars, dependeth altogether upon the credit of those generalities out of which they grow. Albeit therefore every cause admit not such infallible evidence of proof as leaveth no possibility of doubt or scruple behind it; yet they who claim the general assent of the whole world unto that which they teach, and do not fear to give very hard and heavy sentence upon as many as refuse to embrace the same, must have special regard that their first formulations and grounds be more than slender probabilities. This whole question which hath been moved about the kind of Church-regiment we could not but for our own resolution sake endeavour to unrip and sift; following therein as near as we might, the conduct of that judicial method· which serveth best for invention of truth. By means whereof, having found this the head theorem of all their discourses, which plead for the change of

Ecclesiastical Government in England, namely *That the Scripture of God is in such sort the rule of human action, that simply whatsoever we do, and are not by it directed thereunto, the same is sin*; we hold it necessary that the proofs hereof be weighed. Be they of weight sufficient or otherwise, it is not ours to judge and determine; only what difficulties there are which as yet withhold our assent till we be further and better satisfied, I hope, no indifferent amongst them will scorn or refuse to hear. First, therefore, whereas they allege, *That Wisdom* doth teach men *every good way*; and have thereupon inferred that no way is good in any kind of action unless Wisdom do by Scripture lead unto it; see they not plainly how they restrain the manifold ways which Wisdom hath to teach men by unto one only way of teaching, which is by Scripture? The bounds of Wisdom are large, and within them much is contained. Wisdom was Adam's instructor in Paradise. Wisdom endued the Fathers who lived before the Law with the knowledge of holy things; by the Wisdom of the Law of God, David attained to excel others in understanding, and Solomon likewise to excel David by the self-same Wisdom of God, teaching many things besides the Law. The ways of well-doing are in number even as many, as are the kinds of voluntary actions; so that whatsoever we do in this world, and may do it ill, we show ourselves therein by well-doing to be wise. Now if Wisdom did teach men by Scripture not only all the ways that are right and good in some certain kind, according to that of St Paul concerning the use of Scripture, but did simply, without any manner of exception, restraint, or distinction, teach every way of doing well, there is no art but Scripture should teach it, because every art doth teach the way how to do something or other well. To teach men therefore Wisdom professeth, and to teach them every good Way; but not every good way by one way of teaching. Whatsoever either Men on Earth, or the Angels of Heaven do know, it is as a drop of that unemptiable fountain of Wisdom; which Wisdom hath diversely imparted her treasures unto the world. As her ways are of sundry kinds, so her manner of teaching is not merely one and the same. Some things she openeth by the sacred books of Scripture; some things by the glorious works of Nature; with some things she inspireth them from above by spiritual influence; in some things she leadeth and traineth them only by worldly experience and practice. We may not so in any special kind admire her that we disgrace her in any other; but let all her ways be according unto their place and degree adored.

II i 3–4, 288–90

He addresses the question of adiaphora; the many things which are nei-
ther enjoined nor forbidden in Scripture.

They still argue, *That wheresoever faith is wanting, there is sin; and, in*
every action not commanded, faith is wanting; ergo, in every action not
commanded, there is sin; I would demand of them first, forasmuch as
the nature of things indifferent is neither to be commanded nor forbidden, but left free and arbitrary; how there can be anything indifferent,
if for want of faith sin be committed, when anything not commanded
is done? So that of necessity they must add somewhat, and at leastwise
thus set it down: In every action not commanded of God, or permitted
with approbation, faith is wanting, and for want of faith there is sin.
The next thing we are to enquire is what those things be which God
permitteth with approbation, and how we may know them to be permitted? When there are to one end sundry means, as for example, for
the sustenance of our bodies many kinds of food, many sorts of raiment
to clothe our nakedness and so in other things of like condition: here
the end of itself being necessary, but not so any one mean thereunto;
necessary that our bodies should be both fed and clothed, howbeit one
kind of food or raiment necessary; therefore we hold these things free
in their own nature and indifferent. The choice is left to our own discretion, except a principal bond of some higher duty remove the indifferency that such things have in themselves. Their indifferency is removed,
if either we take away our own liberty, as Ananias did, for whom to
have sold or held his possessions it was indifferent till his solemn vow
and promise unto God had strictly bound him one only way; or if God
himself have precisely abridged the same, by restraining us thereunto,
or by barring us from some one or more things of many which otherwise were in themselves altogether indifferent. Many fashions of priestly attire there were, whereof Aaron and his sons might have had their
free choice without sin, but that God expressly tied them unto one. All
meats indifferent unto the Jew, were it not that God by name excepted
some, as swine's flesh. Impossible therefore it is we should otherwise
think, than that what things God doth neither command nor forbid, the
same he permitteth with approbation either to be done or left undone.
All things are lawful unto me, saith the Apostle, speaking as it seemeth
in the person of the Christian Gentile for maintenance of liberty in
things indifferent; whereunto his answer is, that nevertheless, *All things*
are not expedient; in things indifferent there is a choice, they are not
always equally expedient. Now in things although not commanded of
God, yet lawful, because they are permitted, the question is, what light

shall show us the conveniency which one hath above another? For answer, their final determination is that *whereas the Heathen did send*
men for the difference of good and evil to the light of Reason, in such
things the Apostle sendeth us to the school of Christ in his word, which
only is able through faith to give us assurance and resolution in our
doings. Which word *only*, is utterly without possibility of ever being
proved. For what if it were true concerning things indifferent, that unless the word of the Lord had determined of the free use of them, there
could have been no lawful use of them at all; which notwithstanding
is untrue; because it is not the Scripture's setting down such things
as indifferent, but their not setting down as necessary that doth make
them to be indifferent; yet this to our present purpose serveth nothing
to all. We enquire not now whether anything be free to be used which
Scripture hath not set down as free; but concerning things known and
acknowledged to be indifferent, whether particularly in choosing any-
one of them before another, we sin, if anything but Scripture direct
us in this our choice. When many meats are set before me, all are indifferent, none unlawful; I take one as most convenient. If Scripture
require me to do so, then is not the thing indifferent, because I must
do what Scripture requireth. They are all indifferent; I might take any;
Scripture doth not require of me to make any special choice of one;
I do notwithstanding make choice of one, my discretion teaching me
so to do. A hard case, that hereupon I should be justly condemned
of sin.

II iv 3–5, 295–7

Scripture needs interpretation, and human judgment must be respect-
ed, in this as in other matters of accepted knowledge. It is a Christian
humanist approach, typical of Renaissance thought and acceptable to
some, but not the more extreme, Reformers.

An earnest desire to draw all things unto the determination of bare and
naked Scripture, hath caused here much pains to be taken in abating
the estimation and credit of man. Which if we labour to maintain as
far as truth and reason will bear, let not any think that we travel about
a matter not greatly needful. For the scope of all their pleading against
man's authority, is to overthrow the orders, laws, and constitutions in
the Church as depending thereupon, if they should therefore be taken
away, would peradventure leave neither face nor memory of Church to
continue long in the world, the world especially being such as now it
is. That which they have in this case spoken, I would for brevity sake

let pass, but that the drift of their speech being so dangerous, their words are not to be neglected. Wherefore to say that simply an argument taken from man's authority doth hold no way, neither affirmatively nor negatively, is hard. By a man's authority we here understand the force which his word hath for the assurance of another's mind that buildeth upon it; as the Apostle somewhat did upon their report of the house of Chloe; and the Samaritans in a matter of far greater moment upon the report of a simple woman. For so it is said in St John's Gospel, *Many of the Samaritans of that city believed in him for the saying of the woman, which testified, He hath told me all things that ever I did.* The strength of man's authority is affirmatively such that the weightiest affairs in the world depend thereon. In judgment and justice are not hereupon proceedings grounded? Saith not the Law, that *in the mouth of two or three witnesses every word shall be confirmed*? This the Law of God would not say, if there were in a man's testimony no force at all to prove any thing. And if it be admitted that in matter of fact there is some credit to be given to the testimony of man, but not in matter of opinion and judgment, we see the contrary both acknowledged and universally practised also throughout the world. The sentences of wise and expert men were never but highly esteemed. Let the title of a man's right be called in question, are we not bold to rely and build upon the judgment of such as are famous for their skill in the Laws of this land? In matter of State, the weight many times of some one man's authority is thought reason sufficient even to sway over whole nations. And this is not only with the simpler sort, but the learneder and wiser we are, the more such arguments in such cases prevail with us. The reason why the simpler sort are moved with authority, is the conscience of their own ignorance; whereby it cometh to pass that, having learned men in admiration, they rather fear to dislike them than know wherefore they should allow and follow their judgments. Contrariwise with them that are skilful, authority is much more strong and forcible; because they only are able to discern how just cause there is why to some men's authority so much should be attributed. For which cause the name of Hippocrates (no doubt) was more effectual to persuade even such men as Galen himself than to move a silly empiric. So that the very self-same argument in this kind which doth but induce the vulgar sort to like, may constrain the wiser to yield. And therefore not orators only with the people, but even the very profoundest disputers in all faculties have thereby often with the best learned prevailed most. As for arguments taken from human authority, and that negatively, for example sake, if we should think the assembling of the people of God together by the sound of a bell, the presenting of infants at the holy font by such as we commonly call their Godfathers, or any other the like received custom, to be impious, because some men of whom we think very reverently have in their books and writings nowhere mentioned or taught that such things should be in the Church, this reasoning were subject unto just reproof it were but feeble, weak, and unsound. Notwithstanding even negatively an argument from human authority may be strong, as namely thus: the Chronicles of England mention no more than only six Kings bearing the name of Edward since the time of the last conquest; therefore it cannot be there should be more. So that if the question be of the authority of a man's testimony, we cannot simply avouch either that affirmatively it doth not any way hold, or that it hath only force to induce the simpler sort and not to constrain men of understanding and ripe judgment to yield assent; or that negatively it hath in it no strength at all. For unto every of these the contrary is most plain. Neither doth that which is alleged concerning the infirmity of men overthrow or disprove this. Men are blinded with ignorance and error; many things escape them; and in many things they may be deceived; yea, those things which they do know, they may either forget, or upon sundry indirect considerations let pass; and although themselves do not err, yet may they through malice or vanity even of purpose deceive others. Howbeit, infinite cases there are wherein all these impediments and lets are so manifestly excluded, that there is no show or colour whereby any such exception may be taken, but that the testimony of man will stand as a ground of infallible assurance. That there is a city of Rome, that Pius Quintus and Gregory the Thirteenth and others have been Popes of Rome, I suppose we are certainly enough persuaded. The ground of our persuasion, who never saw the place nor persons before named, can be nothing but man's testimony. Will any man here notwithstanding allege those mentioned human infirmities as reasons why these things should be mistrusted or doubted of? Yea, that which is more, utterly to infringe the force and strength of man's testimony were to shake the very fortress of God's truth. For whatsoever we believe concerning salvation by Christ, although the Scripture be therein the ground of our belief; yet the authority of man is, if we mark it, the key which openeth the door of entrance into the knowledge of the Scripture. The Scripture doth not teach us the things that are of God, unless we did credit men who have taught us that the words of Scripture do signify those things. Some way therefore, notwithstanding man's infirmity, yet his authority may enforce assent.

II vii 1–3, 318–21

Despite the foregoing argument, individual human opinions should not prevail against Reason. There is danger in private interpretations of Scripture as practised by some Puritan individuals and groups.

That authority of men should prevail with men either against or above Reason, is no part of our belief. Companies of learned men, be they never so great and reverend, are to yield unto Reason, the weight whereof is by no whit prejudiced by the simplicity of his person which doth allege it but being found to be sound and good, the bare opinion of men to the contrary must of necessity stoop and give place. Irenaeus writing against Marcion, which held one God author of the Old Testament and another of the New, to prove that the Apostles preached the same God which was known before to the Jews, he copiously allegeth sundry their sermons and speeches uttered concerning that matter and recorded in Scripture. And lest any should be wearied with such store of allegations, in the end he concludeth, *While we labour for these demonstrations out of Scripture, and do summarily declare the things which many ways have been spoken, be contented quietly to hear, and do not think my speech tedious. Because demonstrations that are in Scripture may not otherwise be showed, than by citing them out of the Scriptures themselves where they are.* Which words make so little unto the purpose, that they seem, as it were, offended at him which hath called them thus solemnly forth to say nothing. And concerning the verdict of St Jerome, if no man, be he never so well learned, have after the Apostles any authority to publish new doctrine as from Heaven, and to require the world's assent as unto truth received by prophetical revelation; doth this prejudice the credit of learned men's judgments in opening that truth, which by being conversant in the Apostles' writings, they have themselves it from thence learned? St Augustine exhorted not to hear men, but to hearken what God speaketh. His purpose is (I think) that we should stop our ears against his own exhortation, and therefore he cannot mean simply that audience should be altogether be denied unto men; but either that if men speak one thing, and God himself teach another, then he, not they, is to be obeyed; or if they both speak the same thing, yet then also man's speech is unworthy of hearing, not simply, but in comparison of that which proceedeth from the mouth of God. Yea, but we doubt what the will of God is. Are we in this case forbidden to hear what men of judgment think it to be? If not, then the allegation also might very well have been spared. In that ancient strife which was between the Catholic Fathers and Arians, Donatists and others of like perverse and froward disposition, as long as to Fathers or Councils alleged on the one side, the like by the contrary side were opposed, impossible it was that ever the question should by this means grow unto any issue or end. The Scripture they both believed; the Scripture they knew could not give sentence on both sides; by Scripture the controversy between them was such as might be determined. In this case what madness was it with such kinds of proofs to nourish their contention when there were such effectual means to end all controversy that was between them? Hereby therefore it doth not as yet appear that an argument of authority of man affirmatively is in matters divine nothing worth. Which opinion being once inserted into the minds of the vulgar sort, what it may grow unto God knoweth. Thus much we see, it hath already made thousands so headstrong even in gross and palpable errors that a man whose capacity will scarce serve him to utter five words in sensible manner, blusheth not, in any doubt concerning matter of Scripture to think his own bare *Yea*, as good as the *Nay* of all the wise, grave, and learned judgments that are in the whole world: which insolency must be repressed, or it will be the very bane of Christian religion.

II vii 6, 325–7

He ends the Second Book with a denial of the right to add rules and authority to Scripture, a response to the Roman claims for Church tradition. More particularly he rejects the Puritan way of regarding as sinful anything not specifically in Scripture. Not all done through Natural Law and Reason without Scriptural warrant is sin.

What the Scripture purposeth, the same in all points it doth perform. Howbeit, that here we swerve not in judgment, one thing especially we must observe, namely, that the absolute perfection of Scripture is seen by relation unto that end whereto it tendeth. And even hereby it cometh to pass, that first such as imagine the general drift of the body of sacred Scripture not to be so large as it is, nor that God did thereby intend to deliver, as in truth he doth, a full instruction in all things unto salvation necessary, the knowledge whereof man by nature could not otherwise in this life attain unto; they are by this very mean induced either still to look for new revelations from Heaven, or else dangerously to add to the word of God uncertain traditions, that so the doctrine of man's salvation may be complete. Which doctrine we constantly hold in all respect with any such thing added to be so complete, that we utterly refuse as much as once to acquaint ourselves with anything further. Whatsoever to make up the doctrine of man's salvation is added as in supply of the Scripture's unsufficiency, we reject it. Scripture purposing this hath perfectly and fully done it. Again, the scope and purpose of God in delivering the Holy Scripture, such as do take more largely than behoveth, they on the contrary side racking and stretching it further than by him was meant, are drawn into sundry as great inconveniences. Those pretending the Scripture's perfection, infer thereupon that in Scripture all things lawful to be done must needs be contained. We count those things perfect which want nothing requisite of the end whereto they were instituted. As therefore God created every part and particle of man exactly perfect, that is to say, in all points sufficient unto that use for which he appointed it; so the Scripture, yea, every sentence thereof, is perfect, and wanteth nothing requisite unto that purpose for which God delivered the same. So that if hereupon we conclude, that because the Scripture is perfect, therefore all things lawful to be done are comprehended in the Scripture; we may even as well conclude so of every sentence, as of the whole sum and body thereof, unless we first of all prove that it was the drift, scope, and purpose of Almighty God in Holy Scripture to comprise all things which man may practise. But admit this, and mark, I beseech you what would follow. God in delivering Scripture to his Church should clean have abrogated amongst them the Law of Nature, which is an infallible knowledge imprinted in the minds of all the children of men, whereby both general principles for directing of human actions are comprehended, and conclusions derived from them; upon which conclusions groweth in particularity the choice of good and evil in the daily affairs of this life. Admit this, and what shall the Scripture be but a snare and a torment to weak consciences, filling them with infinite perplexities, scrupulosities, doubts insoluble, and extreme despairs? Not that the Scripture itself doth cause any such thing, (for it tendeth to the clean contrary, and the fruit thereof is resolute assurance and certainty, in that it teacheth) but the necessities of this life urging men to do that which the light of Nature, common discretion; and judgment of itself directeth them unto; on the other side, this doctrine teaching them that so to do were to sin against their own souls, and that they put forth their hands to iniquity whatsoever they go about and have not first the sacred Scripture of God for direction; how can it choose but bring the simple a thousand times to their wits' end? How can it choose but vex and amaze them? For in every action of common life to find out some sentence clearly and infallibly setting before our eyes what we ought to do (seem we in Scripture never so expert) would trouble us more than we are aware. In weak and tender minds we little know what misery this strict opinion would breed, besides the stops it would make in the whole course of all men's lives and actions. Make all things sin which we do by direction of Nature's light and by the rule of common discretion without thinking at all upon Scripture; admit this position, and parents shall cause their children to sin as oft as they cause them to do anything before they come to years of capacity, and be ripe for knowledge in the Scripture. Admit this, and it shall not be with masters as it was with him in the Gospel; but servants *being commanded to go*, shall stand still till they have their errand warranted unto them by Scripture. Which, as it standeth with Christian duty in some cases, so in common affairs to require it were most unfit. Two opinions therefore there are concerning sufficiency of Holy Scripture, each extremely opposite unto the other, and both repugnant unto truth. The schools of Rome teach Scripture to be unsuffficient, as if, except traditions were added, it did not contain all revealed and supernatural truth which absolutely is necessary for the children of men in this life to know that they may in the next be saved. Others, justly condemning this opinion, grow likewise unto a dangerous extremity, as if Scripture did not only contain all things in that kind necessary, but all things simply, and in such sort that to do any thing according to any other Law were not only unnecessary, but even opposite unto salvation, unlawful and sinful. Whatsoever is spoken of God, or things appertaining to God, otherwise than as the truth is, though it seem an honour, it is an injury. And as incredible praises given unto men do often abate and impair the credit of their deserved commendation; so we must likewise take great heed lest, in attributing unto Scripture more than it can have, the incredibility of that do cause even those things which indeed it hath most abundantly to be less reverently esteemed. I therefore leave it to themselves to consider, whether they have in this first point overshot themselves or not; which, God doth know, is quickly done, even when our meaning is most sincere, as I am verily persuaded theirs in this case was.

II viii 5–7, 333–6

5

BOOK THREE

That which the general principles and rules of Scripture potentially claim

'Concerning their second assertion, that in Scripture there must be of necessity contained a form of Church-polity, the Laws whereof may in no wise be altered.'

After his contention that the authority of Scripture does not exclude other gifts of discernment given by God, Hooker comes to the issue which was particularly disturbing the ecclesiastical establishment: the claim that Scripture had laid down immutable rules for the structure and government of the Church. The visible Church in this world needs clear laws of polity.

Many are members of the visible Church admitted by baptism, even if they have fallen away from their profession. The invisible, spiritual Church is beyond our understanding.

Albeit the substance of those controversies whereinto we have begun to wade, be rather of outward things appertaining to the Church of Christ, than of anything wherein the nature and being of the Church consisteth: yet because the subject or matter which this position concerneth is a form of Church Government, or Church-polity; it therefore behoveth us so far forth to consider the nature of the Church, as is requisite for men's more clear and plain understanding in what respects of polity or Government are necessary thereunto. That Church of Christ, which we properly term his body mystical, can be but one; neither can that one be sensibly discerned by any man, inasmuch as the parts thereof are some in heaven already with Christ, and the rest that are on earth (albeit their natural persons be visible) we do not discern under this property whereby they are truly and infallibly of that body. Only our minds by intellectual conceit are able to apprehend that such a real body there is, a body collective, because it containeth an huge multitude; a body mystical, because the mystery of their conjunction is removed altogether from sense. Whatsoever we read in Scripture concerning the endless love and the saving mercy which God showeth towards his Church, the only proper subject thereof is this Church. Concerning this flock it is that our Lord and Saviour hath promised, *I give unto them eternal life, and they shall never perish, neither shall any pluck them out from my hand.* They who are of this society have such marks and notes of distinction from all others, as are not objects unto our sense; only unto God who seeth their hearts, and understandeth all their secret cogitations, unto him they are clear and manifest. All men knew Nathanael to be an Israelite; but our Saviour piercing deeper giveth further testimony of him than men could have done, with such certainty as he did; *Behold indeed an Israelite, in whom there is no guile.* If we profess as Peter did, that we love the Lord and profess it in the hearing of men, Charity is prone to believe all things, and therefore charitable we are likely to think we do so, as long as they see no proof to the contrary. But that our love is sound and sincere, that it cometh from *a pure heart, a good conscience, and a faith unfeigned*, who can pronounce, saving only the Searcher of all men's hearts, who alone intuitively doth know in this kind who are his? And as those everlasting promises of love, mercy, and blessedness, belong to the mystical Church; even so on the other side, when we read of any duty which the Church of God is bound unto, the Church whom this doth concern is a sensible known company. And this visible Church in like sort is but one, continued from the first beginning of the world to the last end. Which company being divided into two moieties, the one before, the other since the coming of Christ, that part which since the coming of Christ partly hath embraced and partly shall hereafter embrace the Christian Religion, we term, as by a more proper name, the Church of Christ. And therefore the Apostle affirmeth plainly of all men Christian, that be they Jews or Gentiles, bond or free, they are all incorporated into one company, they all make but *one body*. The unity of which visible Body and Church of Christ consisteth in that uniformity which all several persons thereunto belonging have by reason of that *one Lord*, whose servants they all profess themselves; that *one Faith*, which they all acknowledge; that *one Baptism*, wherewith they are all initiated. The visible Church of Jesus Christ is therefore one, in outward profession of those things which supernaturally appertain to the very essence of Christianity, and are necessarily required in every particular Christian man. [. . .] Now although we know the Christian Faith, and allow of it, yet in this respect we are but entering; entered we are not into the visible Church before our admittance by the door of Baptism. Wherefore immediately upon the acknowledgment of Christian Faith, the Eunuch (we see) was baptized by Philip, Paul by Ananias, by Peter a huge multitude containing three thousand souls; which being once baptized, were reckoned in the number of souls added to the visible Church. As for those virtues which belong unto moral righteousness and honesty of life, we do not mention them, because they are not proper unto Christian men, as they are Christians, but do concern them as they are men. True it is, the want of these virtues excludeth from salvation. So doth much more the absence of inward belief of heart; so doth despair and lack of hope; so emptiness of Christian love and charity. But we speak now of the visible Church, whose children are signed with this mark, *One Lord, one Faith, one Baptism.* In whomsoever these things are, the Church doth acknowledge them for her children; them only she holdeth for aliens and strangers, in whom these things are not found. For want of these it is, that Saracens, Jews, and Infidels are excluded out of the bounds of the Church. Others we may not deny to be of the visible Church, as long as these things are not wanting in them. For apparent it is, that all men are of necessity either Christians, or not Christians. If by external profession they be Christians, then they are of the visible Church of Christ; and Christians by external profession they are all, whose marks of recognizance hath in it those things which we have mentioned, yea, although they be impious Idolaters, wicked Heretics, persons excommunicable, yea, and cast out for notorious improbity. Such withal we deny not to be the imps and limbs of Satan, even as long as they continue such. Is it then possible, that the self-same men should belong both to the Synagogue of Satan, and to the Church of Jesus Christ? Unto that Church which is his mystical body, not possible; because that body consisteth of none but only true Israelites, true sons of Abraham, true servants and saints of God. Howbeit of the visible Body and Church of Jesus Christ, those may be, and oftentimes are, in respect of the main parts of their outward profession, who in regard of their inward disposition of mind, yea, of external conversation, yea, even of some parts of their very profession, are most worthily both hateful in the sight of God himself, and in the eyes of the sounder part of the visible Church most execrable. Our Saviour therefore compareth the *kingdom of heaven to a net* whereunto all which cometh neither is nor seemeth fish; his Church he compareth unto a field, where tares manifestly known and seen by all men do grow, intermingled with good corn; and even so shall continue till the final consummation of the world. God hath had ever, and ever shall have, God's Church visible upon earth.

III i 1–8, 338–43

The claim of the Church of England to be Catholic and Reformed. Luther did not begin a new church. The Church of England is part of the continuing universal Church. Heretics are not totally cut off from the Church, nor are Roman Catholics, a concession which seems embarrassingly arrogant today but was not unusual at the time.

They ask us where our Church did lurk, in what cave of the earth it slept for so many hundreds of years together, before the birth of Martin Luther? As if it were of opinion, that Luther did erect a new Church of Christ. No, the Church of Christ which was from the beginning is, and continueth unto the end: of which Church all parts have not been always equally sincere and sound. [. . .] In St Paul's time the integrity of Rome was famous; Corinth many ways reproved; they of Galatia much more out of square. In St John's time, Ephesus and Smyrna in far better state than Thyatira and Pergamus were. We hope therefore, that to reform ourselves, if at any time we have done amiss, is not to sever ourselves from the Church we were of before. In the Church we were, and we are so still. Other difference between our estate before and now we know none, but only such as we see in Judah; which having sometime been idolatrous, became afterwards more soundly religious, by renouncing idolatry and superstition. [. . .] The indisposition therefore of the Church of Rome to reform herself, must be no stay unto us from performing our duty to God; even as desire of retaining conformity with them would be no excuse if we did not perform that duty. Notwithstanding so far as lawfully we may, we have held and do hold fellowship with them. For even as the Apostle doth say of Israel, that they are in one respect enemies, but in another beloved, of God; in like sort with Rome, we dare not communicate concerning sundry her gross and grievous abominations; yet touching those main parts of Christian truth wherein they constantly still persist, we gladly acknowledge them to be of the family of Jesus Christ; and our hearty prayer unto God Almighty is, that being conjoined so far forth with them, they may at the length (if it be his will) so yield to frame and reform themselves, that no distraction remain in anything, but that *we all may with one heart and one mouth glorify God the Father of our Lord and Saviour*, whose Church we are. As there are which make the Church of Rome utterly no church at all, by reason of so many, so grievous errors in their doctrines; so we have them amongst us, who, under pretence of imagined corruptions in our discipline, do give even as hard a judgment of the Church of England itself. But whatsoever either the one sort or the other teach, we must acknowledge even Heretics themselves to be, though, a maimed part, yet a part of the visible Church. If an Infidel should pursue to death an Heretic, professing Christianity only for Christian profession sake, could we deny unto him the honour of martyrdom? Yet this honour all men know to be proper unto the Church. Heretics therefore are not utterly cut off from the visible Church of Christ.

III i 10–11, 346–8

The Church is not an assembly, but a society. All churches require ecclesiastical polity, and no form of polity is set down in Scripture as necessary for all.

For preservation of Christianity there is not anything more needful, than that such as are of the visible Church have mutual fellowship and society one with another. In which consideration, as the main body of the sea being one, yet within divers precincts hath divers names; so the Catholic Church is in like sort divided into a number of distinct societies, every of which is termed a Church within itself. In this sense the Church is always a visible society of men; not an assembly, but a society. For although the name of the Church be given unto Christian assemblies, although any number of men congregated may be termed by the name of a Church, yet assemblies properly are rather things that belong to a Church. Men are assembled for performance of public actions; which actions being ended, the assembly dissolveth itself, and is no longer in being; whereas the Church which was assembled doth no less continue afterwards than before. *Where but three are, and they of the laity also*, saith Tertullian, *yet there is a Church*; that is to say, a Christian assembly. But a Church, as now we are to understand it, is a society; that is, a number of men belonging unto some Christian fellowship, the place and limits whereof are certain. That wherein they have communion, is the public exercise of such duties as those mentioned in the Apostles' Acts, *Instruction, breaking of bread, and prayer*. As therefore they that are of the mystical body of Christ, have those inward graces and virtues wherein they differ from all others which are not of the same body; again, whosoever appertain to the visible body of the Church, they have also the notes of external profession, whereby the world knoweth what they are: after the same manner, even the several

societies of Christian men, unto every of which the name of a Church
is given, with addition betokening severally, as the Church of Rome,
Corinth, Ephesus, England, and so the rest, must be endued with correspondent general properties belonging unto them as they are public
Christian societies. And of such properties common unto all societies
Christian, it may not be denied that one of the very chiefest is Ecclesiastical Polity. Which word I therefore the rather use, because the name
of government, as commonly men understand it in ordinary speech,
doth not comprise the largeness of that whereunto in this question it
is applied. For when we speak of government, what doth the greatest part conceive thereby, but only the exercise of superiority peculiar
unto rulers and guides of others? To our purpose therefore the name of
Church-polity will better serve, because it containeth both government,
and also whatsoever besides belongeth to the ordering of the Church in
public. Neither is any thing in this degree more necessary than Church-
polity, which is a form of ordering the public spiritual affairs of the
Church of God.

But we must note, that he which affirmeth speech to be necessary
amongst all men throughout the world doth not thereby import that
all men must necessarily speak one kind of language; even so the necessity of Polity and Regiment in all Churches may be held without holding any one certain form to be necessary in them all; nor is it possible
that any form of Polity, much less of Polity Ecclesiastical, should be
good, unless God himself be the author of it. *Those things that are not
of God*, (saith Tertullian) *they can have no other than God's adversary
for their author*. Be it whatsoever in the Church of God, if it be not of
God, we hate it. Of God it must be; either as those things sometimes
were, which God supernaturally revealed, and so delivered them unto
Moses for government of the commonwealth of Israel; or else as those
things which men find out by help of that light which God hath given
them unto that end; The very Law of Nature itself, which no man can
deny but God hath instituted, is not of God, unless that be of God
whereof God is the author as well this latter way as the former. But
forasmuch as no form of Church-polity is thought by them to be lawful, or to be of God, unless God be so the author of it that it be also set
down in Scripture; they should tell us plainly, whether their meaning
be that it must be there set down in whole, or in part. For if wholly, let
them show what one form of Polity ever was so. Their own to be taken
out of Scripture they will not affirm; neither deny they that in part,
even this which they so much oppugn is also from thence taken. Again,
they should tell us, whether only that be taken out of Scripture which

is actually and particularly there set down; or else that also which the general principles and rules of Scripture potentially contain. The one way they cannot so much as pretend, that all the parts of their own discipline are in Scripture; and the other way their mouths are stopped, when they would plead against all other forms besides their own; seeing their general principles are such as do not particularly prescribe any one, but sundry may equally be consonant unto the general axioms of the Scripture.

III i 14 — ii 1, 351–3

We do not impugn or disobey Scripture by Church organization not explicitly enjoined in it. Anglicans are as faithful as any to the authority of Scripture.

Now it can be to Nature no injury that of her we can say the same which diligent beholders of her works have observed; namely, that she provideth for all living creatures nourishment that may suffice; that she bringeth forth no kind of creature whereto she is wanting in that which is needful: although we do not so far magnify her exceeding bounty, as to affirm that she bringeth into the world the sons of men adorned with gorgeous attire, or maketh costly buildings to spring up out of the earth for them; so I trust that to mention what the Scripture of God leaveth unto the Church's discretion in some things, is not in anything to impair the honour which the Church of God yieldeth to the sacred Scriptures' perfection. Wherein seeing that no more is by us maintained, than only that Scripture must needs teach the Church whatsoever is in such sort necessary as hath been set down; and that it is no more disgrace for Scripture to have left a number of other things free to be ordered at the discretion of the Church, than for Nature to have left it to the wit of man to devise his own attire, and not to look for it as the beasts of the field have theirs: if neither this can import, nor any other proof sufficient be brought forth, that we either will at any time or ever did affirm the sacred Scripture to comprehend no more than only those bare necessaries; if we acknowledge that as well for particular application to special occasions, as also in other manifold respects, infinite treasures of wisdom are over and besides abundantly to be found in the Holy Scripture; yea, that scarcely there is any noble part of knowledge worthy the mind of man but from thence it may have some direction and light; yea, that although there be no necessity it should of purpose prescribe any one particular form of Church-government, yet touching the manner of governing in general, the precepts that Scripture setteth down are not few, and the examples many, which it proposeth for all Church governors even in particularities to follow; yea, that those things, finally, which are of principal weight in the very particular form of Church-polity, (although not that form which they imagine, but that which we against them uphold) are in the self-same Scriptures contained; if all this be willingly granted by us, which are accused to pin the Word of God in so narrow a room as that it should be able to direct us but in principal points of our Religion; or as though the substance of Religion, or some rude and unfashioned matter of building the Church were uttered in them, and those things left out that should pertain to the form and fashion of it; let the cause of the accused be referred to the accuser's own conscience, and let that judge whether this accusation be deserved where it hath been laid.

III iv 1, 357–8

Reason is not an enemy of faith, and if properly applied is to be used and honoured in Christian teaching. This is an important passage which comes to the heart of one of Hooker's principal disagreements with the Puritans.

An opinion hath spread itself very far in the world; as if the way to be ripe in Faith were to be raw in wit and judgment; as if Reason were an enemy unto Religion, childish Simplicity the mother of ghostly and divine Wisdom. The cause why such declamations prevail so greatly is, for that men suffer themselves in two respects to be deluded. One is, that the wisdom of man being debased in comparison with that of God, or in regard of some special thing exceeding the reach and compass thereof, it seemeth to them (not marking so much) as if simply it were condemned. Another, that learning, knowledge or wisdom falsely so termed, usurping a name whereof they are not worthy, and being under that name controlled; their reproof is by so much the more easily misapplied, and through equivocation wrested against those things whereunto so precious names do properly and of right belong. This, duly observed, doth to the former allegations of itself make sufficient answer. Howbeit, for all men's plainer and fuller satisfaction; first, concerning the inability of Reason, to search out and to judge of things divine, if they be such as those properties of God and those duties of men towards him which may be conceived by attentive consideration of heaven and earth; we know that of mere natural men, the Apostle testifieth, *How they knew both God, and the Law of God.* Other things of God there be, which are neither so found, nor, though they be showed can ever be approved without the special operation of God's good Grace and Spirit. Of such things sometime spake the Apostle St Paul, declaring how Christ had called him to be a witness of his death and resurrection from the dead, according to that which the prophets and Moses had foreshowed. Festus, a mere natural man, an Infidel a Roman, one whose ears were unacquainted with such matter, heard him, but could not reach unto that whereof he spake; the suffering, and the rising of Christ from the dead, he rejected as idle superstitious fancies not worth the hearing; The Apostle that knew them by the Spirit, and spake of them with power of the Holy Ghost, seemed in his eyes but learnedly mad. Which example maketh manifest what elsewhere the same Apostle teacheth, namely, that Nature hath need of Grace, whereunto I hope we are not opposite, by holding that Grace hath use of Nature. Secondly, Philosophy we are warranted to take heed of; not that Philosophy which is true and sound knowledge attained by natural discourse of Reason; but that Philosophy which to bolster Heresy or Error casteth a fraudulent show of Reason upon things which are indeed unreasonable; and by that mean, as by a stratagem, spoileth the simple which are not able to withstand such cunning. *Take heed lest any spoil you through Philosophy and vain deceit.* He that exhorteth to beware of an enemy's policy, doth not give counsel to be impolitic; but rather to use all prudent foresight and circumspection, lest our simplicity be over-reached by cunning sleights. The way not to be inveigled by them that are so guileful through skill is thoroughly to be instructed in that which maketh skilful against guile; and to be armed with that true and sincere Philosophy, which doth teach against that deceitful and vain which spoileth. Thirdly, but many great Philosophers have been very unsound in belief: and many sound in belief have been also great Philosophers. Could secular knowledge bring the one sort unto the love of Christian Faith? Nor Christian Faith, the other sort out of love with secular knowledge. The harm that heretics did, they did it unto such as were unable to discern between sound and deceitful reasoning; and the remedy against it was ever the skill which the ancient Fathers had to discover such deceit. [. . .] Heresy prevaileth only by a counterfeit show of Reason; whereby notwithstanding it becometh invincible, unless it be convicted of fraud by manifest remonstrance, clearly true, and unable to be withstood. When therefore the Apostle requireth ability to convict heretics, can we think he judgeth it a thing unlawful, and not rather needful to use the principal instrument of their conviction, the light of Reason.

III viii 4–8, 366–8

*Continuing his strong defence of Reason; Scripture does not always give
direct command, and Reason must be applied. Human authority may
make laws for the Church, following the light of Reason.*

The operations of the Spirit, especially these ordinary which be common unto all true Christian men, are, as we know, things secret and
undiscernible even to the very soul where they are, because their nature
is of another and an higher kind than that they can be by us perceived
in this life. Wherefore albeit the Spirit lead us into all truth, and direct
us in all goodness; yet because these workings of the Spirit are so privy
and secret, we therefore stand on a plainer ground, when we gather by
Reason from the quality of things believed or done that the Spirit of
God hath directed us in both; than if we settle ourselves to believe or
to do any certain particular thing as being moved thereto by the Spirit.
But of this enough. To go from the books of Scripture, to the sense
and meaning thereof, because the sentences which are by the Apostles
recited out of the Psalms, to prove the resurrection of Jesus Christ, did
not prove it, if so be the Prophet David meant them of himself. This exposition therefore they plainly disprove, and show by manifest Reason
that of David the words of David could not possibly be meant. Exclude
the use of natural reasoning about the sense of Holy Scripture, concerning the Articles of our Faith, and then that the Scripture doth concern
the Articles of our Faith who can assure us? That which by right exposition buildeth up Christian Faith, being misconstrued breedeth error;
between true and false construction, the difference Reason must show.
Can Christian men perform that which Peter requireth at their hands?
Is it possible they should both believe and be able without the use of
Reason, to *render a reason of their belief*, a reason sound and sufficient
to answer them that demand it, be they of the same Faith with us, or
enemies thereunto? May we cause our Faith without Reason to appear
reasonable in the eyes of men? This being required even of learners in
the school of Christ, the duty of their teachers in bringing them unto
such ripeness must needs be somewhat more than only to read the sentences of Scripture, and then paraphrastically to scholy them, to vary
them with sundry forms of speech, without arguing or disputing about
anything which they contain. This method of teaching may commend
itself unto the world by that easiness and facility which is in it; but
a law or a pattern it is not, as some do imagine, for all men to follow that will do good in the Church of Christ. Our Lord and Saviour
himself did hope by disputation to do some good, yea, by disputation
not only of, but against the truth, albeit with purpose for the truth.

That Christ should be the Son of David, was truth; yet against this truth, our Lord in the Gospel objecteth: *If Christ be the Son of David, how doth David call him Lord?* There is as yet no way known how to dispute, or to determine of things disputed, without the use of natural Reason. If we please to add unto Christ their example, who followed him as near in all things as they could, the sermon of Paul and Barnabas, set down in the Acts, where the people would have offered unto them sacrifice; in that sermon what is there, but only natural Reason to disprove their act? *O men, why do ye these things? We are men even subject to the self-same passions, with you: we preach unto you to leave these vanities, and to turn to the living God, the God that hath not left himself without witness; in that he hath done good to the world, giving rain and fruitful seasons, filling our hearts with joy and gladness.* Neither did they only use Reason in winning such unto a Christian belief, as were yet thereto unconverted, but with believers themselves they followed the self-same course. In that great and solemn assembly of believing Jews, how doth Peter prove that the Gentiles were partakers of the grace of God, as well as they, but by Reason drawn from those effects which were apparently known amongst them: *God, which knoweth the hearts, hath borne them witness in giving unto them the Holy Ghost, as unto you.* The light therefore, which the star of natural Reason and wisdom casteth, is too bright to be obscured by the mist of a word or two uttered to diminish that opinion which justly hath been received concerning the force and virtue thereof, even in matters that touch most nearly the principal duties of men and the glory of the eternal God. In all which hitherto hath been spoken, touching the force and use of man's Reason in things divine, I must crave that I be not so understood or construed, as if any such thing, by virtue thereof, could be done without the aid and assistance of God's most blessed Spirit. The thing we have handled according to the question moved about it; which question is, whether the light of Reason be so pernicious, that, in devising Laws for the Church, men ought not by it to search what may be fit and convenient? For this cause therefore we have endeavoured to make it appear, how in the nature of Reason itself there is no impediment, but that the self-same Spirit which revealeth the things that God hath set down in his Law, may also be thought to aid and direct men in finding out by the light of Reason what Laws are expedient to be made for the guiding of his Church, over and besides them that are in Scripture. Herein therefore we agree with those men, by whom human Laws are defined to be ordinances, which such as have lawful authority given them for that purpose do probably draw from the Laws of Nature and

God, by discourse of Reason aided with the influence of divine grace: for that cause, it is not said amiss touching Ecclesiastical Canons, *That by instinct of the Holy Ghost they have been made, and consecrated by the reverend acceptation of the world.*

Laws for the Church are not made as they should be, unless the makers follow such direction as they ought to be guided by; wherein that Scripture standeth not the Church of God in any stead, or serveth nothing at all to direct, but may be let pass as needless to be consulted with, we judge it profane, impious, and irreligious to think. For although it were in vain to make Laws which the Scripture hath already made, because what we are already there commanded to do, on our parts there resteth nothing, but only that it be executed; yet because both in that which we are commanded, it concerneth the duty of the Church by Law to provide, that the looseness and slackness of men may not cause the commandments of God to be unexecuted; and a number of things there are, for which the Scripture hath not provided by any Law, but left to the careful discretion of the Church; we are to search how the Church in these cases may be well directed to make that provision by Laws which is most convenient and fit. And what is so in these cases, partly Scripture, and partly Reason must teach to discern. Scripture comprehending Examples and Laws; Laws, some natural, and some positive; Examples neither are there for all cases which require Laws to be made, and when there are, they can but direct as precedents only. Natural Laws direct in such sort, that in all things we must for ever do according unto them; positive so, that against them in no case we may do anything, as long as the will of God is, that they should remain in force. Howbeit, when Scripture doth yield us precedents, how far forth they are to be followed; when it giveth natural Laws, what particular order is thereunto most agreeable, when positive, which way to make Laws unrepugnant unto them; yea, though all these should want, yet what kind of ordinances would be most to the good of the Church which is aimed at, all this must be by Reason found out.

III viii 15 — ix 1, 378–81

The rule of faith cannot be changed, but there may be changes in order and discipline, for which the Church has power to make laws. The claim that all such matters are ordained in Scripture is an innovation by present opponents of the Church.

There is no reason in the world wherefore we should esteem it as necessary always to do, as always to believe the same things; seeing every man knoweth that the matter of Faith is constant, the matter contrariwise of Action daily changeable, especially the matter of Action belonging unto Church-polity. Neither can I find that men of soundest judgment have any otherwise taught, than that Articles of Belief, and things which all men of necessity do to the end they may be saved, are either expressly set down in Scripture or else plainly thereby to be gathered. But touching things which belong to Discipline and outward polity the Church hath authority to make Canons, Laws and Decrees, even as we read that in the Apostles' times it did. Which kind of Laws (forasmuch as they are not in themselves necessary to salvation) may, after they are made, be also changed as the difference of times or places all require. Yea, it is not denied, I am sure, by themselves that certain things in Discipline are of that nature as they may be varied by times, places, persons, and the like circumstances. Whereupon I demand, are those changeable points of Discipline commanded in the Word of God, or no? If they be not commanded, and yet may be received in the Church, how can their former position stand, condemning all things in the Church which in the Word are not commanded? If they be commanded, and yet may suffer change, how can this latter stand, affirming all things immutable which are commanded of God? Their distinction touching matters of substance and circumstance, though true, will not serve. For be they great things, or be they small, if God have commanded them in the Gospel, and his commanding them in the Gospel do make them unchangeable, there is no reason we should more change the one than we may the other. If the authority of the Maker do prove unchangeableness in the Laws which God hath made, then must all Laws which he hath made be necessarily for ever permanent, though they be but of circumstance only, and not of substance. I therefore conclude, that neither God's being author of Laws for Government of his Church, nor his committing them unto Scripture, is any reason sufficient wherefore all Churches should forever be bound to keep them without change. But of one thing we are here to give them warning by the way: for whereas in this discourse, we have oftentimes professed that many parts of Discipline or Church-polity are delivered in Scripture, they may perhaps imagine that we are driven to confess their Discipline to be delivered in Scripture; and that having no other means to avoid it, we are fain to argue for the changeableness of Laws ordained even by God himself, as if otherwise theirs of necessity should take place, and that under which we live be abandoned. There is no remedy therefore, but to abate this error in them, and directly to let them know, that if they fall into any such a conceit, they do but a little flatter their own cause. As for us, we think in no respect so highly of it. Our persuasion is, that no age ever had knowledge of it but only ours; that they which defend it, devised it; that neither Christ nor his Apostles at any time taught it, but the contrary. If therefore we did seek to maintain that which most advantageth our own cause, the very best way for us, and the strongest against them, were to hold even as they do, that in Scripture there must needs be found some particular form of Church-polity which God hath instituted, and which for that very cause belongeth to all Churches, to all times. But with any such partial eye to respect ourselves, and by cunning to make those things seem the truest which are the fittest to serve our purpose, is a thing which we neither like nor mean to follow. Wherefore, that which we take to be generally true concerning the mutability of Laws, the same we have plainly delivered, as being persuaded of nothing more than we are of this; that whether it be in matter of speculation or of practice, no untruth can possibly avail the patron and defender long, and that things most truly, are also most behovefully spoken.

III x 6–8, 389–91

The argument that not all Church-polity is commanded in Scripture, and that the Church has power to make Laws, is developed further. Some things are indeed allowed in Scripture but not directly commanded by God. The Church of England has not gone against the commands of Christ in this.

In the matter of external Discipline or Regiment itself, we do not deny but there are some things whereto the Church is bound till the world's end. So as the question is only, how far the bounds of the Church's liberty do reach. We hold, that the power which the Church hath lawfully to make Laws and Orders for itself doth extend unto sundry things of Ecclesiastical jurisdiction, and such other matters, whereto their opinion is, that the Church's authority and power doth not reach. Whereas therefore in disputing against us about this point they take their compass a great deal wider than the truth of things can afford, producing reasons and arguments by way of generality, to prove that Christ hath set down all things belonging any way unto the form of ordering his Church, and hath absolutely forbidden change by addition or diminution, great or small (for so their manner of disputing is): we are constrained to make our defence by showing, that Christ hath not deprived his Church so far of all liberty in making Orders and Laws for itself, and that they themselves do not think he hath so done. For are they able to show that all particular customs, rites, and orders of reformed

Churches, have been appointed by Christ himself? No: they grant, that in matter of circumstance they alter that which they have received; but in things of substance they keep the Laws of Christ without change. If we say the same in our own behalf, (which surely we may do with a great deal more truth) then must they cancel all that hath been before alleged, and begin to enquire afresh, whether we maintain the Laws that Christ hath delivered concerning matters of substance, yea or no. For our constant persuasion in this point is as theirs, that we have no-where altered the Laws of Christ farther than in such particularities only as have the nature of things changeable, according to the differ-ence of times, places, persons, and other the like circumstances. Christ hath commanded prayers to be made, sacraments to be ministered, his Church to be carefully taught and guided. Concerning every of these somewhat Christ hath commanded, which must be kept till the world's end. On the contrary side, in every of them somewhat there may be added, as the Church shall judge it expedient. So that if they will speak to purpose, all which hitherto hath been disputed of, they must give over, and stand upon such particulars only as they can show we have either added or abrogated otherwise than we ought in the matter of Church-polity. Whatsoever Christ hath commanded for ever to be kept in his Church, the same we take not upon us to abrogate; and whatso-ever our Laws have thereunto added besides, of such quality we hope it is as no Law of Christ doth anywhere condemn. Wherefore, that all may be laid together and gathered into a narrow room: first so far forth as the Church is the mystical body of Christ and his invisible spouse, it needeth no external Polity. That very part of the Law divine which teacheth faith and works of righteousness, is itself alone sufficient for the Church of God in that respect. But as the Church is a visible soci-ety and body politic, Laws of Polity it cannot want. Secondly, whereas therefore it cometh in the second place to be enquired, what Laws are fittest and best for the Church; they who first embraced that rigorous and strict opinion, which depriveth the Church of liberty to make any kind of Law for herself, inclined (as it should seem) thereunto, for that they imagined all things which the Church doth without command-ment of Holy Scripture, subject to that reproof which the Scripture itself useth in certain cases, when divine authority ought alone to be followed. Hereupon they thought it enough for the cancelling of any kind of or-der whatsoever, to say, *The Word of God teacheth it not, it is a device of the brain of man, away with it therefore out of the Church.* [. . .] If all things must be commanded of God which may be practised of his Church, I would know what commandment the Gileadites had to erect that Altar which is spoken of in the Book of Joshua. Did not congruity of Reason induce them thereunto, and suffice for defence of their fact? I would know what commandment the women of Israel had yearly to mourn and lament in the memory of Jephthah's daughter; what commandment the Jews had to celebrate their feast of Dedication, never spoken of in the Law, yet solemnized even by our Saviour himself; what commandment, finally, they had for the ceremony of odours used about the bodies of the dead, after which custom notwithstanding (sith it was their custom) our Lord was contented that his own most precious body should be entombed. Wherefore to reject all orders of the Church which men have established, is to think worse of the Laws of men in this respect, than either the judgment of wise men alloweth, or the Law of God itself will bear. Howbeit, they which had once taken upon them to condemn all things done in the Church, and not commanded of God to be done, saw it was necessary for them (continuing in defence of this their opinion) to hold that needs there must be in Scripture set down a complete particular form of Church-polity, a form prescribing how all the affairs of the Church must be ordered, a form in no respect lawful to be altered by mortal men. For reformation of which oversight and error in them, there were that thought it a part of Christian love and charity to instruct them better, and to open unto them the difference between matters of perpetual necessity to all men's salvation, and matters of Ecclesiastical Polity: the one both fully and plainly taught in Holy Scripture; the other not necessary to be in such sort there prescribed; the one not capable of any diminution or augmentation at all by men, the other apt to admit both. Herein the authors of the former opinion were presently seconded by other wittier and better learned, who being loth that the form of Church-polity which they sought to bring in should be otherwise than in the highest degree accounted of, took first an exception against the difference between Church-polity and matters of necessity to salvation. Secondly against the restraint of Scripture, which (they say) receiveth injury at our hands, when we teach that it teacheth not as well matters of Polity, as of Faith and Salvation. Thirdly, constrained thereby we have been, therefore, both to maintain that distinction as a thing not only true in itself, but by them likewise so acknowledged, though unawares. Fourthly, and to make manifest, that from Scripture we offer not to derogate the least thing that truth thereunto doth claim in as much by us it is willingly confessed, that the Scripture of God is a storehouse abounding with inestimable treasures of wisdom and knowledge in many kinds, over and above things in this one kind barely necessary; yea, even that matters of Ecclesiastical Polity are not therein omitted, but taught also, albeit not so taught as those other things before mentioned. For so perfectly are those things taught, that nothing ever can need be added, nothing ever cease to be necessary: these, on the contrary side, as being of a far other nature and quality not so strictly or everlastingly commanded in Scripture but that unto the complete form of Church-polity, much may be requisite which the Scripture teacheth not; and much which it hath taught become unrequisite, sometimes because we need not use it, sometimes also because we cannot.

III xi 13–16, 405–9

Concluding Book Three Hooker replies to those who claim to make their own Church-polity and appoint new types of ministers and church officials not known to Church tradition. He affirms the necessity of the threefold Apostolic order and makes a summary defence of what has been done in the Church of England.

Now these things of greater moment, what are they? Forsooth, *Doctors, Pastors, Lay-elders, Elderships compounded of these three: Synods, consisting of many Elderships; Deacons, Women-church-servants, or Widows; free consent of the people unto actions of greatest moment, after they be by Churches or Synods orderly-resolved.* All this form of Polity (if yet we may term that a form of building, when men have laid a few rafters together, and those not all of the soundest neither) but howsoever, all this form they conclude is prescribed in such sort, that to add to it anything as of like importance, (for so I think they mean) or to abrogate of it anything at all, is unlawful. In which resolution if they will firmly and constantly persist, I see not but that concerning the polities which hitherto have been disputed of, they must agree that they have molested the Church with needless opposition; and henceforward, as we said before, betake themselves wholly unto the trial of particulars, whether every of those things which they esteem as principal be either so esteemed of, or at all established for perpetuity in Holy Scripture; and whether any particular thing in our Church-polity be received other than the Scripture alloweth of, either in greater things, or in smaller. The matters wherein Church-polity is conversant are the public religious duties of the Church, as the administration of the Word and Sacraments, Prayers, spiritual Censures, and the like. To these the Church standeth always bound. Laws of Polity are Laws which appoint in what manner these duties shall be performed. In performance whereof, because all that are of the Church cannot jointly and equally work, the first thing in Polity required is a difference of persons in the Church, without which difference these functions cannot be executed. Hereupon we hold that God's Clergy are a state, which hath been and will be as long as there is a Church upon earth, necessarily by the plain Word of God himself; a state whereunto the rest of God's people must be subject, as touching things that appertain to their soul's health. For where Polity is, it cannot but appoint some to be leaders of others, and some to be led, by others. *If the blind lead the blind, they both perish.* It is with the Clergy, if their persons be respected, even as it is with other men; their quality many times far beneath that which the dignity of their place requireth. Howbeit, according to the order of Polity, they being *the lights of the world*, others (though better and wiser) must that way be subject unto them. Again, forasmuch as where the Clergy are any great multitude, order doth necessarily require that by degrees they be distinguished; we hold there have ever been, and ever ought to be in such case, at leastwise, two sorts of Ecclesiastical persons, the one subordinate unto the other, as to the Apostles in the beginning, and to the Bishops always since, we find plainly both in Scripture, and in all Ecclesiastical records, other ministers of the Word and Sacraments have been. Moreover, it cannot enter into any man's conceit to think it lawful, that every man which listeth should take upon him charge in the Church; and therefore a solemn admittance is of such necessity, that without it there can be no Church-polity. A number of particularities there are, which make for the more convenient being of these principal and perpetual parts in Ecclesiastical Polity, but yet are not of such constant use, and necessity in God's Church. Of this kind are time and places appointed for the exercise of religion; specialties belonging to the public solemnity of the Word, the Sacraments, and Prayer; the enlargement or abridgement of functions ministerial, depending upon those two principal before mentioned: to conclude, even whatsoever doth by way of formality and circumstance concern any public action of the Church. Now although that which the Scripture hath of things in the former kind be for ever permanent, yet in the latter both much of that which the Scripture teacheth is not always needful; and much the Church of God shall always need which the Scripture teacheth not. So as the form of Polity by them set down for perpetuity is three ways faulty. Faulty in omitting some things which in Scripture are of that nature, as namely, the difference that ought to be of Pastors, when they grow to any great multitude; faulty in requiring Doctors, Deacons, Widows, and such like, as things of perpetual necessity by the Law of God, which in truth are nothing less: faulty also in urging some things by Scripture immutable; as their Lay-elders, which the Scripture neither maketh immutable, nor at all teacheth, for anything either we can as yet find, or they have hitherto been able to prove. But hereof more in the books that follow. As for those marvellous discourses whereby they adventure to argue, that God must needs have done the thing which they imagine was to be done; I must confess I have often wondered at their exceeding boldness herein. When the question is, whether God have delivered in Scripture (as they affirm he hath) a complete particular immutable form of Church-polity; why take they that other both presumptuous and superfluous labour to prove he should have done it; there being no way in this case to prove the deed of God, saving only by producing that evidence wherein he hath done it? But if there be no such thing apparent upon record, they do as if one should demand a legacy by force and virtue of some written testament, wherein there being no such thing specified, he pleadeth that there it must needs be, and bringeth arguments from the love or good-will which always the testator bore him, imagining that these or the like proofs will convict a testament to have that in it which other men can nowhere by reading find. In matters which concern the actions of God, the dutiful way on our part is to search what God hath done, and with meekness to admire that, rather than to dispute what he in congruity of Reason ought to do. The ways which he hath whereby to do all things for the greatest good of his Church, are more in number than we can search; other in Nature than that we should presume to determine, which of many should be the fittest for him to choose, till such time as we see he hath chosen of many some one; which one we then may boldly conclude to be the fittest, because he hath taken it before the rest. When we do otherwise, surely we exceed our bounds; who, and where we are, we forget. And therefore needful it is, that our pride in such cases be controlled, and our disputes beaten back with those demands of the blessed Apostle, *How unsearchable are his judgments, and his ways past finding out! Who hath made known the mind of the Lord, or who was his counsellor?*

III xi 19–21, 412–5

6

BOOK FOUR

To alter unnecessarily the ancient received custom of the whole Church

'Concerning their third Assertion, That our form of Church-polity is corrupted with Popish Orders, Rites and Ceremonies, banished out of certain Reformed Churches, whose example therein we ought to have followed.'

The fourth book opens with a defence of outward ceremonies as derived from the earliest Christian practice, and has some important observations about words and matter in the sacraments. The Puritans gave great weight to the words of worship and distrusted any set rules about physical gestures and positions. This passage could be seen as a commentary and support for the preface 'Of Ceremonies', included in the First Book of Common Prayer in 1549 and in all subsequent revisions.

Such was the ancient simplicity and softness of spirit which sometimes prevailed in the world, that they whose words were even as oracles amongst men seemed evermore loth to give sentence against anything publicly received in the Church of God, except it were wonderfully apparently evil; for that they did not so much incline to that severity which delighteth to reprove the least things it seeth amiss, as to that charity which is unwilling to behold anything that duty bindeth it to reprove. The state of this present age wherein zeal hath drowned charity, and skill meekness, will not now suffer any man to marvel, whatsoever he shall hear reproved, by whomsoever. Those Rites and Ceremonies of the Church therefore, which are the self-same now that they were when holy and virtuous men maintained them against profane and deriding adversaries, her own children have at this day in derision: whether justly or not it shall then appear, when all things are heard which they have to allege against the outward received orders of this Church. Which inasmuch as themselves do compare unto *mint* and *cumin*, granting them to be no part of those things which in the matter of Polity are weightier, we hope that for small things their strife will neither be earnest nor long. The sifting of that which is objected against the orders of the Church in particular, doth not belong unto this place. Here we are to discuss only those general exceptions, which have been taken at any time against them. First therefore, to the end that their nature, and use whereto they serve, may plainly appear; and so afterwards their quality the better be discerned; we are to note, that in every grand or main public duty which God requireth at the hands of his Church, there is, besides that matter and form wherein the essence thereof consisteth, a certain outward fashion whereby the same is in decent sort administered. The substance of all religious actions is delivered from God himself in few words. For example sake in the Sacraments. *Unto the element let the Word be added and they both do make a Sacrament*, saith St Augustine. Baptism is given by the element of Water and that prescript form of words which the Church of Christ doth use: the Sacrament of the Body and Blood of Christ is administered in the elements of Bread and Wine, if those mystical Words be added thereunto. But the due and decent form of administering those holy Sacraments doth require a great deal more. The end which is aimed at in setting down the outward form of any religious actions is the edification of the Church. Now men are edified, when either their understanding is taught somewhat whereof, in such actions, it behoveth all men to consider, or when their hearts are moved with any affection suitable thereunto; when their minds are in any sort stirred up unto that reverence, devotion, attention, and due regard which in those cases seemeth requisite. Because therefore unto this purpose not only speech, but sundry sensible means besides have always been thought necessary, and especially those means which being object to the eye, the liveliest and the most apprehensive sense of all other, have in that respect seemed the fittest to make a deep and strong impression; from hence have risen not only a number of prayers, readings, questionings, exhortings, but even of visible signs also, which being used in performance of holy actions, are undoubtedly most effectual to open such matter as men when they know and remember carefully must needs be a great deal the better informed to what effect such duties serve. We must not think but that there is some ground of Reason even in Nature, whereby it cometh to pass that no nation under Heaven either doth or ever did suffer some public actions which are of weight, whether they be evil and temporal, or else spiritual and sacred, to pass without some visible solemnity: the very strangeness whereof and difference from that which is common, doth cause popular eyes to observe and to mark the same. Words, both because they are common and do not so strongly move the fancy of man, are for the most part but slightly heard; and therefore with singular wisdom it hath been provided, that the deeds of men which are made in the presence of witnesses should pass not only with words, but also with certain sensible actions, the memory whereof is far more easy and durable than the memory of speech can be. The things which so long experience of all ages hath confirmed and made profitable, let not us presume to condemn as follies and toys because we sometimes know not the cause and reason of them.

IV i 1–3, 417–9

A reply to the charge that the Church of England has retained some Romish customs and practices. In the context of the period, it is an unusual acceptance of Roman Catholics as neighbours among whom we live.

Let the Church of Rome be what it will, let them that are of it be the people of God and our Fathers in the Christian Faith, or let them be otherwise; hold them for Catholics, or hold them for Heretics, it is not a thing either one way or other in this present question greatly material. Our conformity with them in such things as have been proposed is not proved as yet unlawful by all this. St Augustine hath said, yea and we have allowed his saying, *that the custom of the people of God, and the decrees of our forefathers are to be kept, touching those things whereof the Scripture hath neither one way nor the other given us any charge.* What then? Doth it then therefore follow, that they being neither the people of God, nor our forefathers, are for that cause in nothing, to be followed? This consequent were good, if so be it were granted, that only the custom of the people of God and the decrees of our forefathers are in such case to be observed. But then should no kind of latter Laws in the Church be good, which were a gross absurdity to think. St Augustine's speech therefore doth import, that where we have no divine precept, if yet we have the custom of the people of God, or a decree of our forefathers, this is a Law, and must be kept. Notwithstanding it is not denied, but that we lawfully may observe the positive Constitutions of our own Churches, although the same were but yesterday made by ourselves alone. Nor is there any thing in this to prove, that the Church of England might not by Law receive Orders, Rites, or Customs from the Church of Rome, although they were neither the People of God nor yet our forefathers. How much less, when we have received from them nothing but that which they did themselves receive from such as we cannot deny to have been the people of God, yea such as either we must acknowledge for our own forefathers, or else disdain the race of Christ?

The Rites and Orders wherein we follow the Church of Rome are of no other kind than such as the Church of Geneva itself doth follow them in. We follow the Church of Rome in more things; yet they in some things of the same nature about which our present controversy is: so that the difference is not in the kind, but in the number of Rites only wherein they and we do follow the Church of Rome. The use of wafer-cakes, the custom of godfathers and godmothers in baptism, are things not commanded nor forbidden in the Scripture, things which have been of old, and are retained in the Church of Rome even at this very hour. Is conformity with Rome in such things a blemish unto the Church of England, and unto Churches abroad an ornament? Let them, if not for the reverence they owe unto this Church, (in the bowels whereof they have received, I trust, that precious and blessed vigour which shall quicken them to eternal life) yet at the leastwise for the singular affection which they do bear towards others, take heed how they strike, lest they wound whom they would not. For undoubtedly it cutteth deeper than they are aware of, when they plead that even such Ceremonies of the Church of Rome as contain in them nothing which is not of itself agreeable to the Word of God, ought nevertheless to be abolished, and that neither the Word of God, nor reason, nor the examples of the eldest Churches, do permit the Church of Rome to be therein followed. Heretics they are, and they are our neighbours. By us and amongst us they lead their lives. But what then? Therefore is no Ceremony of theirs lawful for us to use? We must yield and will, that none are lawful if God himself be a precedent against the use of any. But how appeareth it that God is so? [. . .] The cause of more careful separation from the nearest nations {*in the Old Testament*} was the greatness of danger to be specially by it infected. Now, Papists are to us as those nations were unto Israel. Therefore if the wisdom of God be our guide, we cannot allow conformity with them, no not in any such indifferent Ceremonies. Our direct answer hereunto is, that for any thing here alleged we may still doubt whether the Lord in such indifferent Ceremonies as those whereof we dispute did frame his people of set purpose unto any utter dissimilitude, either with Egyptians, or with any other nation else. And if God did not forbid them all such indifferent Ceremonies, then our conformity with the Church of Rome in some such is not hitherto as yet disproved, although Papists were unto us, as those Heathens were unto Israel.

IV v 1 – vi 2, 432–4

The Puritans say that we should repudiate anything connected with Romish practice, but this would be to abandon good usage because of some corruptions. His attack on the 'Arians' in Poland refers to the followers of Fausto Sozzini (1539–1604), an Italian who had preached Unitarian doctrine in that country.

When God did by his good Spirit put it into our hearts, first to reform ourselves, (whence grew our separation) and then by all good means to seek also their reformation; had we not only cut off their corruptions, but also estranged ourselves from them in things indifferent, who seeth not how greatly prejudicial this might have been to so good a cause, and what occasion it had given them to think (to their greater obduration in evil) that, through a forward or wanton desire of innovation, we did unconstrainedly those things for which conscience was pretended? Howsoever, the cause doth stand, as Juda had been rather to choose conformity in things indifferent with Israel when they were nearest opposites, than with the farthest removed Pagans; so we in like cases, much rather with Papists than with Turks. I might add farther, for a more full and complete answer, so much concerning the large odds between the case of the eldest Churches in regard of those Heathens, and ours in respect of the Church of Rome, that very cavillation itself should be satisfied, and have no shift to fly unto.

But that no one thing may detain us over long, I return to their reasons against our conformity with the policy of that Church. That extreme dissimilitude which they urge upon us, is now commended as our best and safest policy for establishment of sound Religion. The ground of which politic position is That *evils must be cured by their contraries*; and therefore the cure of the Church infected with the poison of Antichristianity must be done by that which is thereunto as contrary as may be: a meddled estate of the orders of the Gospel and the ceremonies of Popery, is not the best way to banish Popery. We are contrariwise of opinion, that he which will perfectly recover a sick and restore a diseased body to health, must not endeavour so much to bring it to a state of simple contrariety, as of fit proportion in contrariety unto those evils which are to be cured. He that will take away extreme heat by setting the body in extremity of cold, shall undoubtedly remove the disease, but together with it the diseased too. The first thing therefore in skilful cures is the knowledge of the part affected; the next is of the evil which doth affect it; the last is not only of the kind, but also of the measure of contrary things whereby to remove it. They which measure Religion by dislike of the Church of Rome, think every man so much the more sound, by how much he can make the corruptions thereof to seem more large. And therefore some there are, namely the Arians in reformed Churches of Poland, which imagine the canker to have eaten so far into the very bones and marrow of the Church of Rome, as if it had been not so much as a sound belief, no, not concerning God himself, but that the very belief of the Trinity were a part of Antichristian corruption; and that the wonderful providence of God did bring to pass that the Bishop of the See of Rome should be famous for his triple crown, a sensible mark whereby the world might know him to be that mystical Beast spoken of in the Revelation, to be that great and notorious Antichrist in no one respect so much as in this, that he maintaineth the Doctrine of the Trinity. Wisdom therefore and skill is requisite to know what parts are sound in that Church, and what corrupted. Neither is it to all men apparent, which complain of unsound parts, with what kind of unsoundness every such part is possessed. They can say, that in Doctrine, in Discipline, in Prayers, in Sacraments, the Church of Rome hath (as it hath indeed) very foul and gross corruptions; the nature whereof notwithstanding because they have not for the most part exact skill and knowledge to discern, they think that amiss many times which is not, and the salve of reformation they mightily call for; but where and what the sores are which need it, as they wot full little, so they think it not greatly material to search. Such men's contentment must be wrought by stratagem: the usual method of art is not for them.

IV vii 6–viii 2, 441–3

Further response to the accusation that the Church of England had retained some Romish practices. Some of these are to be found also in other Reformed Churches, and are things indifferent. The dispute about wafer bread arose again in the nineteenth century and was one of the six points of catholic usage condemned by the Purchas Judgment in 1871; it is now general in the Church of England.

In the meanwhile sorry we are that any good and godly mind should be grieved with that which is done. But to remedy their grief lieth not so much in us as in themselves. They do not wish to be made glad with the hurt of the Church; and to remove all out of the Church whereat they show themselves to be sorrowful, would be, as we are persuaded, hurtful, if not pernicious thereunto. Till they be able to persuade the contrary, they must and will, I doubt not, find out some other good mean to cheer up themselves. Amongst which means the example of Geneva may serve for one. Have not they the old Popish custom of using god-fathers and godmothers in baptism? The old Popish custom of administering the blessed Sacrament of the holy Eucharist with wafer-cakes? These things then the godly there can digest. Wherefore should not the godly here learn to do the like, both in them and in the rest of the like nature? Some farther mean, peradventure, it might be to assuage their grief, if so be they did consider the revenge they take on them which have been, as they interpret it, the workers of their continuance in so great grief so long. For if the maintenance of Ceremonies be a corrosive to such as oppugn them, undoubtedly to such as maintain them it can be no great pleasure, when they behold how that which they reverence is oppugned. And therefore they that judge themselves martyrs when they are grieved, should think withal what they are whom they grieve. For we are still to put them in mind, that the cause doth make no difference; for that it must be presumed as good at the least on our part as on theirs till it be in the end decided who have stood for truth and who for error. So that till then the most effectual medicine, and withal the most sound to ease their grief, must not be (in our opinion) the taking away of those things whereat they are grieved, but the altering of that persuasion which they have concerning the same. For this we therefore both pray and labour; the more because we are also persuaded, that it is but conceit in them to think that those Romish Ceremonies, whereof we have hitherto spoken, are like leprous clothes, infectious to the Church, or like soft and gentle poisons the venom whereof being insensibly pernicious, worketh death, and yet is never felt working. Thus they say: but because they say it only, and the world hath not yet had so great experience of their art in curing the diseases of the Church, that the bare authority of their worship should persuade in a cause so weighty, they may not think much if it be required at their hands to show first, by what means so deadly infection can grow from similitude between us and the Church of Rome in these things indifferent; secondly, for that it were infinite, if the Church should provide against every such evil as may come to pass, it is not sufficient that they show possibility of dangerous event, unless there appear some likelihood also of the same to follow in us, except we prevent it. Nor is this enough, unless it be moreover made plain, that there is no good and sufficient way of prevention but by evacuating clean, and by emptying the Church of every such rite and ceremony as is presently called in question. Till this be done, their good affection towards the safety of the Church is acceptable, but the way they prescribe us to preserve it by must rest in suspense. And lest hereat they take occasion to turn upon us the speech of the prophet Jeremy used against Babylon, *Behold we have done our endeavour to cure the diseases of Babylon, but she through her wilfulness doth rest uncured*; let them consider into what straits the Church might drive itself in being guided by this their counsel. Their axiom is that the sound believing Church of Jesus Christ may not be like Heretical Churches in any of those indifferent things which men make choice of and do not take by prescript appointment of the Word of God. In the Word of God the bread is prescribed as a thing without which the Eucharist may not be celebrated; but as for the kind of bread, it is not denied to be a thing indifferent. Being indifferent of itself, we are by this axiom of theirs to avoid the use of unleavened bread in that Sacrament, because such bread the Church of Rome being heretical useth. But doth not the self-same axiom bar us even from leavened bread also, which the Church of the Grecians useth, the opinions whereof are in a number of things the same for which we condemn the Church of Rome, and in some things erroneous, where the Church of Rome is acknowledged to be sound, as namely, in the Article of the Holy Ghost's proceeding? And lest here they should say that because the Greek Church is farther off and the Church of Rome nearer, we are in that respect rather to use that which the Church of Rome useth not, let them imagine a reformed Church in the city of Venice, where a Greek Church and Popish both are; and when both these are equally near, let them consider what the third shall do. Without leavened or unleavened bread it can have no Sacrament; the Word of God doth tie it to neither; and their axiom doth exclude it from both. If this constrain them, as it must, to grant that their axiom is not to take any place save in those things only where the Church hath larger scope; it resteth that they search out some stronger reason than they have as yet alleged; otherwise they constrain not us to think that the Church is tied unto any such rule or axiom, not then when she hath the widest field to walk in and the greatest store of choice.

IV x 1–3, 449–52

An extended defence of what has been retained and what changed in the Church of England, appealing to the universal usage of the early Church. A truly Anglican desire for moderation, but not for the loss of precedent and authority. Even if Hooker cannot be claimed as the creator of the Anglican via media, he lays a good foundation for it.

To leave reformed Churches therefore and their actions for him to judge of, in whose sight they are as they are; and our desire is that they may even in his sight be found such, as we ought to endeavour by all means that our own may likewise be; somewhat we are inforced to speak by way of simple declaration, concerning the proceedings of the Church of England in these affairs, to the end that men whose minds are free from those partial constructions, whereby the only name of difference from some other Churches is thought cause sufficient to condemn ours, may the better discern whether that we have done be reasonable, yea or no. The Church of England being to alter her received laws concerning such orders rites and ceremonies, as had been in former times an hindrance unto piety and Religious service of God, was to enter into consideration first, that the change of laws, especially concerning matter of Religion, must be warily proceeded in. Laws, as all other things human, are many times full of imperfection, and that which is supposed behoveful unto men, proveth often times most pernicious. The wisdom which is learned by tract of time, findeth the laws that have been in former ages established, needful in later to be abrogated. Besides, that which sometime is expedient doth not always so continue: and the number of needless laws unabolished doth weaken the force of them that are necessary. But true withal it is, that alteration though it be from worse to better hath in it inconveniences, and those weighty, unless it be in such laws as have been made upon special occasions, which occasions ceasing, laws of that kind do abrogate themselves. But when we abrogate a law as being ill made, the whole cause for which it was made still remaining; do we not herein revoke our very own deed and upbraid ourselves with folly, yea, all that were makers of it with oversight and with error? Farther, if it be a law which the custom and continual practice of many ages or years hath confirmed in the minds of men, to alter it must needs be troublesome and scandalous. It amazeth them, it causeth them to stand in doubt whether anything be in itself by nature either good or evil, and not all things rather such as men at this or that time agree to accompt of them, when they behold even those things disproved, disanulled, rejected, which use had made in a manner natural. What have we to induce men unto the willing obedience and observation of laws, but the weight of so many men's judgment, as have with deliberate advice assented thereunto, the weight of that long experience, which the world hath had thereof with consent and good liking? So that to change any such law must needs with the common sort impair and weaken the force of those grounds, whereby all laws are made effectual. Notwithstanding we do not deny alteration of laws to be sometimes a thing necessary, as when they are unnatural, or impious, or otherwise hurtful unto the public community of men, and against that good for which human societies were instituted. When the Apostles of our Lord and Saviour were ordained to alter the laws of heathenish Religion received throughout the whole world; chosen I grant they were (Paul excepted) the rest ignorant, poor, simple, unschooled altogether and unlettered men; howbeit extraordinarily endued with ghostly wisdom from above before they ever undertook this enterprise, yea their authority confirmed by miracle, to the end it might plainly appear that they were the Lord's Ambassadors, unto whose Sovereign power for all flesh to stoop, for all the kingdoms of the earth to yield them selves willingly conformable in whatsoever should be required, it was their duty. In this case therefore their oppositions in maintenance of public superstition against Apostolic endeavours, that they might not condemn the ways of their ancient predecessors, that they must keep *Religiones traditas*, the rites which from age to age had descended, that the ceremonies of Religion had been ever accounted by so much holier as elder, these and like allegations in this case were vain and frivolous. Not to stay longer therefore in speech concerning this point we will conclude, that as the change of such laws as have been specified is necessary, so the evidence that they are such must be great. If we have neither voice from heaven that so pronounceth of them, neither sentence of men grounded upon such manifest and cleared proof, that they in whose hands it is to alter them may likewise infallibly even in heart and conscience judge them so; upon necessity to urge alteration is to trouble and disturb without necessity. As for arbitrary alterations, when laws in themselves not simply bad or unmeet are changed for better and more expedient; if the benefit of that which is newly better devised be but small, sith the custom of easiness to alter and change is so evil, no doubt but to bear a tolerable sore is better then to venture on a dangerous remedy. Which being generally thought upon as a matter that touched nearly their whole enterprise, whereas change was notwithstanding concluded necessary, in regard of the great hurt which the Church did receive by a number of things then in use, whereupon a great deal of that which had been was now to be taken away and removed out of the Church; yet sith there are diverse ways of abrogating things established, they saw it best to cut off presently such things, as might in that sort be extinguished without danger, leaving the rest to be abolished by disusage through tract of time. And as this was done for the manner of abrogation: so touching the stint or measure thereof, rites and ceremonies and other external things of like nature being hurtful unto the Church, either in respect of their quality or in regard of their number; in the former there could be no doubt or difficulty what should be done, their deliberation in the latter was more hard. And therefore in as much as they did resolve to remove only such things of that kind as the Church might best spare, retaining the residue; their whole counsel is in this point utterly condemned, as having either proceeded from the blindness of those times, or from negligence, or from desire of honour and glory, or from an erroneous opinion that such things might be tolerated for a while, or if it did proceed (as they which would seem most favourable are content to think it possible) from a purpose *partly the easier to draw Papists unto the Gospel*, by keeping so many orders still the same with theirs, *and partly to redeem peace thereby, the breach whereof they might fear would ensue upon more thorough alteration*, or howsoever it came to pass, the thing they did is judged evil. But such is the lot of all that deal in public affairs whether of Church or Commonwealth, that which men list to surmise of their doings be it good or ill, they must beforehand patiently arm their minds to endure. Wherefore to let go private surmises, whereby the thing in itself is not made either better or worse, if just and allowable reasons might lead them to do as they did, then are these censures all frustrate. Touching ceremonies harmless therefore in themselves, and hurtful only in respect of number: was it amiss to decree, that those things which were least needful and newliest come should be the first that were taken away, as in the abrogating of a number of Saints' days and of other the like customs it appeareth they did, till afterwards the form of common prayer being perfited, articles of sound Religion and Discipline agreed upon, Catechisms framed for the needful instruction of youth, Churches purged of things that indeed were burdensome to the people or to the simple offensive and scandalous, all was brought at the length unto that wherein now we stand? Or was it amiss, that having this way eased the Church as they thought of superfluity, they went not on till they had plucked up even those things also, which had taken a great deal stronger and deeper root; those things which to abrogate without constraint of manifest harm thereby arising, had been to alter unnecessarily (in their judgments) the ancient received custom of the whole Church, the universal practice of the people of God, and those very decrees of our fathers, which were not only set down by agreement of general councils, but had accordingly been put in ure and so continued in use till that very time present? True it is that neither councils nor customs, be they never so ancient and so general, can let the Church from taking away that thing which is hurtful to be retained. Where things have been instituted which being convenient and good at the first, do afterwards in process of time wax otherwise; we make no doubt but they may be altered, yea, though councils or customs general have received them. And therefore it is but a needless kind of opposition which they make who thus dispute, *If in those things, which are not expressed in the Scripture, that is to be observed of the Church, which is the custom of the people of God and decree of our forefathers; then how can these things at any time be varied, which heretofore have been once ordained in such sort?* Whereto we say, that things so ordained are to be kept, howbeit not necessarily any longer, than till there grow some urgent cause to ordain the contrary. For there is not any positive law of men, whether it be general or particular, received by formal expressed consent, as in councils; or by secret approbation, as in customs it cometh to pass, but the same may be taken away if occasion serve. Even as we all know, that many things generally kept heretofore are now in like sort generally unkept and abolished everywhere. Notwithstanding till such things be abolished, what exception can there be taken against the judgment of St Augustine who saith, *That of things harmless whatsoever there is, which the whole Church doth observe throughout the world; to argue for any man's immunity from observing the same, it were a point of most insolent madness.* And surely odious it must needs have been for one Christian Church to abolish that, which all had received and held for the space of many ages, and that without any detriment unto Religion so manifest and so great, as might in the eyes of unpartial men appear sufficient to clear them from all blame of rash and inconsiderate proceeding, if in fervour of zeal they had removed such things. Whereas contrariwise so reasonable moderation herein used hath freed us from being deservedly subject unto that bitter kind of obloquy, whereby as the Church of Rome doth under the colour of love towards those things which be harmless, maintain extremely most hurtful corruptions; so we peradventure might be upbraided, that under colour of hatred towards those things that are corrupt, we are on the other side as extreme, even against most harmless ordinances. And as they are obstinate to retain that, which no man of any conscience is able well to defend, so we might be reckoned fierce and violent to tear away that, which if our own mouths did condemn, our consciences would storm and repine thereat.

IV xiv 1–6, 480–5

7

BOOK FIVE

The general maintenance and defence of our whole Church service

'Concerning their fourth Assertion, That touching several public duties of Christian Religion, there is amongst us much superstition retained in them: and concerning persons, which for performance of those duties are endowed with the power of Ecclesiastical Order, our Laws and proceedings according thereunto are many ways therein also corrupted.'

In the longest of the Books, Hooker makes a detailed defence of the order, discipline and practice of the Church of England, replying more specifically to some objections raised in the previous Books, and introducing many new matters.

He begins with his basic premise that true religion is the root of all virtues and the stay of all well-ordered commonwealths.

Few there are of so weak capacity, but public evils they easily espy; fewer so patient, as not to complain, when the grievous inconveniences thereof work sensible smart. Howbeit to see wherein the harm which they feel consisteth, the seeds from which it sprang, and the method of curing it, belongeth to a skill, the study whereof is so full of toil, and the practice so beset with difficulties, that wary and respective men had rather seek quietly their own, and wish that the world may go well, so it be not long of them, than with pain and hazard make themselves advisers for the common good. We which thought it at the very first a sign of cold affection towards the Church of God, to prefer private ease before the labour of appeasing public disturbance, must now, of necessity, refer events to the gracious providence of almighty God, and, in discharge of our duty towards him, proceed with the plain and impartial defence of a common cause. Wherein our endeavour is not so much to overthrow them with whom we contend, as to yield them just and reasonable causes of those things, which for want of due consideration heretofore they misconceived, accusing Laws for men's oversights, impugning evils grown through personal defects unto that which is not evil, framing to some sores unwholesome plasters, and applying other some where no sore is. To make therefore our beginning that which to both parts is most acceptable, we agree that pure and unstained religion ought to be the highest of all cares appertaining to public regiment: as well in regard of that aid and protection, which they who faithfully serve God confess they receive at his merciful hands; as also for the force which religion hath to qualify all sorts of men, and to make them in public affairs the more serviceable, governors the apter to rule with conscience, inferiors for conscience sake the willinger to obey. It is no peculiar conceit, but a matter of sound consequence, that all duties are by so much the better performed, by how much the men are more religious from whose habilities the same proceed. For if the course of politic affairs cannot in any good sort go forward without fit instruments, and that which fitteth them be their virtues, let polity acknowledge itself indebted to religion, godliness being the chiefest top and wellspring of all true virtues, even as God is of all good things. So natural is the union of Religion with Justice, that we may boldly deny there is either, where both are not. For how should they be unfeignedly just, whom religion doth not cause to be such; or they religious, which are not found such by the proof of their just actions? If they which employ their labour and travail, about the public administration of justice, follow it only as a trade, with unquenchable and unconscionable thirst of gain, being not in heart persuaded that justice is God's own work, and themselves his agents in this business, the sentence of right God's own verdict, and themselves his priests to deliver it; formalities of justice do but serve to smother right, and that, which is necessarily ordained for the common good, is through shameful abuse made the cause of common misery. The same piety which maketh them that are in authority desirous to please and resemble God by justice, inflameth every way men of action with zeal to do good (as far as their place will permit) unto all: for that, they know, is most noble and divine. Whereby, if no natural or casual inhability cross their desires, they always delighting to inure themselves with actions most beneficial to others cannot but gather from thence great experience, and through experience more wisdom, because conscience and the fear of swerving

from that which is right maketh them diligent observers of circumstances, the loose regard whereof is the nurse of vulgar folly, no less
than Solomon's attention thereunto was of natural furtherances the
most effectual to make him eminent above others. For he gave good
heed, and pierced every thing to the very ground, and by that mean
became the author of many parables. Concerning fortitude, sith evils
great and unexpected (the true touchstone of constant minds) do cause
oftentimes even them to think upon divine power with fearefullest sus-
picions, which have been otherwise the most secure despisers thereof,
how we should look for any constant resolution of mind in such cases
saving only where unfeigned affection to Godward hath bred the confidence to be assisted by his hand? For proof whereof let but the Acts of
the ancient Jews be indifferently weighed; from whose magnanimity, in
cases of most extreme hazard, those strange and unwonted resolutions
have grown, which for all circumstances no people under the roof of
heaven did ever hitherto match. And that which did always so animate
them was their mere Religion. Without which, if so be it were possible
that all other ornaments of mind might be had in their full perfection,
nevertheless the mind that should possess them divorced from piety
could be but a spectacle of commiseration; even as that body is, which
adorned with sundry other admirable beauties, wanteth eyesight, the
chiefest grace that nature hath in that kind to bestow. They which commend so much the felicity of that innocent world, wherein it is said,
that men of their own accord did embrace fidelity and not for fear of
the magistrate, or because revenge was before their eyes, if at any time
they should do otherwise, but that which held the people in awe was
the shame of ill doing, the love of equity and right itself a bar against
all oppressions which greatness of power causeth, they which describe
unto us any such state of happiness amongst men, though they speak
not of religion, do notwithstanding declare that which is in truth her
only working. For if religion did possess sincerely and sufficiently the
hearts of all men there would need no other restraint from evil. This
doth not only give life and perfection to all endeavours wherewith it
concurreth: but what event soever ensue, it breedeth, if not joy and
gladness always, yet always patience, satisfaction, and reasonable contentment of mined. Whereupon it hath been set down as an axiom of
good experience, that all things religiously taken in hand are prosper-
ously ended, because whether men in the end have that which religion
did allow them to desire, or that which it teacheth them contentedly to
suffer, they are in neither event infortunate.

V i 1–2, 13–16

The folly and danger of atheism. We think of the sixteenth century as a time of universal, though divided, Christian faith, but there were some instances of complete unbelief.

They of whom God is altogether unapprehended are but few in number, and for grossness of wit such, that they hardly and scarcely seem to hold the place of human being. These we should judge to be of all others most miserable but that a wretcheder sort there are, on whom whereas nature hath bestowed riper capacity, their evil disposition seriously goeth about therewith to apprehend God as being not God. Whereby it cometh to pass that of these two sorts of men, both godless, the one having utterly no knowledge of God, the other study how to persuade themselves that there is no such thing to be known. The fountain and wellspring of which impiety is a resolved purpose of mined to reap in this world what sensual profit or pleasure soever the world yieldeth, and not to be barred from any whatsoever means available thereunto. And that this is the very radical cause of their Atheism, no man I think will doubt which considereth what pains they take to destroy those principal spurs and motives unto all virtue, the creation of the world, the providence of God, the Resurrection of the dead, the joys of the Kingdom of heaven and the endless pains of the wicked, yea above all things the authority of Scripture, because on these points it evermore beareth, and the Soul's immortality, which granted, draweth easily after it the rest as a voluntary train. Is it not wonderful that base desires should so extinguish in men the sense of there own excellency, as to make them willing that their souls should be like to the souls of beasts, mortal and corruptible with their bodies? Till some admirable or unusual accident happen (as it hath in some) to work the beginning of a better alteration in their minds, disputation about the knowledge of God with such kind of persons commonly prevaileth little. For how should the brightness of wisdom shine, where the windows of the soul are of very set purpose closed? True religion hath many things in it the only mention whereof galleth and troubleth their minds. Being therefore loath that inquiry into such matters should breed a persuasion in the end contrary unto that they embrace, it is mere endeavour to banish as much as in them lieth quite and clean from their cogitation whatsoever may sound that way. But it cometh many times to pass (which is their torment) that the thing they shun doth follow them, truth as it were even obtruding itself into their knowledge and not permitting them to be so ignorant as they would be. Whereupon inasmuch as the nature of man is unwilling to continue doing that wherein it shall always condemn itself, they continuing still obstinate to follow the course which they have begun, are driven to devise all the shifts that wit can invent for the smothering of this light, all that may but with any the least show of possibility stay their minds from thinking that true, which they heartily wish were false, but cannot think it so without some scruple and fear of the contrary. Now because that judicious learning, for which we commend most worthily the ancient sages of the world, doth not in this case serve the turn, these trencher-mates (for such the most of them be) frame to themselves a way more pleasant, a new method they have of turning things that are serious into mockery, an art of contradiction by way of scorn, a learning wherewith we were long sithence forewarned that the miserable times whereinto we are fallen should abound. This they study, this they practise, this they grace with wanton superfluity of wit, too much insulting over the patience of more virtuously disposed minds. For towards these so forlorn creatures we are (it must be confessed) too patient. In zeal to the glory of God Babylon hath excelled Sion. We want that decree of Nebuchodonosor; the fury of this wicked brood hath the reins much at liberty, their tongues walk at large, the spit venom of their poisoned hearts breaketh out to the annoyance of others, what their untamed lust suggesteth the same their licentious mouths do everywhere set abroach. With our contentions their irreligious humour also is much strengthened. Nothing pleaseth them better, than these manifold oppositions about the matter of religion; as well for that they have hereby the more opportunity to learn on one side how another may be oppugned, and so to weaken the credit of all unto themselves; as also because by this hot pursuit of lower controversies amongst men professing religion and agreeing in the principal foundations thereof, they conceive hope that about the higher principles themselves time will cause altercation to grow.

V ii 1–2, 19–21

He repeats his reason for writing this reply to critics. The Church is fully reformed, but has not cast out all usages from the past. Reverence and dignity in worship must not be confused with superstition. The phrase 'Signs must resemble the things they signify' is highly relevant to Anglican practice.

Howsoever superstition do grow, that wherein unsounder times have done amiss, the better ages ensuing must rectify, as they may. I now come to those accusations brought against us by pretenders of reformation, the first in the rank whereof is such, that if so be the Church of England did at this day justly deserve to be touched, as they in this cause have imagined it doth, rather would I exhort all sorts to seek pardon even with tears at the hands of God, than meditate words of defence for our doings, to the end that men might think favourably of them. For as the case of this world, especially now, doth stand, what other stay or succour have we to lean unto, saving the testimony of our conscience and the comfort we take in this, that we serve the living God (as near as our wits can reach unto the knowledge thereof) even according to his own will, and do therefore trust that his mercy shall be our safeguard against those enraged powers abroad which principally in that respect are become our enemies? But sith no man can do ill with a good conscience, the consolation which we herein seem to find is but a mere deceitful pleasing of ourselves in error, which at the length must needs greater grief, if that which we do to please God most be for the manifold defects thereof offensive unto him. For so it is judged, our prayers, our sacraments, our fasts, our time and places of public meeting together for the worship and service of God, our marriages, our burials, our functions, elections and ordinations ecclesiastical, almost whatsoever we do in the exercise of our religion according to laws for that purpose established, all things are some way or other thought faulty, all things are stained with superstition. Now although it may be the wiser sort of men are not greatly moved hereat, considering how subject the very best things have been always unto cavil, when wits possessed either with disdain or dislike thereof have set them up as their mark to shoot at: safe notwithstanding it were not therefore to neglect the danger which from hence may grow, and that especially in regard of them, who desiring to serve God as they ought, but being not so skilful as in every point to unwind themselves when the snares of glosing speech do lie to entangle them, are in mind not a little troubled, when they hear so bitter invectives against that which this Church hath taught them to reverence as holy, to approve as lawful, and to observe as behoveful for the exercise of Christian duties. It seemeth therefore, at the least for their sakes, very meet that such as blame us in this behalf be directly answered, and they which follow us informed plainly in the reasons of that we do. On both sides the end intended between us, is to have laws and ordinances such, as may rightly serve to abolish superstition and to establish the service of God with all things thereunto appertaining in some perfect form. There is an inward reasonable, and there is an outward serviceable worship belonging unto God. Of the former kind are all manner virtuous duties that each man in reason and conscience to Godward oweth. Solemn and serviceable worship we name, for distinction sake, whatsoever belongeth to the Church or public society of God by way of external adoration. It is the latter of these two whereupon our present question groweth. Again this latter being ordered, partly, and as touching principal matters, by none but precepts divine only; partly, and as concerning things of inferior regard, by ordinances as well human as divine: about the substance of Religion wherein God's only law must be kept, there is here no controversy, the crime now intended against us is that our laws have not ordered those inferior things as behoveth, and that our customs are either superstitious or otherwise amiss, whether we respect the exercise of public duties in religion or the functions of persons authorized thereunto.

It is with teachers of Mathematical sciences usual, for us in this present question necessary, to lay down first certain reasonable demands which in most particulars following are to serve as principles whereby to work, and therefore must be beforehand considered. The men whom we labour to inform in the truth, perceive that so to proceed is requisite. For to this end they also propose touching customs and rites indifferent their general axioms, some of them subject unto just exceptions, and as we think, more meet by them to be farther considered than assented unto by us. As that, *In outward things belonging to the service of God, reformed Churches ought by all means to shun conformity with the Church of Rome*; that, *The first reformed should be a pattern whereunto all that come after ought to conform themselves*; that *Sound religion may not use the things which being not commanded of God have been either devised or abused unto superstition.* These and the rest of the same consort we have in the book going before examined. Other things they allege and rules not unworthy of approbation, as *That in all such things the glory of God and the edification or ghostly good of his people must be sought*; that *Nothing should be undecently or unorderly done.* But for as much as all the difficulty is in discerning what things do glorify God and edify his Church, what not; when we should think them decent and fit, when otherwise: because these rules being too general come not near enough unto the matter which we have in hand; and the former principles being nearer the purpose are too far from truth, we must propose unto all men certain petitions incident and very material in causes of this nature, such as no man of moderate judgment hath cause to think unjust or unreasonable.

The first thing therefore which is of force to cause approbations with good conscience towards such customs or rites as publicly are established, is when there riseth from the due consideration of those customs and rites in themselves apparent reason, although not always to prove them better, than any other that might possibly be devised, (for who did ever require this in man's ordinances?) yet competent to show their convenience and fitness, in regard of the use for which they should serve. Now touching the nature of religious services and the manner of their due performance, thus much generally we know to be most clear, that whereas the greatness and dignity of all manner actions is measured by the worthiness of the subject from which they proceed and of the object whereabout they are conversant, we must of necessity in both respects acknowledge, that this present world affordeth not any thing comparable unto the public duties of religion. For if the best things have the perfectest and best operations, it will follow that seeing man is the worthiest creature upon earth, and every society of men more worthy than any man, and of societies that most excellent which we call the Church; there can be in this world no work performed equal to the exercise of true religion, the proper operation of the Church of God. Again forasmuch as religion worketh upon him who in majesty and power is infinite, as we ought we accompt not of it, unless we esteem it even according to that very height of excellence which our hearts conceive when divine sublimity itself is rightly considered. In the powers and faculties of our souls God requireth the uttermost which our unfeigned affection towards him is able to yield. So that if we affect him not far above and before all things, our religion hath not that inward perfection which it should have, neither do we indeed worship him as our God. That which inwardly each man should be, the Church outwardly ought to testify. And therefore the duties of our religion which are seen must be such as that affection which is unseen ought to be. Signs must resemble the things they signify. If religion bear the greatest sway in our hearts, our outward religious duties must show it, as far as the Church hath outward hability. Duties of religion performed by whole societies of men ought to have in them according to our power a sensible excellence, correspondent to the majesty of him whom we worship. Yea then are the public duties of religion best ordered when the militant Church doth resemble by sensible means, as it may in such cases, that hidden dignity and glory wherewith the Church triumphant in heaven is beautified. Howbeit even as the very heat of the sun itself which is the life of the whole world was to the people of God in the Desert a grievous annoyance, for ease whereof his extraordinary providence ordered a cloudy pillar to overshadow them: So things of general use and benefit (for in this world what is so perfect that no inconvenience doth ever follow it?) may by some accident be incommodious to a few. In which case, for such private evils remedies there are of like condition, though public ordinances, wherein the common good is respected, be not stirred. Let our first demand be therefore, that in the external form of religion such things as are apparently, or can be sufficiently proved effectual and generally fit to set forward godliness, either as betokening the greatness of God, or as beseeming the dignity of religion, or as concurring with celestial impressions in the minds of men, may be reverently thought of; some few rare, casual, and tolerable, or otherwise curable inconveniences notwithstanding.

V iv 1 — vi 2, 26–30

The right and indeed the duty of private judgment in matters of religion was a tenet of the Reformers. Hooker does not deny it, but says that it has often been abused and should not be set against authority and tradition.

Where the Word of God leaveth the Church to make choice of her own Ordinances, if against those things which have been received with great reason or against that which the ancient practice of the Church hath continued time out of mind, or against such Ordinances as the power and authority of that Church under which we live hath in itself devised for the public good, or against the discretion of the Church in mitigating sometimes with favourable equity that rigour which otherwise the literal generality of Ecclesiastical Laws hath judged to be more convenient and meet; if against all this it should be free for men to reprove, to disgrace, to reject at their own liberty what they see done and practised according to order set down; if in so great variety of ways as the wit of man is easily able to find out towards any purpose and in so great liking as all men especially have unto those inventions, whereby some one may seem to have been more enlightened from above than many thousands, the Church did give every man licence to follow what himself imagineth that God's Spirit did reveal unto him, or what he supposed that God is likely to have revealed to some special person whose virtues deserve to be highly esteemed; what other effect could hereupon ensue, but the utter confusion of his Church under pretence of being taught, led, and guided by his Spirit, the gifts and graces whereof do so naturally all tend unto common peace, that where such singularity is, they whose hearts it possesseth ought to suspect it the more; inasmuch as if it did come of God and should for that cause prevail with others, the same God which revealeth it to them would also give them power of confirming it to others, either with miraculous operation, or with strong and invincible remonstrance of sound Reason, such as whereby it might appear that God would indeed have all men's judgments give place unto it; whereas now the error and unsufficiency of their arguments do make it on the contrary side against them a strong presumption, that God hath not moved their hearts to think such things as he hath not enabled them to prove.

V x 1, 40–1

The Puritans generally disliked consecrated buildings being set apart for worship. In defending the practice, he shows himself, here and elsewhere, as adept as his opponents in citing biblical support.

Solemn duties of public service to be done unto God must have their places set and prepared in such sort as beseemeth actions of that regard. Adam even during the space of his small continuance in Paradise, had where to present himself before the Lord. Adam's sons had out of Paradise in like sort whither to bring their sacrifices. The Patriarchs used altars and mountains and groves to the self-same purpose. In the vast wilderness, when the people of God had themselves no settled habitation, yet a moveable tabernacle they were commanded of God to make. The like charge was given them against the time they should come to settle themselves in the land which had been promised unto their fathers, *Ye shall seek that place which the Lord your God shall choose.* When God had chosen Jerusalem, and in Jerusalem Mount Moriah, there to have his standing habitation made, it was in the chiefest of David's desires to have performed so good a work. His grief was no less that he could not have the honour to build God a temple, than their anger is at this day who bite asunder their own tongues with very wrath, that they have not as yet the power to pull down the temples which they never built, and to level them with the ground. It was no mean thing which he purposed. To perform a work so majestical and stately was no small charge. Therefore he incited all men unto bountiful contribution, and procured towards it with all his power, gold, silver, brass, iron, wood, precious stones, in great abundance. Yea moreover, *Because I have* (saith David) *a joy in the House of my God, I have of my own gold and silver, besides all that I have prepared for the House of the sanctuary, given to the House of my God three thousand talents of gold, even the gold of Ophir, seven thousand talents of fined silver.* After the overthrow of this first House of God, a second was instead thereof erected; but with so great odds, that they wept which had seen the former, and beheld how much this latter came behind it, the beauty whereof notwithstanding was such that even this was also the wonder of the whole world. Besides which temple, there were both in other parts of the land, and even in Jerusalem, by process of time, no small number of synagogues for men to resort unto. Our Saviour himself, and after him the Apostles, frequented both the one and the other. The Church of Christ which was in Jerusalem, and held that profession, which had not the public allowance and continuance of authority, could not so long use the exercise of Christian Religion but in private only. So that as Jews they had access to the temples and synagogues where God was served after the custom of the Law; but for that which they did as Christians they were of necessity forced otherwhere to assemble themselves. And as God gave increase to his Church, they sought out both there and abroad for that purpose not the fittest (for so the times would not suffer them to do) but the safest places they could. In process of time, some whiles by sufferance, some whiles by special leave and favour, they began to erect to themselves oratories; not in any sumptuous or stately manner, which neither was possible by reason of the poor estate of the Church and had been perilous in regard of the world's envy towards them. At the length, when it pleased God to raise up Kings and Emperors favouring sincerely the Christian truth, that which the Church before either could not or durst not do, was with all alacrity performed. Temples were in all places erected, no cost was spared, nothing judged too dear which that way should be spent. The whole world did seem to exult, that it had occasion of pouring out gifts to so blessed a purpose. That cheerful devotion which David this way did exceedingly delight to behold, and wish that the same in the Jewish people might be perpetual, was then in Christian people everywhere to be seen. Their actions, till this day always accustomed to be spoken of with great honour, are called openly into question. They, and as many as have been followers of their example in that thing, we especially that worship God either in temples which their hands made, or which other men sithence have framed by the like pattern, are in that respect charged no less than with the very sin of idolatry. Our Churches in the foam of that good spirit which directeth such fiery tongues, they term spitefully the temples of Baal, idle synagogues, abominable sties.

V xi 1–3, 42–4

He continues and develops his argument for the holiness of churches and the reverence due to them.

Our opinion concerning the force and virtue which such places have, is, I trust, without any blemish or stain of heresy. Churches receive, as everything else, their chief perfection from the end whereunto they serve. Which end being the public worship of God, they are in consideration houses of greater dignity than any provided for meaner purposes. For which cause they seem after a sort even to mourn, as being injured and defrauded of their right, when places not sanctified as they are, prevent them unnecessarily in that pre-eminence and honour. Whereby also it doth come to pass, that the service of God hath not then itself such perfection of grace and comeliness, as when the dignity of place which it wisheth for doth concur. Again, albeit the true worship of God be to God in itself acceptable, who respecteth not so much in what place, as with what affection he is served; and therefore Moses in the midst of the sea, Job on the dunghill, Ezekiah in bed, Jeremiah in mire, Jonas in the whale, Daniel in the den, the Thief on the cross, Peter and Paul in prison, calling unto God were heard, as St Basil noteth: manifest notwithstanding it is, that the very majesty and holiness of the place where God is worshipped hath in regard of us great virtue, force, and efficacy, for that it serveth as a sensible help to stir up devotion; and in that respect, no doubt, bettereth even our holiest and best actions in this kind. As therefore we everywhere exhort all men to worship God; even so, for performance of this service by the people of God assembled, we think not any place so good as the Church, neither any exhortation so fit as that of David, O *worship the Lord in the beauty of holiness*.

V xvi 1–2, 57–8

One of the strengths of the Book of Common Prayer is that if is firmly based in Scripture. If the two lessons at Morning and Evening Prayer according to the original lectionary are read daily, most of the Old Testament will be read once, and nearly all the New Testament twice, every year. This was an achievement for its compilers, and should have pleased all who affirmed the Reformed principle of the importance and sufficiency of Scripture. However, some of the Puritans objected to the reading of lessons without commentary, and maintained that the Word of God could be expounded only by sermons based in Scripture. Hooker defends this practice for instruction and edification. He notes some of the problems, still argued today, about different translations. The 'reverend prelate' refers to St Paul (Acts 15.21).

Moses and the Prophets, Christ and his Apostles, were in their times all preachers of God's truth; some by word, some by writing, some by both. This they did partly as faithful witnesses, making mere relation what

God himself had revealed unto them; and partly as careful expounders, teachers, persuaders thereof. The Church in like case preacheth still, first publishing by way of testimony or relation the truth which from them she hath received even in such sort as it was received written in the sacred volumes of Scripture; secondly by way of explication discovering the mysteries which lie hid therein. The Church as a witness preacheth his mere revealed truth by reading publicly the sacred Scripture, so that a second kind of preaching is the reading of holy writ. For this we may the boldlier speak being strengthened with the example of so reverend a Prelate as saith, that Moses from the time of ancient generations and ages long since past, had amongst the cities of the very Gentiles them that preached him, in that he was read every Sabbath day. For so of necessity it must be meant, inasmuch as we know that the Jews have always had their weekly readings of the Law of Moses; but that they always had in like manner their weekly sermons upon some part of the Law of Moses, we nowhere find. Howbeit still we must here remember, that the Church by her public reading of the book of God preacheth only as a witness. Now the principal thing required in a witness is fidelity. Wherefore as we cannot excuse that Church, which either through corrupt translations of Scripture delivereth instead of divine speeches anything repugnant unto that which God speaketh; or, through falsified additions proposeth that to the people of God as Scripture, which is in truth no Scripture; so the blame which in both these respects hath been laid upon the Church of England is surely altogether without cause. Touching translations of Holy Scripture, albeit we may not disallow of their painful travels herein who strictly have tied themselves to the very original letter; yet the judgment of the Church, as we see by the practice of all nations, Greeks, Latins, Persians, Syrians, Ethiopians, Arabians, hath been ever, that the fittest for public audience are such as following a middle course between the rigour of literal translators, and the liberty of paraphrasts, do with greatest shortness and plainness deliver the meaning of the Holy Ghost. Which being a labour of so great difficulty, the exact performance thereof we may rather wish than look for. So that, except between the words of translation and the mind of the Scripture itself there be contradiction, every little difference should not seem an intolerable blemish necessarily to be sponged out. Whereas therefore the prophet David in a certain Psalm doth say concerning Moses and Aaron, that they were obedient to the Word of God, and in the self-same place our allowed translation saith, they were not obedient, we are for this cause challenged as manifest gainsayers of Scripture, even in that which we read for Scripture unto the people. But forasmuch as words are resemblances of that which the mind of the speaker conceiveth, and conceits are images representing that which is spoken of, it followeth that they who will judge of words, should have recourse to the things themselves from whence they rise. In setting down that miracle, at the sight whereof Peter fell down astonished before the feet of Jesus, and cried, *Depart, Lord, I am a sinner,* the Evangelist St Luke saith, the store of the fish which they took was such, that the net they took it in brake, and the ships which they loaded, therewith sunk: St John recording the like miracle saith, that albeit the fishes in number were so many, yet the net with so great a weight was not broken. Suppose they had written both of one miracle; although there be in their words a manifest show of jar, yet none, if we look upon the difference of matter, with regard whereunto they might have both spoken of one miracle, the very same which they spake of divers, the one intending thereby to signify that the greatness of the burden exceeded the natural ability of the instruments which they had to bear it; the other, that the weakness thereof was supported by a supernatural and miraculous addition of strength. The nets as touching themselves brake, but through the power of God they held. Are not the words of the prophet Micah touching Bethlehem, *Thou Bethlehem the least*? And doth not the very Evangelist translate these words, *Thou Bethlehem not the least*? The one regarding the quantity of the place, the other the dignity. Micah attributeth unto it smallness in respect of circuit; Matthew greatness in regard of honour and estimation, by being the native soil of out Lord and Saviour Christ. Sith therefore speeches which gainsay one another must of necessity be applied both unto one and the self-same subject; sith they must also the one affirm, the other deny the self-same thing; what necessity of contradiction can there be between the letter of the prophet David and our authorized translation thereof, if he, understanding Moses and Aaron, do say, *They were not disobedient*; we, applying our speech to Pharaoh and the Egyptians, do say of them, *They were not obedient*? Or (which the matter itself will easily enough likewise suffer) if the Egyptians being meant by both, it be said that they, in regard of their offer to let go the people when they saw the fearful darkness, disobeyed not the word of the Lord; and yet that they did not obey his word, inasmuch as the sheep and cattle at the self-same time they withheld. Of both translations the better I willingly acknowledge that which cometh nearer to the very letter of the original verity; yet so, that the other may likewise safely enough be read, without any peril at all of gainsaying as much as the least jot or syllable of God's most sacred and precious truth.

V xix 1–3, 64–8

He continues his argument against the claim that sermons expound-
ing the Word of God are the only true preaching and that there is not
the same value in reading biblical passages. The Puritans objected to
the Apocrypha as not being the perfect Word of God; the Church of
England gave them partial recognition and included some extracts from
them in its lectionary.

We marvel the less that our reading of books not canonical is so much
impugned, when so little is attributed unto the reading of canonical
Scripture itself, that now it hath grown to be a question, Whether the
Word of God be any ordinary mean to save the souls of men, in that it
is either privately studied or publicly read and so made known, or else
only as the same is preached that is to say *explained by a lively voice* and
applied to the people's use *as the speaker in his wisdom* thinketh meet.
For this alone is it which they use to call preaching. The public reading
of the Apocrypha they condemn altogether as a thing effectual unto
evil; the bare reading in like sort of whatsoever, yea even of Scriptures
themselves, they mislike, as a thing uneffectual to do that good, which
we are persuaded may grow by it. Our desire is in this present controversy, as in the rest, not to be carried up and down with the waves of
uncertain arguments, but rather positively to lead on the minds of the
simpler sort by plainer and easy degrees, till the very nature of the thing
itself do make manifest what is truth. First therefore because whatsoever is spoken concerning the efficacy or necessity of God's word, the
same they tie and restrain only unto sermons, howbeit not sermons read
neither (for such they also abhor in the Church) but sermons without
book, sermons which spend their life in their birth and may have public
audience but once: for this cause to avoid ambiguities, wherewith they
often intangle themselves, not marking what doth agree to the word of
God in itself, and what in regard of outward accidents which may be-
fall it, we are to know that the word of God is his heavenly truth touching matters of eternal life revealed and uttered unto men; unto prophets
and apostles by immediate divine inspiration, from them to us by their
books and writings. We therefore have no Word of God but the Scripture. Apostolic sermons were unto such as heard them his word even as
properly as to us their writings are. Howbeit not so our own sermons,
the expositions which our discourse of wit doth gather and minister out
of the Word of God. For which cause in this present question we are,
when we name the Word of God, always to mean the Scripture only.
The end of the word of God is to save, and therefore we term it the
word of life. The way for all men to be saved is by the knowledge of

that truth which the word hath taught. And sith eternal life is a thing of itself communicable unto all, it behoveth that the word of God the necessary mean thereunto be so likewise. Wherefore the word of life hath been always a treasure, though precious, yet easy as well to attain as to find, lest any man desirous of life should perish through the difficulty of the way. To this end the word of God no otherwise serveth then only in the nature of a doctrinal instrument. It saveth because it maketh wise to salvation. Wherefore the ignorant it saveth not, they which live by the word must know it. And being the instrument which God hath purposely framed, thereby to work the knowledge of salvation in the hearts of men, what cause is there wherefore it should not of itself be acknowledged a most apt and a likely mean to leave an apprehension of things divine in our understanding, and in the mind an assent thereunto? For touching the one, sith God, who knoweth and discloseth best the rich treasures of his own wisdom, hath by delivering his word made choice of the Scriptures, as the most effectual means, whereby those treasures might be imparted unto the world, it followeth that to man's understanding the Scripture must needs be even of itself intended as a full and perfect discovery, sufficient to imprint in us the lively character of all things necessarily required for that attainment of eternal life. And concerning our assent to the mysteries of heavenly truth, seeing that the word of God for the author's sake hath credit with all that confess it (as we all do) to be his word, every proposition of Holy Scripture, every sentence being to us a principle, if the principles of all kinds of knowledge else have that virtue in themselves whereby they are able to procure our assent unto such conclusions as the industry of right discourse doth gather from them, we have no reason to think the principles of that truth which tendeth unto man's everlasting happiness less forcible than any other, when we know that of all other they are for their certainty the most infallible. But as everything of price, so this doth require travail. We bring not the knowledge of God with us into the world. And the less our own opportunity or hability in that way, the more we need the help of other men's judgments to be our direction herein. Nor doth any man ever believe, into whom the doctrine of belief is not instilled by instruction some way received at the first from others. Wherein whatsoever fit means there are to notify the mysteries of the word of God, whether publicly (which we call preaching) or in private howsoever, the word by *every* such mean even ordinarily doth save, and not only by being delivered unto men in sermons. *Sermons* are not the only preaching which doth save souls. For concerning the use and sense of this word preaching which they shut up in so close a

prison, although more than enough spoken to redeem the liberty thereof, yet because they insist so much and so proudly insult thereon, we
must a little inure their ears with hearing how others whom they more
regard are in this case accustomed to use the self-same language with
us whose manner of speech they deride. Justin Martyr doubteth not
to tell the Grecians that even in certain of their writings the very judgment to come is preached; nor the Council of Vaus to insinuate that
presbyters absent through infirmity from their churches might be said
to preach by those deputies who in their stead did read homilies; nor
the Council of Toledo to call the usual public reading of the Gospels in
the Church preaching; nor others long before these our days to write,
that by him who but readeth a lesson in the solemn assembly as part of
divine service the very office of preaching is so far forth executed. Such
kind of speeches were then familiar, those phrases seemed not to them
absurd, they would have marvelled to hear the outcries which we do,
because we think that the apostles in writing and others in reading to
the Church those books which the apostles wrote are neither untruly
nor unfitly said to preach. For although men's tongues and their pens
differ, yet to one and the self-same general if not particular effect they
may both serve. It is no good argument, St Paul could not write with his
tongue, therefore could he neither preach with his pen. For preaching
is a general end whereunto writing and speaking do both serve. Men
speak not with the instruments of writing, neither write with the instruments of speech and yet things recorded with the one and uttered with
the other may be preached well enough with both. By their patience
therefore be it spoken, the apostles preached as well when they wrote
as when they spake the gospel of Christ, and our usual public reading
of the Word of God for the people's instruction is preaching. Nor about
words would we ever contend, were not their purpose so restraining
the same injurious to God's most sacred word and Spirit. It is on both
sides confessed that the word of God outwardly administered (his Spirit
inwardly concurring therewith) converteth, edifieth, and saveth souls.
Now whereas the external administration of his word is as well by
reading barely the Scripture, as by explaining the same when sermons
thereon be made, in the one they deny that the finger of God hath ordinarily certain principal operations, which we most steadfastly hold and
believe that it hath in both.

V xxi 1–5, 84–8

*After affirming the great importance of preaching, he further defends
the practice of direct reading from Scripture. The present age has the*

blessing of easier access to the sacred texts, a fact which had been welcomed by all the Reformers and which the Puritan opposition could hardly deny.

So worthy a part of divine service we should greatly wrong, if we did not esteem preaching as the blessed ordinance of God, sermons as keys to the Kingdom of Heaven, as wings to the soul, as spurs to the good affections of man, unto the sound and healthy as food, as physic unto diseased minds. Wherefore, how highly soever it may please them with words of truth to extol sermons, they shall not herein offend us. We seek not to derogate from anything which they can justly esteem, but our desire is to uphold the just estimation of that from which it seemeth unto us that they derogate more than becometh them. That which offendeth us is first, the great disgrace which they offer unto our custom of bare reading the Word of God and to his gracious Spirit, the principal virtue whereof thereby manifesting itself for the endless good of men's souls, even the virtue which it hath to convert, to edify, to save souls, this they mightily strive to obscure: and secondly, the shifts wherewith they maintain their opinion of sermons, whereunto while they labour to appropriate the saving power of the Holy Ghost, they separate from all apparent hope of life and salvation thousands whom the goodness of Almighty God doth not exclude. Touching therefore the use of Scripture, even in that it is openly read, and the inestimable good, which the Church of God by that very means hath reaped; there was, we may very well think, some cause which moved the Apostle St Paul to require that any one Church's affairs gave particular occasion to write, might, for the instruction of all be published, and that by reading. When the very having of the books of God was a matter of no small charge and difficulty, inasmuch as they could not be had otherwise than only in written copies, it was the necessity not of preaching things agreeable with the Word, but of reading the Word itself at large to the people, which caused Churches throughout the world to have public care that the sacred Oracles of God, being procured by common charge, might with great sedulity be kept both entire and sincere. If then we admire the providence of God in the same continuance of Scripture, notwithstanding the violent endeavours of Infidels to abolish, and the fraudulence of Heretics always to deprave the same, shall we set light by that custom of reading from whence so precious a benefit hath grown?

The voice and testimony of the Church, acknowledging Scripture to be the Law of the living God, is for the truth and certainty thereof no mean evidence. For if with reason we may presume upon things which a few men's depositions do testify, suppose we that the minds of men are not, both at their first access to the school of Christ exceedingly moved, yea and for ever afterwards also confirmed much, when they consider the main consent of all the Churches in the whole world witnessing the sacred authority of Scriptures, ever sithence the first publication thereof even till this present day and hour? And that they all have always so testified, I see not how we should possibly wish a proof more palpable than this manifest received and everywhere continued custom of reading them publicly as the Scriptures. The reading therefore of the Word of God, as the use hath ever been, in open audience, is the plainest assent and acknowledgment that it is his Word.

V xxii 1, 88–9

He continues to affirm the importance of hearing the Word of God without intermediary, and addresses the criticism that Scripture may be too hard for unaided understanding.

Touching hardness, which is the second pretended impediment as against homilies, being plain, it is no bar, so neither doth it infringe the efficacy, no not of Scriptures, although but read. The force of reading, how small soever they will have it, must of necessity be granted sufficient to notify that which is plain or easy to be understood. And of things necessary to all men's salvation, we have been hitherto accustomed to hold (especially sithence the publishing of the Gospel of Jesus Christ, whereby the simplest having now a key unto knowledge which the Eunuch in the Acts did want, our children may of themselves by reading understand that which he without an interpreter could not) they are in Scripture plain and easy to be understood. As for those things which at the first are obscure and dark, when memory hath laid them up for a time, judgment afterwards growing explaineth them. Scripture therefore is not so hard, but that the only reading thereof may give life unto willing hearers. The easy performance of which holy labour is, in like sort, a very cold objection to prejudice the virtue thereof. For what though an Infidel, yea though a child, may be able to read; there is no doubt, but the meanest and worst amongst the people under the Law had been as able as the priests themselves were to offer sacrifice; did this make sacrifice of no effect unto that purpose for which it was instituted? In Religion some duties are not commended so much by the hardness of their execution, as by the worthiness and dignity of that acceptation wherein they are held with God. We admire the goodness of God in Nature; when we consider how he hath provided, that things most needful to preserve this life should be most prompt and easy for all living creatures to come by. Is it not as evident a sign of his wonderful providence over us, when the food of eternal life, upon the utter want whereof our endless death and destruction necessarily ensueth, is prepared and always set in such a readiness that those very means, than which nothing is more easy, may suffice to procure the same? Surely, if we perish it is not the lack of scribes and learned expounders that can be our just excuse. The Word which saveth our souls is near us; we need for knowledge but to read and live. The man which readeth the Word of God, the Word itself doth pronounce blessed if he also observe the same. Now all these things being well considered, it shall be no intricate matter for any man to judge with indifferency on which part the good of the Church is most conveniently sought; whether on ours, whose opinion is such as hath been showed, or else on theirs who leaving no ordinary way of salvation for them unto whom the Word of God is but only read, do seldom name them but with great disdain and contempt who execute that service in the Church of Christ. By means whereof it hath come to pass, that Churches which cannot enjoy the benefit of usual preaching are judged as it were even forsaken of God, forlorn and without either hope or comfort: contrariwise, those places which every day, for the most part, are at sermons as the flowing sea, do by their emptiness at times of reading, and by other apparent tokens show to the voice of the living God, this way sounding in the ears of men, a great deal less reverence than were meet. But if no other evil were known to grow thereby, who can choose but think them cruel which doth hear them so boldly teach, that if God, (as to him there is nothing impossible) do haply save any such as continue where they have all other means of instruction, but are not taught by continual preaching, yet this is miraculous, and more than the fitness of so poor instruments can give any man cause to hope for; that Sacraments are not effectual to salvation, except men be instructed by preaching before they be made partakers of them; yea, that both Sacraments and prayers also, where sermons are not, *do not only not feed, but are ordinarily to further condemnation*; what man's heart doth not rise but at the mention of these things?

V xxii 14–17, 106–9

Hooker, an experienced and noted preacher, raises questions about the nature and effect of sermons. The Church had authorized two Books of Homilies to be read in churches, particularly, but not only, by clergy not licensed to preach their own sermons. The Homilies had status as *teaching sound doctrine, but the Puritans objected to the reading of set words.*

If preaching be most profitable to man's salvation, then is not reading; if reading be, then preaching is not. Are they resolved then at the leastwise, if preaching be the only ordinary mean whereby it pleaseth God to save our souls, what kind of preaching it is which doth save? Understand they how or in what respect there is that force or virtue in preaching? We have reason wherefore to make these demands; for that, although their pens run all upon preaching and sermons, yet when themselves do practise that whereof they write, they change their dialect, and those words they shun as if there were in them some secret sting. It is not their phrase to say they preach, or to give to their own instructions and exhortations the name of sermon; the pain they take themselves in this kind is either opening, or lecturing, or reading, or exercising, but in no case preaching. And in this present question, they also warily protest that what they ascribe to the virtue of preaching, they still mean it of good preaching. Now one of them saith that a good sermon must expound and apply a large portion of the text of Scripture at one time. Another giveth us to understand, that sound preaching *is not to do as one did at London, who spent most of his time in invectives against good men, and told his audience how the magistrate should have an eye to such as troubled the peace of the Church.* The best of them hold it for no good preaching, *when a man endeavoureth to make a glorious show of eloquence and learning, rather than to apply himself to the capacity of the simple.* But let them shape us out a good preacher by what pattern soever pleaseth them best; let them exclude and inclose whom they will with their definitions, we are not desirous to enter into any contention with them about this, or to abate the conceit they have of their own ways, so that when once we are agreed what sermons shall currently pass for good, we may at length understand from them, what that is in a good sermon which doth make it the Word of Life unto such as hear. If substance of matter, evidence of things, strength and validity of arguments and proofs, or if any other virtue else which words and sentences may contain; of all this, what is there in the best sermons being uttered, which they lose by being read? But they utterly deny that the reading either of Scriptures or homilies and sermons, can ever by the ordinary grace of God save any soul. So that although we had all the sermons word for word which James, Paul, Peter, and the rest of the Apostles made, some one of which sermons was of power to convert thousands of the hearers unto Christian Faith; yea, although we had all the instructions, exhortations, consolations which came from the gracious lips of our Lord Jesus Christ himself, and should read them ten thousand times over, to Faith and Salvation no man could hope hereby to attain. Whereupon it must of necessity follow that the vigour and vital efficacy of sermons doth grow from certain accidents, which are not in them, but in their master: his virtue, his gesture, his countenance, his zeal, the motion of his body, and the inflection of his voice, who first uttereth them as his own, is that which giveth them the form, the nature, the very essence of instruments available to eternal life. If they like neither that nor this, what remaineth but that their final conclusion be, *Sermons we know are the only ordinary means to Salvation, but why or how we cannot tell?* Wherefore to end this tedious controversy, wherein the too great importunity of our over-eager adversaries hath constrained us much longer to dwell than the barrenness of so poor a cause could have seemed at the first likely either to require or to admit, if they which without partialities and passions are accustomed to weigh all things and accordingly to give their sentence, shall here sit down to receive our audit, and cast up the whole reckoning on both sides, the sum which truth amounteth unto will appear to be but this; that as medicines, provided of nature and applied by art for the benefit of bodily health, take effect sometime under and sometime above the natural proportion of their virtue, according as the mind and fancy of the patient doth more or less concur with them, so whether we barely read unto men the Scriptures of God, or by homilies concerning matter of belief and conversation seek to lay before them the duties which they owe unto God and man; whether we deliver them books to read and consider of in private at their own best leisure, or call them to the hearing of sermons publicly in the House of God; albeit every of these and the like unto these means do truly and daily effect that in the hearts of men for which they are each and all meant; yet the operation which they have in common being most sensibly and most generally noted in one kind above the rest, that one hath in some men's opinions drowned altogether the rest, and injuriously brought to pass that they have been thought not less effectual than the other, but without the other uneffectual to save souls. Whereas the cause why sermons only are observed to prevail so much, while all means else seem to sleep, and do nothing, is in truth but that singular affection and attention which the people showeth everywhere towards the one and their cold disposition to the other; the reason hereof being partly the art which our adversaries use for the credit of their sermons, to bring men out of conceit with all other teaching besides; partly a custom which men have to let those things carelessly pass by their ears which they have oftentimes heard before, or know they may hear again whenever it pleaseth themselves; partly the especial advantages which sermons naturally have to procure attention, both in that they come always new, and because by the hearer it is still presumed, that if they be let slip for the present, what good soever they contain is lost, and that without all hope of recovery. This is the true cause of odds between sermons and other kinds of wholesome instruction.

V xxii 19–20, 111–4

A vigorous attack on several opposing arguments: the sanctity of churches, the sharing of set forms in public worship, the honourable status of the clergy. These things draw worshippers together within the invisible Church. If the spirit of the early Church prevailed everywhere now, there would be no need for laws against recusancy.

A great part of the cause wherefore religious minds are so inflamed with the love of public devotion, is that virtue, force and efficacy, which by experience they find that the very form and reverend solemnity of common prayer duly ordered hath, to help that imbecility and weakness in us, by means whereof we are otherwise of ourselves the less apt to perform unto God so heavenly a service, with such affection of heart, and disposition in the powers of our soul as is requisite. To this end therefore all things hereunto appertaining have been ever thought convenient to be done with the most solemnity and majesty that the wisest could devise. It is not with public as with private prayer. In this rather secrecy is commended than outward show, whereas that being the public act of a whole society, requireth accordingly the more care to be had of external appearance. The very assembling of men therefore unto this service hath been ever solemn. And concerning the place of assembly, although it serve for other uses as well as this, yet seeing that our Lord himself hath to this, as to the chiefest of all other, plainly sanctified his own Temple, by entitling it *the house of prayer*, what pre-eminence of dignity soever hath been either by the ordinance, or through the special favour and providence of God annexed unto his Sanctuary, the principal cause thereof must needs be in regard of *common* prayer. For the honour and furtherance whereof, if it be as the gravest of the ancient fathers seriously were persuaded, and do oftentimes plainly teach, affirming that the house of prayer is a court beautified with the presence of celestial powers, that there we stand, we pray, we sound forth hymns unto God, having his Angels intermingled as our associates; and that with reference hereunto the apostle doth require so great care to be had of decency for the angels' sake; how can we come to the house of prayer, and not be moved with the very glory of the place itself, so to frame our affections praying, as doth best beseem them, whose suits the Almighty doth there sit to hear, and his angels attend to further? When this was ingrafted in the minds of men, there needed no penal statutes to draw them unto public prayer. The warning sound was no sooner heard, but the Churches were presently filled, the pavements covered with bodies prostrate, and washed with their tears of devout joy. And as the place of public prayer is a circumstance in the outward form thereof, which hath moment to help devotion; so the person much more with whom the people of God do join themselves in this action, as with him that standeth and speaketh in the presence of God for them. The authority of his place, the fervour of his zeal, the piety and gravity of his whole behaviour, must needs accordingly both grace and set forward the service he doth. The authority of his calling is a furtherance, because if God have so far received him into favour, as to impose upon him by the hands of men that office of blessing the people in his name and making intercession to him in theirs, which office he hath sanctified with his own most gracious promise, and ratified that promise by manifest actual performance thereof, when others before in like place have done the same, is not his very ordination a seal as it were to us that the self-same divine love which hath chosen the instrument to work with, will by that instrument effect the thing whereto he ordained it, in blessing his people and accepting the prayers which his servant offereth up unto God for them? It was in this respect a comfortable title which the ancients used to give unto God's ministers, terming them usually *God's most beloved*, which were ordained to procure by their prayers his love and favour towards all. Again if there be not zeal and fervency in him which proposeth for the rest those suits and supplications which they by their joyful acclamations must ratify; if he praise not God with all his might; if he pour not out his soul in prayer; if he take not their causes to heart, and speak not as Moses, Daniel, and Ezra did for their people; how should there be but in them frozen coldness, when his affections seem benumbed from whom theirs should take fire? Virtue and godliness of life are required at the hands of the minister of God, not only in that he is to teach and instruct the people, who for the most part are rather led away by the ill example, than directed aright by the wholesome instruction of them, whose life swerveth from the rule of their own doctrine; but also much more in regard of this other part of his function; whether we respect the weakness of the people, apt to loathe and abhor the sanctuary when they which perform the service thereof are such as the sons of Heli were; or else consider the inclination of God himself, who requireth the lifting up of pure hands in prayers, and hath given the world plainly to understand that the wicked, although they cry, shall not be heard. They are not fit supplicants to seek his mercy on the behalf of others, whose own unrepented sins provoke his just indignation. *Let thy priests therefore, O Lord, be evermore clothed with righteousness, that thy saints may* thereby with more devotion *rejoice and sing*! But of all helps for due performance of this service, the greatest is that very set and standing order itself, which framed with common advice, hath both for matter and form prescribed whatsoever is herein publicly done. No doubt from God it hath proceeded, and by us it must be acknowledged a work of singular care and providence, that the Church hath evermore held a prescript form of Common Prayer, although not in all things everywhere the same, yet for the most part retaining still the same analogy. So that if the Liturgies of all ancient Churches throughout the world be compared amongst themselves, it may be easily perceived they had all one original mould, and that the public prayer of the people of God in Churches thoroughly settled, did never use to be voluntary dictates, proceeding from any men's extemporal wit. To him which considereth the grievous and scandalous inconveniences whereunto they make themselves daily subject, with whom any blind and secret corner is judged a fit house of Common Prayer; the manifold confusions which they fall into, where every man's private spirit and gift (as they term it) is the only bishop that ordaineth him to his ministry; the irksome deformities whereby through endless and senseless effusions of undigested prayers, they oftentimes disgrace in most unsufferable manner the worthiest part of Christian duty towards God, who herein are subject to no certain order, but pray both what and how they list; to him, I say, which weigheth duly all these things, the reasons cannot be obscure why God doth in public prayer so much respect the solemnity of places where the authority and calling of persons by whom, and the precise appointment even with what words or sentences, his name should be called on amongst his people.

V xxv 1–5, 118–21

He follows with a more precise defence of set liturgy, one of the chief Puritan objections, justifying it by biblical reference. He refers specifically to the three biblical canticles used in Morning and Evening Prayer.

No man hath hitherto been so impious, as plainly and directly to condemn prayer. The best stratagem that Satan hath, who knoweth his kingdom to be no one way more shaken than by the public devout prayers of God's Church, is by traducing the form and manner of them to bring them into contempt; and so to shake the force of all men's devotion towards them. From this, and from no other forge, hath proceeded a strange conceit, that to serve God with any set form of Common Prayer is superstitious. As though God himself did not frame to his priests the very speech wherewith they were charged to bless the people; or as if our Lord, even of purpose to prevent this fancy of extemporal and voluntary prayers, had not left us of his own framing one which might both remain as a part of the Church Liturgy, and serve as a pattern whereby to frame all other prayers with efficacy, yet without superfluity of words. If prayers were no otherwise accepted of God than being conceived always new, according to the exigence of present occasions; if it be right to judge him by our own bellies, and to imagine that he doth loathe to have the self-same supplications often iterated, even as we do to be every day fed without alteration or change of diet; if prayers be actions which ought to waste away themselves in the making; if being made to remain that they may be resumed and used again as prayers, they be but instruments of superstition; surely we cannot excuse Moses, who gave such occasion of scandal to the world by not being contented to praise the name of Almighty God according to the usual naked simplicity of God's Spirit, for that admirable victory given them against Pharaoh, unless so dangerous a precedent were left for the casting of prayers into certain poetical moulds, and for the framing of prayers which might be repeated often, although they never had again the same occasions which brought them forth at the first. For that very hymn of Moses grew afterwards to be a part of the ordinary Jewish Liturgy; not only that, but sundry other sithence invented. Their books of Common Prayer contained partly hymns taken out of the Holy Scripture, partly benedictions, thanksgivings, supplications, penned by such as have been from time to time the governors of that synagogue. These they sorted into their several times and places, some to begin the service of God with, and some to end, some to go before, and some to follow, and some to be interlaced between the divine readings of the Law and Prophets. Unto their custom of finishing the Passover with certain Psalms, there is not anything more probable, than that the holy Evangelist doth evidently allude, saying, That after the cup delivered by our Saviour unto his Apostles, they sung, and went forth to the mount of Olives. As the Jews had their songs of Moses, and David, and the rest; so the Church of Christ from the very beginning hath both used the same, and besides them other of like nature; the song of the Virgin Mary, the song of

Zachary, the song of Simeon, such hymns as the Apostle doth often speak of, saying, *I will pray and sing with the Spirit.* Again, *in Psalms, hymns, and songs, making melody unto the Lord, and that heartily.* Hymns and Psalms are such kinds of prayer as are not wont to be conceived upon a sudden; but are framed by meditation beforehand, or else by prophetical illumination are inspired, as at that time it appeareth they were, when God by extraordinary gifts of the Spirit enabled men to all parts of service necessary for the edifying of his Church.

V xxvi 1–3, 121–4

Some of the more moderate Puritans were disposed to accept the idea of a set liturgy, but found fault with the Prayer Book as having too many traces of Roman tradition. Hooker denies this, reducing the argument close to absurdity by detailed listing of objections ranging from serious to trivial.

Now, albeit the admonitioners did seem at the first to allow no prescript form of prayer at all, but thought it the best that their minister should always be left to pray as his own discretion did serve; yet because this opinion upon better advice they afterwards retracted, their defender and his associates have sithence proposed to the world a form such as themselves like and, to show their dislike of ours, have taken against it those exceptions, which whosoever doth measure by number, must needs be greatly out of love with a thing that hath so many faults; whosoever by weight cannot choose but esteem very highly of that wherein the wit of so scrupulous adversaries hath not hitherto observed any defect which themselves can seriously think to be of moment. Gross errors and manifest impiety they grant we have taken away; Yet many things in it they say are amiss; many instances they give of things in our Common Prayer, not agreeable, as they pretend, with the Word of God. It hath in their eye too great affinity with the form of the Church of Rome; it differeth too much from that which Churches elsewhere reformed allow and observe; our attire disgraceth it; it is not orderly read nor gestured as beseemeth; it requireth nothing to be done which a child may not lawfully do; it hath a number of short cuts or shreddings, which may be better called wishes than prayers; it intermingleth prayings and readings in such manner as if supplicants should use in proposing their suits unto mortal princes, all the world would judge them mad; it is too long, and by that mean abridgeth preaching; it appointeth the people to say after the minister; it spendeth time in singing and in reading the Psalms by course from side to side; it useth the Lord's Prayer too oft;

the songs of *Magnificat, Benedictus,* and *Nunc Dimittis,* it might very well spare; it hath the Litany, the Creed of Athanasius, and *Gloria Patri,* which are superfluous; it craveth earthly things too much; for deliverance from those evils against which we pray it giveth no thanks; some things it asketh unseasonably, when they need not to be prayed for, as deliverance from thunder and tempest, when no danger is nigh; some in too abject and diffident a manner, as that God would give us that which we for our unworthiness dare not ask; some which ought not to be desired, as the deliverance from sudden death, riddance from all adversity, and the extent of saving mercy towards all men. These and such like are the imperfections whereby our form of Common Prayer is thought to swerve from the Word of God. A great favourer of that part, but yet (his error that way excepted) a learned, painful, a right virtuous and good man, did not fear sometime to undertake, against Popish detractors, the general maintenance and defence of our whole Church service, as having in it nothing repugnant to the Word of God: and even they which would file away most from the largeness of that offer do notwithstanding in more sparing terms acknowledge little less. For when those opposite judgments which never are wont to con- strue things doubtful to the better, those very tongues which are always prone to aggravate whatsoever hath but the least show whereby it may be suspected to savour of, or to sound towards any evil, do by their own voluntary sentence clearly free us from gross and from manifest impiety herein; who would not judge us to be discharged of all blame, which are confessed to have no great fault, even by their very word and testimony in whose eyes no fault of ours hath ever hitherto been accus- tomed to seem small? Nevertheless, what they seem to offer us with one hand, the same with the other they pull back again. They grant we err not in palpable manner, we are not openly, and notoriously impious; yet errors we have, which the sharp insight of these wisest men espy; there is hidden impiety, which the profounder sort are able enough to disclose. Their skilful ears perceive certain harsh and unpleasant dis- cords in the sound of our Common Prayer, such as the rules of divine harmony, such as the Laws of God cannot bear.

V xxvii 1–2, 124–7

After justifying the use of the surplice, claiming that 'there is no one sentence in all the Scriptures of God which doth control the wearing of it in such manner, and to such purpose, as the Church of England alloweth', he meets objections to set places and positions during the service. These were all matters which would continue to be disputed but

*which were becoming part of the Anglican formation. This passage is
instructive about the details and rationale of Church practice in the late
sixteenth century.*

Having thus disputed whether the surplice be a fit garment to be used
in the service of God, the next question whereinto we are drawn is,
whether it be a thing allowable or no that the minister should say service in the Chancel, or turn his face at any time from the people, or
before service ended move from the place where it was begun? By them
which trouble us with those doubts, we would willingly be resolved of
a greater doubt; whether it be not a kind of taking God's name in vain
to debase Religion with such frivolous disputes, as will bestow time and
labour about them? Things of such mean regard and quality, although
necessary to be considered, are notwithstanding very unsavoury when
they come to be disputed of; because disputation presupposeth some
difficulty in the matter which is argued, whereas in things of this nature
they must be either very simple or very froward, who need to be taught
by disputation what is meet. When we make profession of our Faith, we
stand; when we acknowledge our sins, or seek unto God for favour, we
fall down; because the gesture of constancy becometh us best in the one,
in the other the behaviour of humility. Some parts of our Liturgy consist in the reading of the Word of God, and the proclaiming of his Law,
that the people may thereby learn what their duties are towards him;
some consist in words of praise and thanksgiving whereby we acknowledge unto God what his blessings are towards us; some are such as albeit
they serve to singular good purpose even when there is no Communion
administered, nevertheless being devised at the first for that purpose,
are at the Table of the Lord for that cause also commonly read; some
are uttered as from the people, some as with them unto God, some as
from God unto them, all as before his sight whom we fear, and whose
presence to offend with any the least unseemliness we be surely as
loath as they who most reprehend or deride that we do. Now, because
the Gospels which are weekly read do all historically declare something
which our Lord Jesus Christ himself either spake, did, or suffered in his
own person; it hath been the custom of Christian men then especially in
token of the greater reverence to stand, to utter certain words of accla-
mation, and at the name of Jesus to bow. Which harmless Ceremonies,
as there is no man constrained to use; so we know no reason wherefore
any man should yet imagine it an unsufferable evil. It showeth a reverend
regard to the Son of God above other messengers, although speaking
as from God also. And against Infidels, Jews, Arians, who derogate

from the honour of Jesus Christ, such Ceremonies are thus profitable. As for any erroneous estimation, advancing the Son above the Father and the Holy Ghost, seeing that the truth of his equality with them is a mystery so hard for the wits of mortal men to rise unto, of all heresies that which may give him superiority above them is least to be feared. But to let go this as a matter scarce worth the speaking of, whereas if fault be in these things anywhere justly found, Law hath referred the whole disposition and redress thereof to the Ordinary of the place; they which elsewhere complain that disgrace and injury is offered even to the meanest parish minister when the magistrate appointed him what to wear, and leaveth not so small a matter as that to his own discretion, being presumed a man discreet and trusted with the care of the people's souls, do think the gravest Prelates in the land no competent judges to discern and appoint where it is fit for the minister to stand, or which way convenient to look. From their Ordinary therefore they appeal to themselves, finding great fault that we neither reform the thing against the which they have long since given sentence, nor yet make answer unto what they bring, Which is, that Saint Luke declaring how *Peter stood up in the midst of the Disciples*, did thereby deliver an unchangeable rule, that whatsoever is done in the Church, ought to be done in the midst of the Church; and therefore not baptism to be administered in one place, marriage solemnized in another, the Supper of the Lord received in a third, in a fourth sermons, in a fifth prayers to be made; that the custom which we use is Levitical, absurd, and such as hindereth the understanding of the people; that if it be meet for the minister, at some time to look towards the people, if the body of the Church be a fit place for some part of divine service, it must needs follow, that whensoever his face is turned any other way, or anything done any other where, it hath absurdity. All these reasons, they say, have been brought, and were hitherto never answered; besides a number of merriments and jests unanswered likewise, wherewith they have presently moved much laughter at our manner of serving God. Such is their evil hap to play upon dull spirited men. We are still persuaded that a bare denial is answer sufficient to things which mere fancy objecteth; and that the best apology to words of scorn and petulancy, is Isaac's apology to his brother Ishmael, the apology which patience and silence maketh. Our answer therefore to their reasons is, No; to their scoffs, nothing.

V xxx 1–4, 138–42

In a passage of resistance to the Puritan excessive emphasis on personal ability in worship, he meets objections that reading set services

*needs no skill or inspiration in the minister. He then turns to more ma-
terial affairs, complaining of secular appropriation of church property
and the meanness of endowments, and other disincentives to seeking
ordination.*

When they object that our book requireth nothing to be done which
a child may not do as *lawfully and as well as that man wherewith
the book contenteth itself,* is it their meaning that the service of God
ought to be a matter of great difficulty, a labour which requireth great
learning and deep skill, or else that the book containing it should teach
what men are fit to attend upon it, and forbid either men unlearned or
children to be admitted thereunto? In setting down the form of common prayer, there was no need that the book should mention either the
learning of a fit, or the fitness of an ignorant minister, more than that he
which describeth the manner how to pitch a field should speak of moderation and sobriety in diet. And concerning the duty itself, although
the hardness thereof be not such as needeth much art, yet surely they
seem to be very far carried besides themselves to whom the dignity of
public prayer doth not discover somewhat more fitness in men of gravity
and ripe discretion than in children of *ten years of age,* for the decent
discharge and performance of that office. It cannot be that they who
speak thus should thus judge. At the board and in private it very well
becometh children's innocence to pray, and their elders to say Amen.
Which being a part of their virtuous education, serveth greatly both
to nourish in them the fear of God, and to put us in continual remembrance of that powerful grace which openeth the mouths of infants to
sound his praise. But public prayer, the service of God in the solemn
assembly of Saints, is a work though easy yet withal so weighty and of
such respect, that the great facility thereof is but a slender argument to
prove it may be as well and as lawfully committed to children as to men
of years, howsoever their hability of learning be but only to do that in
decent order wherewith the book contenteth itself. The book requireth
but orderly reading. As in truth what should any prescript form of
prayer framed to the minister's hand require, but only so to be read as
behoveth? We know that there are in the world certain voluntary overseers of ill books, whose censure in this respect would fall as sharp on
us as it hath done on many others, if delivering but a form of prayer,
we should either express or include anything more then doth properly
concern prayer. The minister's greatness or meanness of knowledge to
do other things, his aptness or insufficiency otherwise than by reading
to instruct the flock standeth in this place as a stranger with whom our

form of common prayer hath nothing to do. Wherein their exception against easiness, as if that did nourish ignorance, proceedeth altogether of a needless jealousy. I have often heard it inquired of by many, how it might be brought to pass that the Church should everywhere have able preachers to instruct the people; what impediments there are to hinder it, and which were the speediest way to remove them. In which consultations the multitude of parishes, the paucity of schools, the manifold discouragements which are offered unto men's inclination that way, the penury of the ecclesiastical estate, the irrecoverable loss of so many livings of principal value clean taken away from the Church long sithence by being appropriated, the daily bruises that spiritual promotions use to take by often falling, the want of somewhat in certain statutes which concern the state of the Church, the too great facility of many Bishops, the stony hardness of too many patrons' hearts not touched with any feeling in this case: such things oftentimes are debated and much thought upon by them that enter into any discourse concerning defect of knowledge in the clergy. But whosoever be found guilty, the communion book hath surely deserved least to be called in question for this fault. If all the clergy were as learned as themselves are that most complain of ignorance in others, yet our book of prayer might remain the same; and remaining the same it is, I see not how it can be a let unto any man's skill in preaching. Which thing we acknowledge to be God's good gift, howbeit no such necessary element that every act of religion should be thought imperfect and lame wherein there is not somewhat exacted that none can discharge but an able preacher.

V xxxi 1–4, 142–4

There were further objections to prayers for material as well as spiritual benefits, and repetition of the Lord's Prayer. These matters continue to arouse occasional criticism; Hooker's reply is still valid.

In vain we labour to persuade them that anything can take away the tediousness of prayer, except it be brought to the very same, both measure and form, which themselves assign. Whatsoever therefore our Liturgy hath more than theirs, under one devised pretence or another they cut it off. We have of prayers for earthly things in their opinion too great a number; so oft to rehearse the Lord's prayer in so small a time is as they think a loss of time; the people praying after the minister they say both wasteth time, and also maketh an unpleasant sound; the Psalms they would not have to be made (as they are) a part of our common prayer, nor to be sung or said by turns, nor such music to be used with them; those evangelical hymns they allow not to stand in our Liturgy; the Litany, the Creed of Athanasius, the sentence of Glory wherewith we use to conclude Psalms, these things they cancel, as having been instituted in regard of occasions peculiar to the times of old, and as being therefore now superfluous. Touching prayers for things earthly, we ought not to think that the Church hath set down so many of them without cause. They peradventure, which find this fault, are of the same affection with Solomon, so that if God should offer to grant them whatsoever they ask, they would neither crave riches, nor length of days, nor yet victory over their enemies, but only an understanding heart, for which cause themselves having eagles' wings are offended to see others fly so near the ground. But the tender kindness of the Church of God it very well beseemeth to help the weaker sort which are by so great odds more in number, although some few of the perfecter and stronger may be therewith for a time displeased. Ignorant we are not, that of such as resorted to our Saviour Christ being present on earth, there came not any unto him with better success for the benefit of their souls' everlasting happiness, than they whose bodily necessities gave them the first occasion to seek relief, where they saw willingness and hability of doing every way good unto all. The graces of the spirit are much more precious than worldly benefits; our ghostly evils of greater importance then any harm which the body feeleth. Therefore our desires to heavenward should both in measure and number no less exceed than their glorious object doth every way excel in value. These things are true and plain in the eye of a perfect judgment. But yet it must be withal considered, that the greatest part of the world are they which be farthest from perfection. Such being better able by sense to discern the wants of this present life than by spiritual capacity to apprehend things above sense, which tend to their happiness in the world to come, are in that respect the more apt to apply their minds even with hearty affection and zeal at the least unto those branches of public prayer, wherein their own particular is moved. And by this mean there stealeth upon them a double benefit; first because that good affection, which things of smaller accompt have once set on work, is by so much the more easily raised higher; and secondly in that the very custom of seeking so particular aid and relief at the hands of God doth by a secret contradiction withdraw them from endeavouring to help themselves by those wicked shifts, which they know can never have his allowance, whose assistance their prayer seeketh. These multiplied petitions of worldly things in prayer have therefore, besides their direct use a service whereby the Church underhand, through a kind of heavenly fraud, taketh therewith the souls of men as with certain baits. If then their calculation be true (for so they reckon) that a full third of our prayers be allotted unto earthly benefits, for which our Saviour in his platform hath appointed but one petition amongst seven, the difference is without any great disagreement; we respecting what men are, and doing which is meet in regard of the common imperfection; our Lord contrariwise proposing the most absolute proportion that can be in men's desires, the very highest mark whereat we are able to aim. For which cause also our custom is both to place it in the front of our prayers as a guide, and to add it in the end of some principal limbs or parts as a complement which fully perfecteth whatsoever may be defective in the rest. Twice we rehearse it ordinarily, and oftener as occasion requireth more solemnity or length in the form of divine service, not mistrusting, till these new curiosities sprang up, that ever any man would think our labour herein misspent, the time wastefully consumed, and the service itself made worse by so repeating that which otherwise would more hardly be made familiar to the simpler sort, for the good of whose souls there is not in Christian religion any thing of like continual use and force throughout every hour and moment of their whole lives. I mean not only because prayer, but because this very prayer is of such efficacy and necessity. For that our Saviour did but set men a bare example how to contrive or devise prayers of their own, and no way bind them to use this, is no doubt an error. John the Baptist's disciples which had been always brought up in the bosom of God's Church from the time of their first infancy till they came to the school of John, were not so brutish that they could be ignorant how to call upon the name of God, but of their master they had received a form of prayer amongst themselves, which form none did use saving his disciples, so that by it as by a mark of special difference they were known from others. And of this the Apostles having taken notice, they request that as John had taught his, so Christ would likewise teach them to pray.

V xxxv 1–3, 152–5

Puritans objected to the Psalms being observed separately from the rest of Scripture. The Psalter annexed to the Prayer Book is worked through continuously every month. In common with others of his time and later, Hooker assumes Davidic authorship of the Psalms. He is also of his age in loving music and finding it an aid to worship.

The complaint which they make about Psalms and hymns might as well be overpast without any answer, as it is without any cause brought forth. But our desire is to content them, if it may be, and to yield them a just reason even of the least things, wherein undeservedly they have but as much as dreamed or suspected that we do amiss. They seem sometimes so to speak, as if it greatly offended them that such hymns and Psalms as are Scripture should in Common Prayer be otherwise used than the rest of the Scripture is wont; sometimes displeased they are at the artificial music which we add unto Psalms of this kind, or of any other nature else; sometime the plainest and the most intelligible rehearsal of them yet they savour not, because it is done by interlocution; and with a mutual return of sentences from side to side. They are not ignorant what difference there is between other parts of Scripture and Psalms. The choice and flower of all things profitable in other books, the Psalms do both more briefly contain, and more movingly also express, by reason of that poetical form wherewith they are written. The ancients, when they speak of the Book of Psalms, use to fall into large discourses, showing how this part above the rest doth of purpose set forth and celebrate all the considerations and operations which belong to God; it magnifieth the holy meditations and actions of divine men; it is of things heavenly an universal declaration, working in them whose hearts God inspireth with the due consideration thereof, an habit or disposition of mind whereby they are made fit vessels, both for receipt and for delivery of whatsoever spiritual perfection. What is there necessary for man to know, which the Psalms are not able to teach? They are to beginners an easy and familiar introduction, a mighty augmentation of all virtue and knowledge in such as are entered before, a strong confirmation to the most perfect amongst others. Heroical magnanimity, exquisite justice, grave moderation, exact wisdom, repentance unfeigned, unwearied patience, the mysteries of God, the sufferings of Christ, the terrors of wrath, the comforts of grace, the works of Providence over this world, and the promised joys of that world which is to come, all good necessarily to be either known, or done, or had, this one celestial fountain yieldeth. Let there be any grief or disease incident unto the soul of man, any wound or sickness named, for which there is not in this treasure-house a present comfortable remedy at all times ready to be found. Hereof it is, that we covet to make the Psalms especially familiar unto all. This is the very cause why we iterate the Psalms oftener than any other part of Scripture besides; the cause wherefore we inure the people together with their minister, and not the minister alone, to read them as other parts of Scripture he doth.

Touching musical harmony whether by instrument, or by voice, it being but of high and low in sounds a due proportionable disposition, such notwithstanding is the force thereof, and so pleasing effects it hath in that very part of man which is most divine, that some have been thereby induced to think that the soul itself by nature is, or hath in it harmony; a thing which delighteth all ages, and beseemeth all states; a thing as seasonable in grief as in joy; as decent being added unto actions of greatest weight and solemnity, as being used when men most sequester themselves from action. The reason hereof is an admirable facility which music hath to express and represent to the mind, more inwardly than any other sensible mean, the very standing, rising, and falling, the very steps and inflections every way, the turns and varieties of all passions, whereunto the mind is subject; yea, so to imitate them, that, whether it resemble unto us the same state wherein our minds already are, or a clean contrary, we are not more contentedly by the one confirmed, than changed and led away by the other. In harmony the very image and character even of Virtue and Vice is perceived, the mind delighted with their resemblances, and brought by having them often iterated into a love of the things themselves. For which cause there is nothing more contagious and pestilent than some kinds of harmony; than some, nothing more strong and potent unto good. And that there is such a difference of one kind from another we need no proof but our own experience, inasmuch as we are at the hearing of some more inclined unto sorrow and heaviness, of some more mollified and softened in mind; one kind apter to stay and settle us, another to move and stir our affections; there is that draweth to a marvellous grave and sober mediocrity; there is also that carrieth as it were into ecstasies, filling the mind with an heavenly joy, and for the time in a manner severing it from the body: so that although we lay altogether aside the consideration of ditty or matter, the very harmony of sounds being framed in due sort, and carried from the ear to the spiritual faculties of our souls, is by a native puissance and efficacy greatly available to bring to a perfect temper whatsoever is there troubled, apt as well to quicken the spirits as to allay that which is too eager; sovereign against melancholy and despair, forcible to draw forth tears of devotion, if the mind be such as can yield them, able both to move and to moderate all affections. The prophet David having therefore singular knowledge, not in poetry alone, but in music also, judged them both to be things most necessary for the House of God, left behind him to that purpose a number of divinely indited poems, and was further the author of adding unto poetry melody in public prayer, melody both vocal and instrumental for the raising up of men's hearts and the softening of their affections towards God. In which considerations the Church of Christ, doth likewise at this day retain it as an ornament to God's service, and an help to our own devotion.

V xxxvii 1–2, xxxviii 1–2, 158–61

One of the prayers at the end of the Holy Communion service, to be said when there has been no communion, speaks of 'those things which we for our unworthiness dare not' ask. Cartwright objected that this has 'still the note of the Popish servility'. Hooker replies that reverence and awe are not incompatible with complete trust in the merits of Christ. Respect is due to superiors of all kinds, temporal and spiritual.

Is it credible that the very acknowledgment of our own unworthiness to obtain, and in that respect our professed fearfulness to ask anything otherwise than only for his sake to whom God can deny nothing, that this should be noted for a Popish error; that this should be termed baseness, abjection, error of mind, or servility, is it credible? That which we for our unworthiness are afraid to crave, our prayer is that God for the worthiness of his Son would notwithstanding vouchsafe to grant. May it please them to show us which of these words it is that carrieth the note of Popish and servile fear? In reference to other creatures of this inferior world, man's worth and excellency is admired. Compared with God, the truest inscription wherewith we can circle so base a coin is that of David, *Universa vanitas est omnis homo*: whosoever hath the name of a mortal man, there is in him whatsoever the name of vanity doth comprehend. And therefore what we say of our own unworthiness there is no doubt but truth will ratify; alleged in prayer, it both becometh and behoveth saints. For as humility is in suitors a decent virtue; so the testification thereof by such effectual acknowledgments, not only argueth a sound apprehension of his supereminent glory and majesty before whom we stand, but putteth also into his hands a kind of pledge or bond for security against our unthankfulness, the very natural root whereof is always either ignorance, dissimulation, or pride: ignorance, when we know not the Author from whom our good cometh; dissimulation, when our hands are more open than our eyes upon that we receive; pride, when we think ourselves worthy of that which mere grace and undeserved mercy bestoweth. In prayer, therefore, to abate so vain imaginations with the true conceit of unworthiness, is rather to prevent than commit a fault. It being no error thus to think, no fault thus to speak of ourselves when we pray, is it a fault, that the consideration of our unworthiness maketh us fearful to open our mouths by way of suit? While Job had prosperity and lived in honour, men feared him for his authority's sake, and in token of their fear, when they saw him, they hid themselves. Between Elihu and the rest of Job's familiars, the greatest disparity was but in years: and he, though riper than they in judgment, doing them reverence in regard of age, stood long doubtful and very loth to adventure upon speech in his elders' hearing. If so small inequality between man and man make their modesty a commendable virtue, who respecting superiors, as superiors, can neither speak nor stand before them without fear; that the Publican approacheth not more boldly to God; that when Christ in mercy draweth near to Peter, he in humility and fear craveth distance; that being to stand, to speak, to sue in the presence of so great Majesty, we are afraid, let no man blame us. In which consideration notwithstanding, because to fly altogether from God, to despair that creatures unworthy shall be able to obtain any thing at his hands, and under that pretence to surcease from prayers as bootless or fruitless offices, were to him no less injurious than pernicious to our own souls; even that which we tremble to do we do, we ask those things which we dare not ask. The knowledge of our own unworthiness is not without belief in the merits of Christ. With that true fear which the one causeth, there is coupled true boldness, and encouragement drawn from the other. The very silence which our unworthiness putteth us unto, doth itself make request for us, and that in the confidence of his grace. Looking inward we are stricken dumb; looking upward, we speak and prevail. O happy mixture, wherein things contrary do so qualify and correct the one the danger of the other's excess, that neither boldness can make us presume, as long as we are kept under with the sense of our own wretchedness; nor, while we trust in the mercy of God through Jesus Christ, fear be able to tyrannize over us! As therefore our fear excludeth not that boldness which becometh saints; so if our familiarity with God do not savour of this fear, it draweth too near that irreverent confidence wherewith true humility can never stand.

V xlvii 1–4, 198–200

A consideration of petitionary prayer, our requests and God's response. This was, and remains, the principal part of most people's prayers, and one which raises theological questions about human desires and God's providence.

Petitionary prayer belongeth only to such as are in themselves impotent, and stand in need of relief from others. We thereby declare unto God what our own desire is, that he by his power should effect. It presupposeth therefore in us, first, the want of that which we pray for: secondly, a feeling of that want: thirdly, an earnest willingness of mind to be eased therein: fourthly, a declaration of this our desire in the sight of God; not as if he should be otherwise ignorant of our necessities, but because we this way show we honour him as our God, and are verily persuaded that no good thing can come to pass which he by his omnipotent power effecteth not. Now because there is no man's prayer acceptable whose person is odious, neither any man's person gracious without faith, it is of necessity required that they which pray, do believe. The prayers which our Lord and Saviour made were for his own worthiness accepted; ours God accepteth not but with this condition, if they be joined with belief in Christ. The prayers of the just are accepted always, but not always those things granted for which they pray. For in prayer, if faith and assurance to obtain were both one and the same thing, seeing that the effect of not obtaining is a plain testimony that they which pray were not sure they should obtain; it would follow, that their prayer being without certainty of the event, was also made unto God without faith, and consequently that God abhorred it. Which to think of so many prayers of Saints as we find have failed in particular requests, how absurd were it! His faithful people have this comfort, that whatsoever they rightly ask, the same no doubt but they shall receive, so far as may stand with the glory of God and their own everlasting good; unto either of which two, it is no virtuous man's purpose to seek, or desire to obtain anything prejudicial; and therefore that clause which our Lord and Saviour in the prayer of his agony did express, we in petitions of like nature do always imply. *Pater, si possibile est,* [Father if it is possible] if it may stand with thy will and pleasure: or if not, but that there be secret impediments and causes, in regard whereof the thing we pray for is denied us; yet the prayer itself which we make is a pleasing sacrifice to God, who both accepteth and rewardeth it some other way. So that sinners, in very truth, are denied when they seem to prevail in their supplications, because it is not for their sakes, or to their good, that their suits take place; the faithful contrariwise, because it is for their good oftentimes that their petitions do not take place, prevail even then when they most seem denied. *Our Lord God in anger hath granted some unpatient men's requests; as on the other side the Apostles' suit he hath of favour and mercy not granted* (saith St Augustine). To think we may pray unto God for nothing but what he hath promised in Holy Scripture we shall obtain, is perhaps an error. For of prayer are two uses. It serveth as a mean to procure those things which God hath promised to grant when we ask; and it serveth as a mean to express our lawful desires also towards that, which whether we shall have or no, we know not till we see the event. Things in themselves unholy or unseemly, we may not ask; we may whatsoever, being not forbidden, either Nature or Grace shall reasonably move us to wish as importing the good of men; albeit God himself hath nowhere by promise assured us of that particular which our prayer craveth. To pray for that which is in itself, and of its own nature apparently a thing impossible, were not convenient. Wherefore, though men do without offence wish daily that the affairs which with evil success are past, might have fallen out much better; yet to pray that they may have been any other than they are, this being a manifest impossibility in itself, the rules of Religion do not permit. Whereas contrariwise, when things of their own nature contingent and mutable, are by the secret determination of God appointed one way, though we the other way make our prayers, and consequently ask those things of God, which are by this supposition impossible, we notwithstanding do not hereby in prayer transgress our lawful bounds. That Christ, as the only-begotten Son of God, having no superior, and therefore owing honour unto none, neither standing in any need, should either give thanks or make petition unto God, were most absurd. As man, what could beseem him better, whether we respect his affection to God-ward, or his own necessity, or his charity and love towards men? Some things he knew should come to pass, and notwithstanding prayed for them, because he also knew that the necessary means to effect them were his prayers.

V xlviii 2–5, 201–3

Although his concern is mainly with the polity and usage of the Church, Hooker also addresses matters of doctrine. He does not give as much close attention to sacramental theology as some writers of the Reformation period, but here he addresses the matter vigorously, affirming the importance of the sacraments as uniting us with Christ.

Instruction and prayer whereof we have hitherto spoken are duties which serve as elements, parts or principles to the rest that follow, in which number the sacraments of the Church are chief. The Church is to us that very mother of our new birth in whose bowels we are all bred, at whose breasts we receive nourishment. As many therefore as are apparently to our judgment born of God, they have the seed of their regeneration by the ministry of the Church, which useth to that end and purpose not only the word but the sacraments, both having generative force and virtue. As oft as we mention a sacrament properly understood (for in the writings of the ancient fathers all articles which are peculiar to Christian faith, all duties of religion containing that which sense or natural reason cannot of itself discern are most commonly named sacraments) our restraint of the word to some few principal divine ceremonies importeth in every such ceremony two things, the substance of the ceremony itself which is visible, and besides that somewhat else more secret in reference whereunto we conceive that ceremony to be a sacrament. For we all admire and honour the holy sacraments, not respecting so much the service which we do unto God in receiving them, as the dignity of that sacred and secret gift which we thereby receive from God. Seeing that sacraments therefore consist altogether in relation to some such gift or grace supernatural as only God can bestow, how should any but the Church administer those ceremonies as sacraments which are not thought to be sacraments by any but by the Church? There is in sacraments to be observed their force and their form of administration. Upon their force their necessity dependeth. So that how they are necessary we cannot discern till we see how effectual they are. When sacraments are said to be visible signs of invisible grace, we thereby conceive how grace is indeed the very end for which these heavenly mysteries were instituted, and besides sundry other properties observed in them the matter whereof they consist is such as signifieth, figureth, and representeth their end. But still their efficacy resteth obscure to our understanding, except we search somewhat more distinctly what grace in particular that is whereunto they are referred, and what manner of operation they have towards it. The use of sacraments is but only in this life, yet so that here they concern a far better life than this, and are for that cause accompanied with *grace which worketh salvation*. Sacraments are the powerful instruments of God to eternal life. For as our natural life consisteth in the union of the body with the soul, so our life supernatural in the union of the soul with God. And forasmuch as there is no union of God with man without that mean between both which is both, it seemeth requisite that we first consider how God is in Christ, then how Christ is in us, and how the sacraments do serve to make us partakers of Christ. In other things we may be more brief, but the weight of these requireth largeness.

V l 1–3, 219–20

He also has a profound regard for the Incarnation as giving continual life to the world and drawing the Church into the being of God. Here his contention is not so much with the Puritans as with Anabaptists and Socinians. It is a subtle and in places difficult argument which shows his capacity for philosophical theology and scholastic method. Damascen is St John Damascene or 'Of Damascus' (c.675 – c.749) a Greek theologian who wrote an important work on the doctrine of the Trinity.

The Lord our God is but one God. In which indivisible Unity notwithstanding we adore the Father, as being altogether of himself; we glorify that consubstantial Word which is the Son; we bless and magnify that co-essential Spirit eternally proceeding from both, which is the Holy Ghost. Seeing therefore the Father is of none, the Son is of the Father, and the Spirit is of both, they are by these their several properties really distinguishable each from other. For the substance of God, with this property to be of none, doth make the Person of the Father; the very self-same substance in number with this property to be of the Father, maketh the Person of the Son; the same substance having added unto it the property of proceeding from the other two, maketh the Person of the Holy Ghost. So that in every Person there is implied both the substance of God, which is one; and also that property which causeth the same Person really and truly to differ from the other two. Every Person hath his own subsistence which no other Person hath, although there be others besides that are of the same substance. As no man but Peter can be the person which Peter is, yet Paul hath the self-same nature which Peter hath. Again, Angels have every of them the nature of pure and invisible Spirits; but every Angel is not that Angel which appeared in a dream to Joseph. Now when God became Man, lest we should err in applying this to the Person of the Father or of the Spirit, St Peter's confession unto Christ, was, *Thou art the Son of the living God*; and St John's exposition thereof was plain, that it is the Word which was made Flesh. *The Father and the Holy Ghost* (saith Damascen) *have no communion with the Incarnation of the Word, otherwise than only by approbation and assent.* Notwithstanding, forasmuch as the Word and Deity are one subject, we must beware we exclude not the Nature of God from Incarnation, and so make the Son of God incarnate not to be very God. For undoubtedly, even the Nature of God itself in the only Person of the Son is incarnate and hath taken to itself flesh. Wherefore, Incarnation may neither be granted to any Person but only one, nor yet denied to that Nature which is common unto all three. Concerning the cause of which incomprehensible mystery, forasmuch as it seemeth a thing unconsonant that the world should honour any as the Saviour, but him whom it honoureth as the Creator of the world, and in the wisdom of God it hath not been thought convenient to admit any way of saving man but by man himself, though nothing should be spoken of the love and mercy of God towards man, which this way are become such a spectacle as neither men nor angels can behold without a kind of heavenly astonishment, we may hereby perceive there is cause sufficient why Divine Nature should assume human, that so God might be in Christ reconciling to himself the world. And if some cause be likewise required why rather to this end and purpose the Son than either the Father or the Holy Ghost be made man, could we which are born the children of wrath be adopted the sons of God through grace, otherwise than the natural Son of God being Mediator between God and us? It became therefore him, by whom all things are, to be the way of salvation to all, that the institution and restitution of the world might be both wrought by one hand. The world's salvation was without the Incarnation of the Son of God a thing impossible: not simply impossible, but impossible, it being presupposed that the will of God was no otherwise to have it saved than by the death of his own Son. Wherefore taking to himself our flesh, and by his Incarnation making it his own flesh, he had now of his own, although from us, what to offer unto God for us. And as Christ took manhood, that by it he might be capable of death, whereunto he humbled himself; so because manhood is the proper subject of compassion and feeling pity, which maketh the sceptre of Christ's regency even in the kingdom of Heaven be amiable, he which without our nature could not on earth suffer for the sins of the world, doth now also, by means thereof, both make intercession to God for sinners, and exercise dominion over all men with a true, a natural, and a sensible touch of mercy.

V li 1–3, 220–2

The Incarnation is not just an event in history, but the continuing power of God in the life and salvation of the faithful. He refers to the question of imputed righteousness, a strong tenet of Reformed and particularly of Lutheran doctrine, which says that the merits of Christ are made effective within us, without any righteousness of our own. The catholic doctrine of imparted grace claims that these merits effect a real change in the believer, from sin to a state of grace.

Doth any man doubt but that even from the flesh of Christ our very bodies do receive that life which shall make them glorious at the latter day, and for which they are already accompted parts of his blessed body? Our corruptible bodies could never live the life they shall live, were it not that here they are joined with his which is incorruptible, and that his is in ours as a cause of immortality, a cause by removing through the death and merit of his own flesh that which hindered the life of ours. Christ is therefore both as God and as man that true vine whereof we both spiritually and corporally are branches. The mixture of his substance with ours is a thing which the ancient Fathers disclaim. Yet the mixture of his flesh with ours they speak of, to signify what our very bodies through mystical conjunction receive from that vital efficacy which we know to be in his, and from bodily mixtures they borrow divers similitudes rather to declare the truth then the manner of coherence between his sacred and the sanctified bodies of Saints. Thus much no Christian will deny, that when Christ sanctified his own flesh giving as God and taking as man the Holy Ghost, he did not this for himself only but for our sakes, that the grace of sanctification and life which was first received in him might pass from him to his whole race as malediction came from Adam unto all mankind. Howbeit because the work of his Spirit to those effects is in us prevented by sin and death possessing us before, it is of necessity that as well our present sancti- fication unto newness of life, as the future restoration of our bodies should presuppose a participation of the grace, efficacy, merit or virtue of his body and blood, without which foundation first laid there is no place for those other operations of the Spirit of Christ to ensue. So that Christ imparteth plainly himself by degrees. It pleaseth him in mercy to accompt himself incomplete and maimed without us. But most assured we are that we all receive of his fulness, because he is in us as a moving and working cause, from which many blessed effects are really found to ensue, and that in sundry both kinds and degrees all tending to eternal happiness. It must be confessed that of Christ, working as a creator, and a governor of the world by providence, all are partakers; not all partakers of that grace whereby he inhabiteth whom he saveth. Again as he dwelleth not by grace in all, so neither doth he equally work in all them in whom he dwelleth. Whence is it (saith St Augustine) *that some be holier then others are, but because God doth dwell in some more plentifully then in others*? And because the divine substance of Christ is equally in all, his human substance equally distant from all, it appeareth that the participation of Christ wherein there are many de- grees and differences must needs consist in such effects as being derived from both natures of Christ really into us are made our own, and we by halving them in us are truly said to have him from whom they come, Christ also more or less to inhabit and impart himself as the graces are fewer or more, greater or smaller, which really flow into us from Christ. Christ is whole with the whole Church, and whole with every part of the Church, as touching his person which can no way divide itself or be possessed by degrees and portions. But the participation of Christ importeth, besides the presence of Christ's person, and besides the mystical copulation thereof with the parts and members of his whole Church, a true actual influence of grace whereby the life which we live according to godliness is his, and we receive those perfections wherein our eternal happiness consisteth. Thus we participate Christ partly by imputation, as when those things which he did and suffered for us are imputed unto us for righteousness; partly by habitual and real infusion, as when grace is inwardly bestowed while we are on earth and afterwards more fully both our souls and bodies made like unto his in glory. The first thing of his so infused into our hearts in this life is the spirit of Christ, whereupon because the rest of what kind soever do all both necessarily depend and infallibly also ensue, therefore the Apostles term it sometime the seed of God, sometime the pledge of our heavenly inheritance, sometime the handsell or earnest of that which is to come. From hence it is that they belong to the mystical body of our Saviour Christ and be in number as the stars of heaven, divided successively by reason of their mortal condition into many generations, are notwithstanding coupled every one to Christ their head and all unto every particular person amongst themselves, in as much as the same Spirit, which anointed the blessed soul of our Saviour Christ doth so formalize, unite and actuate his whole race, as if both he and they were so many limbs compacted into one body, by being quickened all with one and the same soul. That wherein we are partakers of Jesus Christ by imputation agreeth equally unto all that have it. For it consisteth in such acts and deeds of his as could not have longer continuance than while they were in doing, nor at any time belong unto any other but to him from whom they came, and therefore how men either then or before or sithence should be made partakers of them, there can be no way imagined but only by imputation. Again a deed must either not be imputed to any but rest altogether in him whose it is, or if at all it be imputed, they which have it by imputation must have it such as it is whole. So that degrees being neither in the personal presence of Christ, nor in the participation of those effects which are ours by imputation only, it resteth that we wholly apply them to the participation of Christ's infused grace, although even in this kind also the first beginning of life, the seed of God, the first fruits of Christ's Spirit be without latitude. For we have hereby only the being of the Sons of God, in which number how far soever one may seem to excel another, yet touching this that all are sons they are all equals, some happily better sons then the rest are, but none any more a son than another. Thus therefore we see how the Father is in the Son and the Son in the Father, how they both are in all things and all things in them, what communion Christ hath with his Church, how his Church and every member thereof is in him by original derivation, and he personally in them by way of mystical association wrought through the gift of the Holy Ghost, which they that are his receive from him, and together with the same what benefit soever the vital force of his body and blood may yield, yea by steps and degrees they receive the complete measure of all such divine grace, as doth sanctify and save throughout, till the day of their final exaltation to a state of fellowship in glory, with him whose partakers they are now in those things that tend to glory. As for any mixture of the substance of his flesh with ours, the participation which we have of Christ includeth no such kind of gross surmise.

V lvi 9–13, 251–5

He turns to baptism, another source of contention at the time. He asserts the value of the ceremonies of the Church, but concedes that some details may be omitted in cases of necessity.

Now even as the soul doth organize the body and give unto every member thereof that substance, quantity and shape which nature seeth most expedient, so the inward grace of sacraments may teach what serveth best for their outward form, a thing in no part of Christian religion, much less here to be neglected. Grace intended by sacraments was a cause of the choice, and is a reason of the fitness of the elements themselves. Furthermore, seeing that the grace which here we receive doth no way depend upon the natural force of that which we presently behold, it was of necessity that words of express declaration taken from the very mouth of our Lord himself should be added unto visible elements, that the one might infallibly teach what the other do most assuredly bring to pass. In writing and speaking of the blessed sacraments we use for the most part under the name of their *substance* not only to comprise that whereof they outwardly and sensibly consist, but also the secret grace which they signify and exhibit. This is the reason wherefore commonly in definitions, whether they be framed larger to augment, or stricter to abridge the number of sacraments we find grace expressly mentioned as their true essential form, elements as the matter whereunto that form doth adjoin itself. But if that be separated which is secret and that considered alone which is seen, as of necessity it must in all those speeches that make distinction of sacraments from sacramental grace, the name of a sacrament in such speeches can imply no more than what the *outward substance* thereof doth comprehend. And to make complete the outward substance of a sacrament there is required an outward form, which form sacramental elements receive from sacramental words. Hereupon it groweth that many times there are three things said to make up the substance of a sacrament, namely the grace which is thereby offered, the element which shadoweth or signifieth grace, and the word which expresseth what is done by the element. So that whether we consider the outward by itself alone, or both the outward and inward substance of any sacrament; there are in the one respect but two essential parts, and in the other but three that concur to give sacraments their full being. Furthermore because definitions are to express but the most immediate and nearest parts of nature whereas other principles farther off, although not specified in defining, are notwithstanding in nature implied and presupposed, we must note that inasmuch as sacraments are actions religious and mystical, which nature they have not unless they proceed from a serious meaning, (and what every man's private mind is, as we cannot know, so neither are we bound to examine) therefore always in these cases the known intent of the Church generally doth suffice, and where the contrary is not manifest we may presume that he which outwardly doth the work hath inwardly the purpose of the Church of God. Concerning all other orders, rites, prayers, lessons, sermons, actions and their circumstances whatsoever they are to the outward substance of baptism but things accessory, which the wisdom of the Church of Christ is to order according to the exigence of that which is principal. Again considering that such ordinances have been made to adorn the sacrament, and not the sacrament to depend on them; seeing also that they are not of the substance of baptism and that baptism is far more necessary then any such incident rite or solemnity ordained for the better administration thereof, if the case be such as permitteth not baptism to have the decent complements of baptism, better it were to enjoy the body without his furniture, than to wait for this till the opportunity of that for which we desire it be lost. Which premises standing, it seemeth to have been no absurd collection, that in cases of necessity which will not suffer delay till baptism be administered with usual solemnities (to speak the least) it may be tolerably given without them, rather than any man without it should be suffered to depart this life.

V lviii 1–4, 259–62

Baptism is necessary for all Christians: assurance of election does not excuse us from receiving it. Here again he has the Anabaptists in his sights. He further explores sacramental doctrine; God's grace is not limited to the sacraments, but we are required to obey him in accepting them as the means of grace. The question of baptismal regeneration was another matter which continued to be disputed through to the nineteenth century. The Valentinians were an early Gnostic sect who taught that only favoured 'spiritual' believers had full knowledge of the Christian mysteries.

All things which either are known causes or set means, whereby any great good is usually procured, or men delivered from grievous evil, the same we must needs confess necessary. And if regeneration were not in this very sense a thing necessary to eternal life, would Christ himself have taught Nicodemus, that to see the kingdom of God is impossible, saving only for those men which are born from above? His words following in the next sentence are a proof sufficient, that to our regeneration his Spirit is no less necessary, than regeneration itself necessary unto life. Thirdly, unless as the Spirit is a necessary outward cause, so water were a necessary outward mean of our regeneration, what construction should we give unto those words wherein we are said to be new born, and that *ex hudati*, even of water? Why are we taught that with water God doth purify and cleanse his Church? Wherefore do the Apostles of Christ term Baptism a bath of regeneration? What purpose had they in giving men advice to receive outward Baptism, and in persuading them it did avail to remission of sins? If outward Baptism were a cause in itself possessed of that power, either natural or supernatural, without the present operation whereof no such effect could possibly grow; it must then follow, that seeing effects do never prevent the necessary causes out of which they spring, no man could ever receive grace before Baptism: which being apparently both known, and also confessed to be otherwise in many particulars, although in the rest we make not Baptism a cause of grace; yet the grace which is given them with their Baptism doth so far forth depend on the very outward Sacrament, that God will have it embraced, not only as a sign or token of what we receive, but also as an instrument or mean whereby we receive grace, because Baptism is a sacrament which God hath instituted in his Church to the end that they which receive the same might thereby be incorporated into Christ; and so through his most precious merit obtain as well that saving grace of imputation which taketh away all former guiltiness, as also that infused divine virtue of the Holy Ghost which giveth to the powers of the soul their first disposition towards future newness of life. There are that elevate too much the ordinary and immediate means of life, relying wholly upon the bare conceit of that eternal election, which notwithstanding includeth a subordination of means, without which we are not actually brought to enjoy what God secretly did intend; and therefore to build upon God's election, if we keep not ourselves to the ways which he hath appointed for men to walk in, is but a self-deceiving vanity. When the Apostle saw men called to the participation of Jesus Christ, after the Gospel of God embraced and the Sacrament of life received, he feareth not then to put them in the number of elect Saints; he then accounteth them delivered from death, and clean purged from all sin. Till then, notwithstanding their preordination unto life, which none could know of, saving God, what were they, in the Apostle's own account, but children of wrath, as well as others, plain aliens, altogether without hope, strangers, utterly without God in this present world? So that by sacraments, and other sensible tokens of grace, we may boldly gather that he whose mercy vouchsafeth to bestow the means hath also long sithence intended us that whereunto they lead. But let us never think it safe to presume of our own last end by bare conjectural collections of his first intent and purpose, the means failing that should come between. Predestination bringeth not to life without the grace of eternal vocation, wherein our Baptism is implied. For as we are not naturally men without birth, so neither are we Christian men in the eye of the Church of God but by new birth; nor according to the manifest ordinary course of divine dispensation new-born, but by that Baptism which both declareth and maketh us Christians. In which respect, we justly hold it to be the door of our actual entrance into God's house, the first apparent beginning of life, a seal perhaps to the grace of election before received; but to our sanctification here, a step that hath not any before it. There were of the old Valentinian heretics some which had knowledge in such admiration that to it they ascribed all, and so despised the Sacraments of Christ, pretending that as ignorance had made us subject to all misery, so the full redemption of the inward man, and the work of our restauration must needs belong unto knowledge only. They draw very near unto this error who, fixing wholly their minds on the known necessity of Faith, imagine that nothing but Faith is necessary for the attainment of all grace. Yet is it a branch of belief, that Sacraments are in their place no less required than belief itself. For when our Lord and Saviour promiseth eternal life, is it any otherwise than as he promiseth restitution of health unto Naaman the Syrian, namely, with this condition, *wash and be clean*? or as to them which were stung of serpents health by beholding the brazen serpent? If Christ himself which giveth salvation do require Baptism, it is not for us that look for salvation to sound and examine him, whether unbaptized men may be saved; but seriously to do that which is required, and religiously to fear the danger which may grow by the want thereof. Had Christ only declared his will to have all men baptized and not acquainted us with any cause why Baptism is necessary, our ignorance in the reason of that he enjoineth might perhaps have hindered somewhat the forwardness of our obedience thereunto; whereas now being taught that Baptism is necessary to take away sin, how have we the fear of God in our hearts, if care of delivering men's souls from sin do not move us to use all means for their Baptism?

V lx 1–4, 264–8

In the course of discussing baptism, he takes the question of unbaptized infants, a source of concern to parents at a time of high infant mortality, and develops a pragmatic and charitable Anglican type of argument. Those deprived of the sacraments by no fault of their own can be saved, but the Church must always be conscientious to provide a sacramental mystery.

Touching infants which die unbaptized, sith they neither have this sacrament itself, nor any sense or conceit thereof, the judgment of many hath gone hard against them. But yet seeing grace is not absolutely tied unto sacraments; and besides, such is the lenity of God, that unto things altogether impossible he bindeth no man, but, where we cannot do what is enjoined us, accepteth our will to do instead of the deed itself; again, forasmuch as there is in their Christian parents, and in the Church of God, a presumed desire, that the sacrament of Baptism might be given them, yea, a purpose also that it shall be given; remorse of equity hath moved divers of the School-Divines in these considerations, ingenuously to grant, that God, all-merciful to such as are not in themselves able to desire Baptism, imputeth the secret desire that others have in their behalf, and accepteth the same as theirs, rather than casteth away their souls for that which no man is able to help. And of the will of God to impart his grace unto infants without Baptism in that case, the very circumstance of their natural birth may serve as a just argument; whereupon it is not to be misliked, that men in charitable presumption do gather a great likelihood of their salvation, to whom the benefit of Christian parentage being given, the rest that should follow is prevented by some such casualty as man hath himself no power to avoid. For, we are plainly taught of God, that the seed of faithful parentage is holy from the very birth. Which albeit we may not so understand, as if the children of believing parents were without sin; or grace from baptized parents derived by propagation; or God, by covenant and promise, tied to save any in mere regard of their parents' belief; yet seeing, that to all professors of the name of Christ this pre-eminence above Infidels is freely given, that the fruit of their bodies bringeth into the world with it a present interest and right to those means wherewith the ordinance of Christ is that his Church shall be sanctified, it is not to be thought that he which, as it were, from Heaven, hath nominated and designed them unto holiness by special privilege of their very birth, will himself deprive them of regeneration and inward grace, only because necessity depriveth them of outward Sacraments. In which case, it were the part of charity to hope, and to make men rather partial than cruel judges, if we had not those fair appearances which here we have. Wherefore a necessity there is of receiving, and a necessity of administering the sacrament of Baptism; the one peradventure not so absolute as some have thought, but out of all peradventure the other more straight and narrow than that the Church which is by office a mother unto such as crave at her hands the sacred mystery of their new birth, should repel them, and see them die unsatisfied of their ghostly desires rather than give them their souls' rights with omission of those things which serve but only for the more convenient and orderly administration thereof. For as on the one side we grant, that those sentences of Holy Scripture which make Sacraments most necessary to eternal life are no prejudice to their salvation that want them by some inevitable necessity, and without any fault of their own; so it ought, in reason, to be likewise acknowledged that, forasmuch as our Lord himself maketh baptism necessary, necessary whether we respect the good received by baptism, or the testimony thereby yielded unto God of that humility and obedience which reposing wholly itself on the authority of his commandment, and on the truth of his heavenly promise, doubteth not but from creatures despicable in their own condition and substance to obtain grace of inestimable value; or rather not from them, but from him, yet by them, as by his appointed means. Howsoever he, by the secret of his own incomprehensible mercy, may be thought to save without Baptism, this cleareth not the Church from guiltiness of blood if, through her superfluous scrupulosity, lets and impediments of less regard should cause a grace of so great moment to be withheld, wherein our merciless strictness may be our own harm, though not theirs towards whom we show it; and we for the hardness of our hearts may perish, albeit they through God's unspeakable mercy do live.

V lx 6–7, 270–3

A particular Puritan objection was to signing with the cross in baptism, which continued to be raised when the Prayer Book was discussed at the Hampton Court and Savoy Conferences. Hooker gives full quotation to the objection, meets it, and has some further remarks about the validity of traditional customs.

In baptism many things of very ancient continuance are now quite and clean abolished; for that the virtue and grace of this Sacrament had been therewith overshadowed, as fruit with too great abundance of leaves. Notwithstanding to them which think that always imperfect reformation that doth but shear and not flay, our retaining certain of those formal rites, especially the dangerous sign of the Cross, hath seemed almost an unpardonable oversight. *The Cross,* (they say,) *sith it is but a mere invention of man, should not therefore at all have been added to the Sacrament of Baptism. To sign children's foreheads with a Cross, in token that hereafter they shall not be ashamed to make profession of the Faith of Christ, is to bring into the Church a new word, whereas there ought to be no doctor heard in the Church but our Saviour Christ. That reason which moved the Fathers to use, should move us not to use the sign of the Cross. They lived with Heathens that had the Cross of Christ in contempt; we with such as adore the Cross; and therefore we ought to abandon it, even as, in like consideration, Hezekiah did of old the brazen serpent.* These are the causes of displeasure conceived against the Cross; a ceremony the use whereof hath been profitable, although we observe it not as the ordinance of God, but of man. *For* (saith Tertullian) *if of this and the like customs thou shouldest require some commandment to be spewed thee out of Scripture, there is none found.* What reason there is to justify tradition, use, or custom in this behalf, *either thou mayest of thyself perceive, or else learn of some other that doth.* Lest therefore the name of tradition should be offensive to any, considering how far by some it hath been and is abused, we mean by traditions, ordinances made in the prime of Christian Religion, established with that authority which Christ hath left to his Church for matters indifferent, and in that consideration requisite to be observed, till like authority see just and reasonable cause to alter them. So that traditions ecclesiastical are not rudely and in gross to be shaken off, because the inventors of them were men. Such as say, they allow no invention of men to be mingled with the outward administration of Sacraments; and under that pretence, condemn our using the sign of the Cross, have belike some special dispensation themselves to violate their own rules. For neither can they indeed decently, nor do they ever baptize any without manifest breach of this their profound axiom, *That men's inventions should not be mingled with Sacraments and institutions of God*. They seem to like very well in Baptism the custom of Godfathers, *because so generally the Churches have received it*. Which custom being of God no more instituted than the other, (howsoever they pretend the other hurtful and this profitable) it followeth that even in their own opinion, if their words do show their minds, there is no necessity of stripping Sacraments out of all such attire of ceremonies as man's wisdom hath at any time clothed them withal; and consequently, that either they must reform their speech as over-general, or else condemn their own practice as unlawful. Ceremonies have more in weight than in sight; they work by commonness of use much, although in the several acts of their usage we scarcely discern any good they do. And because the use which for the most part is not perfectly understood, superstition is apt to impute unto them greater worth than indeed they have. For prevention whereof when we use this ceremony, we always plainly express the whereunto it serveth, namely, for a sign of remembrance to put us in mind of our duty.

V lvi 1–4, 317–9

He ends his defence of the cross in baptism with some wise remarks about excessive scruples and demands for radical change. The typically Anglican call for moderation is sounded.

When Heathens despised Christian Religion because of the sufferings of Jesus Christ, the Fathers, to testify how little such contumelies and contempts prevailed with them, chose rather the sign of the Cross than any other outward mark, whereby the world might most easily discern always what they were. On the contrary side now, whereas they which do all profess the Christian Religion are divided amongst themselves; and the fault of the other part is that in zeal to the sufferings of Christ they admire too much, and over-superstitiously adore the visible sign of his Cross; if you ask what we that mislike them should do, we are here advised to cure one contrary by another. Which art or method is not yet so current as they imagine. For if, as their practice for the most part showeth, it be their meaning that the scope and drift of reformation, when things are faulty, should be to settle the Church in the contrary; it standeth them upon to beware of this rule, because seeing vices have not only virtues, but other also in nature opposite unto them, it may be dangerous in these cases to seek but that which we find contrary to present evils. For in sores and sicknesses of the mind, we are not simply to measure good by distance from evil, because one vice may in some respect be more opposite to another, than either of them to that virtue which holdeth the mean between them both. Liberality and covetousness, the one a virtue and the other a vice, are not so contrary as the vices of covetousness and prodigality. Religion and superstition have more affiance, though the one be light and the other darkness, than superstition and profaneness which both are vicious extremities. By means whereof it cometh also to pass that the mean which is virtue seemeth in the eyes of each extreme an extremity: the liberal-hearted man is by the opinion of the prodigal miserable, and by the judgment of the miserable lavish; impiety for the most part upbraideth religion as superstitious, which superstition often accuseth as impious; both so conceiving thereof, because it doth seem more to participate each extreme than one extreme doth another and is by consequent less contrary to either of them than they mutually between themselves. Now if he that seeketh to reform covetousness or superstition should but labour to induce the contrary, it were but to draw men out of lime into coal-dust: so that their course, which will remedy the superstitious abuse of things profitable in the Church, is not still to abolish utterly the use thereof, because not using at all is most opposite to ill using; but rather, if it may be, to bring them back to a right, perfect, and religious usage, which, albeit less contrary to the present sore, is notwithstanding the better and by many degrees the sounder way of recovery: and unto this effect, that very precedent itself which they propose may be best followed. For as the Fathers, when the Cross of Christ was in utter contempt, did not superstitiously adore the same, but rather declared that they so esteemed it as was meet; in like manner where we find the Cross to have that honour which is due to Christ, is it not as lawful for us to retain it in that estimation which it ought to have, and in that use which it had of old without offence, as by taking it clean away to seem followers of their example which cure wilfully by abscission that which they might both preserve and heal? Touching therefore the sign and ceremony of the Cross, we no way find ourselves bound to relinquish it; neither because the first inventors thereof were but mortal men; nor lest the sense and signification we give unto it should burden us as authors of a new Gospel in the House of God; nor in respect of some cause which the Fathers had more than we have to use the same; nor, finally, for any such offence or scandal as heretofore it hath been subject unto by error, now reformed in the minds of men.

V lvi 20–24, 335–7

He returns to the sacrament of the Eucharist, as necessary for all Christians. Again there is the typically Anglican emphasis on faith and reverence and the avoidance of speculation about 'what happens' in the consecration. His position is that the Real Presence is in the reception. The Eucharist is not a mere individual memorial, but he denies the Roman Catholic doctrine of transubstantiation and the Lutheran of consubstantiation, which teach of an actual change in the elements of bread and wine. However, he also rejects the teaching of the Swiss Reformer Zwingli and the German Oecolampadius that the Eucharist is merely symbolic and confirms the grace already in the recipient. His mention of 'the influence of the heavens' on all created things shows how belief in astrological influence was general in the sixteenth century.

The grace which we have by the holy Eucharist doth not begin but continue life. No man therefore receiveth this sacrament before baptism, because no dead thing is capable of nourishment. That which groweth must of necessity first live. If our bodies did not daily waste, food to restore them were a thing superfluous. And it may be that the grace of baptism would serve to eternal life, were it not that the state of our spiritual being is daily so much hindered and impaired after baptism. In that life therefore where neither body nor soul can decay, our souls shall as little require this sacrament as our bodies corporal nourishment. But as long as the days of our warfare last, during the time that we are both subject to diminution and capable of augmentation in grace the words of our Lord and Saviour Christ will remain forcible, *Except ye eat the flesh of the Son of Man and drink his blood ye have no life in you.* Life being therefore proposed unto all men as their end, they which by baptism have laid the foundation and attained the first beginning of a new life have here their nourishment and food prescribed for *continuance* of life in them. Such as will live the life of God must eat the flesh and drink the blood of the Son of Man, because this is a part of that diet which if we want we cannot live. Whereas therefore in our infancy we are incorporated into Christ, and by baptism receive the grace of his spirit, without any sense or feeling of the gift which God bestoweth, in the Eucharist, we so receive the gift of God, that we know by grace what the grace is which God giveth us, the degrees of our own increase in holiness and virtue we see and can judge of them, we understand that the strength of our life begun in Christ, is Christ, that his flesh is meat, and his blood drink, not by surmised imagination but truly, even so truly that through faith we perceive in the body and blood sacramentally presented the very taste of eternal life, the grace of the sacrament is here as the food which we eat and drink. This was it that some did exceedingly fear, lest Zwingli and Oecolampadius would bring to pass, that men should accompt of this sacrament but only as of a shadow, destitute empty and void of Christ. But seeing that by opening the several opinions which have been held they are grown (for ought I can see) on all sides at the length of a general agreement, concerning that which alone is material, namely the real participation of Christ and of life in his body and blood by means of this sacrament, wherefore should the world continue still distracted, and rent with so manifold contentions, when there remaineth now no controversy saving only about the subject where Christ is? Yea even in this point no side denieth but that the soul of man is the receptacle of Christ's presence. Whereby the question is yet driven to a narrower issue, nor doth any thing rest doubtful but this, whether when the sacrament is administered, Christ be whole within man only, or else his body and blood be also externally seated in the very consecrated elements themselves, which opinion, they that defend, are driven either to consubstantiate and incorporate Christ, with elements sacramental or to transubstantiate and change their substance into his, and so the one to hold him really, but invisibly moulded up with the substance of those elements, the other to hide him under the only visible show of bread and wine, the substance whereof (as they imagine) is abolished and his succeeded in the same room. All things considered and compared with that success, which truth hath hitherto had, by so bitter conflicts with errors in this point, shall I wish that men would more give themselves to meditate with silence what we have by the sacrament, and less to dispute of the manner how? If any man suppose that this were too great stupidity and dullness, let us see whether the apostles of our Lord themselves have not done the like. It appeareth by many examples that they of their own disposition were very scrupulous and inquisitive, yea in other cases of less importance and less difficulty, always apt to move questions. How cometh it to pass that so few words of so high a mystery being uttered, they receive with gladness the gift of Christ and make no show of doubt or scruple? The reason hereof is not dark to them which have any thing at all observed how the powers of the mind are wont to stir when that which we infinitely long for presenteth itself above and besides expectation. Curious and intricate speculations do hinder, they abate, they quench such inflamed motions of delight and joy as divine graces use to raise when extraordinarily they are present. The mind therefore feeling present joy is always marvellous unwilling to admit any other cogitation, and in that case casteth off those disputes whereunto the intellectual part at other times easily draweth. [. . .] When they saw their Lord and Master with hands and eyes lifted up to heaven first bless and consecrate for the endless good of all generations till the world's end the chosen elements of bread and wine, which elements made for ever the instruments of life by virtue of his divine benediction they being the first that were commanded to receive from him, the first which were warranted by his promise that not only unto them at the present time but to whomsoever they and their successors after them did duly administer the same, those mysteries should serve as conducts of life and conveyances of his body and blood unto them, was it possible they should hear that voice *Take, eat, this is my body, Drink ye all of this, this is my blood*; possible that doing what was required and believing what was promised, the same should have present effect in them, and not fill them with a kind of fearful admiration at the heaven which they saw in themselves? They had at that time a sea of comfort and joy to wade in, and we by that which they did are taught that this heavenly food is given for the satisfying of our empty souls, and not for the exercising of our curious and subtle wits. If we doubt what those admirable words may import, let him be our teacher for the meaning of Christ to whom Christ was himself a schoolmaster, let our Lord's Apostle be his interpreter, content we ourselves with his explication, My body, *the communion of my body,* my blood, *the communion of my blood.* Is there anything more expedite clear and easy than that as Christ is termed our life because through him we obtain life, so the parts of this sacrament are his body and blood for that they are so to us who receiving them receive that by them which they are termed? The bread and cup are his body and blood because they are causes instrumental upon receipt whereof the participation of his body and blood ensueth. For that which produceth any certain effect is not vainly nor improperly said to be that very effect whereunto it tendeth. Every cause is in the effect which groweth from it. Our souls and bodies quickened to eternal life are effects the cause whereof is the person of Christ, his body and his blood are the true wellspring out of which this life floweth. So that his body and blood are in that very subject whereunto they minister life not only by effect and operation even as the influence of the heavens is in plants, beasts, men, and in every thing which they quicken, but also by a far more divine and mystical kind of union which maketh us one with him even as he and the Father are one. The real presence of Christ's most blessed body and blood is not therefore to be sought for in the sacrament, but in the worthy receiver of the sacrament. And with this the very order of our Saviour's words agreeth; first *Take and eat*; then *This is my body which is broken for you*: first *Drink ye all of this*, then followeth, *This is my blood of the new testament which is shed for many for the remission of sins*. I see not which way it should be gathered by the words of Christ when and where the bread is his body or the cup his blood but only in the very heart and soul of him which receiveth them.

V lxvii 1–6, 348–52

With a degree of tolerance unusual for his time, he defends Roman Catholics as being Christians, although in error. Puritans, and many of more moderate churchmanship, objected to allowing them to receive the sacrament in the Church of England, although some might be willing to do so. Hooker maintains that the universal Church, even in places where it is weak or mistaken, stands plainly apart from all unbelievers.

Our fault in admitting Popish communicants, is it in that we are forbidden to eat, and therefore much more to communicate with notorious malefactors? The name of a Papist is not given unto any man for being a notorious malefactor: and the crime wherewith we are charged is suffering Papists to communicate; so that, be their life and conversation whatsoever in the sight of man, their Popish opinions are in this case laid as bars and exceptions against them; yea, those opinions which they have held in former times, although they now both profess by word, and offer to show by fact the contrary. All this doth not justify us, which ought not (they say) to admit them in any wise, till their gospel-like behaviour have removed all suspicion of Popery from them, because Papists are *dogs, swine, beasts, foreigners and strangers from the House of* God; in a word, *they are not of the Church*. What the terms of gospel-like behaviour may include is obscure and doubtful; but of the visible Church of Christ in this present world, from which they separate all Papists, we are thus persuaded. Church is a word which art hath devised, thereby to sever and distinguish that society of men, which professeth the true religion, from the rest which profess it not. There have been in the world, from the very first foundation thereof, but three religions, Paganism which lived in the blindness of corrupt and depraved nature; Judaism, embracing the law which reformed heathenish impieties, and taught salvation to be looked for through one, whom God in the last days would send, and exalt to be Lord of all: finally, Christian belief, which yieldeth obedience to the Gospel of Jesus Christ, and acknowledgeth him the Saviour whom God did promise. Seeing then that the Church is a name, which art hath given to professors of true religion; as they which will define a man are to pass by those qualities wherein one man doth excel another, and to take only those essential properties whereby a man doth differ from creatures of other kinds, so he that will teach what the Church is shall never rightly perform the work whereabout he goeth, till in matter of Religion he touch that difference which severeth the Church's Religion from theirs who are not the Church. Religion being therefore a matter partly of contemplation, partly of action; we must define the Church, which is a religious society, by such differences as do properly explain the essence of such things, that is to say, by the object or matter whereabout the contemplations and actions of the Church are properly conversant. For so all knowledges and all virtues are defined. Whereupon, because the only object, which separateth ours from other religions, is Jesus Christ, in whom none but the Church doth believe; and whom none but the Church doth worship; we find that accordingly the Apostles do everywhere distinguish hereby the Church from Infidels and from Jews, *accounting them which call upon the name of our Lord Jesus Christ to be his Church*. If we go lower, we shall but add unto this certain casual and variable accidents, which are not properly of the being, but make only for the happier and better being of the Church of God, either in deed, or in men's opinions and conceits. This is the error of all Popish definitions that hitherto have been brought. They define not the Church by that which the Church essentially is, but by that wherein they imagine their own more perfect than the rest are. Touching parts of eminency and perfection, parts likewise of imperfection and defect in the Church of God, they are infinite, their degrees and differences no way possible to be drawn unto any certain account. There is not the least contention and variance, but it blemisheth somewhat the unity that ought to be in the Church of Christ, which notwithstanding may have not only without offence or breach of concord her manifold varieties in rites and ceremonies of Religion, but also her strifes and contentions many times, and that about matters of no small importance; yea, her schisms, factions, and such other evils whereunto the body of the Church is subject, sound and sick remaining both of the same body, as long as both parts retain by outward profession that vital substance of truth, which maketh Christian Religion to differ from theirs which acknowledge not our Lord Jesus Christ, the blessed Saviour of mankind, give no credit to his glorious Gospel, and have his Sacraments, the seals of eternal life, in derision.

V lxviii 5–6, 346–9

By the late sixteenth century, there were 'Church Papists' who received Holy Communion in the established Church, to fulfil the law and avoid

*the penalty for recusancy, but without sincere commitment to the re-
formed faith. Hooker says that to repel them would be to make their
eventual reconciliation less likely. We must not 'dive into men's consciences'. He then defends the practice of ministering to a small number
of communicants. It was common for many to leave the church after the
first part of the Communion service; they may have good reasons, and
absence is better than unworthy reception.*

While without any cause we fear to profane Sacraments, we shall not
only defeat the purpose of most wholesome laws, but lose or wilfully
hazard those souls from whom the likeliest means of full and perfect
recovery are by our indiscretion withheld. For neither doth God thus
bind us to dive into men's consciences, nor can their fraud and deceit
hurt any man but themselves. To him they seem such as they are; but
of us they must be taken for such as they seem. In the eye of God they
are against Christ, that are not truly and sincerely with him; in our eyes
they must be received as with Christ, that are not to outward show
against him. The case of impenitent and notorious sinners is not like
unto theirs, whose only imperfection is error severed from pertinancy,
error in appearance, content to submit itself to better instruction; error
so far already cured as to crave at our hands that Sacrament, the hatred
and utter refusal whereof was the weightiest point wherein heretofore
they swerved and went astray. In this case therefore they cannot reasonably charge us with remiss dealing, or with carelessness to whom we
impart the mysteries of Christ; but they have given us manifest occasion
to think it requisite that we earnestly advise rather, and exhort them
to consider as they ought their sundry oversights; first, in equalling
undistinctly crimes with errors, as touching force to make uncapable
of this Sacrament; secondly, in suffering indignation at the faults of the
Church of Rome to blind and withhold their judgments from seeing
that which withal they should acknowledge, concerning so much, nevertheless, still due to the same Church, as to be held and reputed a part
of the House of God, a limb of the visible Church of Christ; thirdly,
in imposing upon the Church a burthen, to enter farther into men's
hearts, and to make a deeper search of their conscience than any Law of
God or reason of man enforceth; fourthly and lastly, in repelling, under
colour of longer trial such from the mysteries of heavenly grace, as are
both capable thereof by the Laws of God, for anything we hear to the
contrary, and should in divers considerations be cherished according
to the merciful examples and precepts whereby the Gospel of Christ
hath taught us towards such to show compassion, to receive them with

lenity and all meekness; if anything be shaken in them, to strengthen it; not to quench with delays and jealousies that feeble smoke of conformity which seemeth to breathe from them, but to build wheresoever there is any foundation; to add perfection unto slender beginnings; and that, as by other offices of piety, even so by this very food of life which Christ hath left in his Church, not only for preservation of strength, but also for relief of weakness. But to return to our own selves, in whom the next thing severely reproved is the paucity of communicants. If they require at communions frequency, we wish the same, knowing how acceptable unto God such service is, when multitudes cheerfully concur unto it; if they encourage men thereunto, we also (themselves acknowledge it) are not utterly forgetful to do the like; if they require some public coaction for remedy of that, wherein by milder and softer means little good is done, they know our Laws and Statutes provided in that behalf, whereunto whatsoever convenient help may be added more by the wisdom of man, what cause have we given the world to think that we are not ready to hearken to it, and to use all good means of sweet compulsion to have this high and heavenly banquet largely furnished? Only we cannot so far yield as to judge it convenient, that the holy desire of a competent number should be unsatisfied because the greater part is careless and undisposed to join with them. Men should not (they say) be permitted a few by themselves to communicate when so many are gone away, because this Sacrament is a token of our conjunction with our brethren; and therefore by communicating apart from them, we make an apparent show of distraction. I ask then, on which side unity is broken, whether on theirs that depart, or on theirs who being left behind, do communicate? First, in the one it is not denied but that they may have reasonable causes of departure, and that then even they are delivered from just blame. Of such kind of causes two are allowed, namely, danger of impairing health, and necessary business requiring our presence otherwise. And may not a third cause, which is unfitness at the present time, detain us as lawfully back as either of these two? True it is, that we cannot hereby altogether excuse ourselves, for that we ought to prevent this, and do not. But if we have committed a fault in not preparing our minds before, shall we therefore aggravate the same with a worse: the crime of unworthy participation? He that abstaineth doth want for the time that grace and comfort which religious communicants have; but he that eateth and drinketh unworthily receiveth death; that which is life to others turneth in him to poison. Notwithstanding, whatsoever be the cause for which men abstain, were it reason that the fault of one part should any way abridge their benefit

that are not faulty? There is in all the Scripture of God no one syllable
which doth condemn communicating amongst a few, when the rest are
departed from them.

V lxviii 8–10, 374–7

*Hooker begins a justification of festivals and holy days with reflections
on time, its movement and its destructive power; a regular Renaissance
theme. For the Christian, such thoughts lead to consideration of God's
infinitude and our limitations. Melissus of Samos, a philosopher in the
fourth century BC, taught that reality is infinite and eternal.*

As the substance of God alone is infinite and hath no kind of limitation, so likewise his continuance is from everlasting to everlasting,
and knoweth neither beginning nor end. Which demonstrable conclusion being presupposed, it followeth necessarily that besides him, all
things are finite both in substance and in continuance. If in substance
all things be finite, it cannot be but that there are bounds without the
compass whereof their substance doth not extend; if in continuance
also limited, they all have, it cannot be denied, their set and their certain terms before which they had no being at all. This is the reason why,
first, we do most admire those things which are greatest; and, secondly,
those things which are ancientest; because the one are least distant from
the infinite substance, the other from the infinite continuance of God.
Out of this we gather that only God hath true immortality or eternity,
that is to say, continuance wherein there groweth no difference by addition of hereafter unto now, whereas the noblest and perfectest of all
things besides have continually, through continuance, the time of former continuance lengthened; so that they could not heretofore be said
to have continued so long as now, neither so long as hereafter. God's
own eternity is the hand which leadeth Angels in the course of their
perpetuity; their perpetuity the hand that draweth out celestial motion;
the line of which motion, and the thread of time, are spun together.
Now as nature bringeth forth time with motion; so we by motion have
learned how to divide time, and by the smaller parts of time both to
measure the greater, and to know how long all things else endure. For
time, considered in itself, is but the flux of that very instant wherein the
motion of the heaven began, being coupled with other things; it is the
quantity of their continuance measured by the distance of two instants,
as the time of a man is a man's continuance from the instant of his first
breath till the instant of his last gasp. Hereupon some have defined
time to be the measure of the motion of heaven; because the first thing

which time doth measure is that motion wherewith it began, and by the help whereof it measureth other things; as when the prophet David saith, that a man's continuance doth not commonly exceed threescore and ten years, he useth the help both of motion and number to measure time. They which make time an effect of motion, and motion to be in nature before time, ought to have considered with themselves, that albeit we should deny, as Melissus did, all motion, we might notwithstanding acknowledge time, because time doth but signify the quantity of continuance, which continuance may be all things that rest and are never moved. Besides, we may also consider in rest both that which is past, and that which is present, and that which is future; yea, further, even length and shortness in every of these, although we never had conceit of motion. But to define, without motion, how long or how short continuance is, were impossible. So that herein we must of necessity use the benefit of years, days, hours, minutes, which all grow from celestial motion. Again, for as much as that motion is circular, whereby we make our divisions of time, and the compass of the circuit such that the heavens which are therein continually move and keep in their motions uniform celerity, must needs touch often the same points, they cannot choose but bring unto us by equal distances frequent return of the same times. Furthermore, whereas time is nothing but a mere quantity of that continuance which all things have, that are not, as God is, without beginning, that which is proper unto all quantities agreeth also to this kind; so that time doth but measure other things, and neither worketh in them any real effect, nor is itself ever capable of any. And therefore when commonly we use to say, that time doth eat or fret out all things; that time is the wisest thing in the world, because it bringeth forth all knowledge; and that nothing is more foolish than time, which never holdeth any thing long, but whatsoever one day learneth, the same another day forgetteth again; that some men see prosperous and happy days and that some men's days are miserable; in all these and the like speeches that which is uttered of the time is not verified of time itself, but agreeth unto those things which are in time, and do by means of so near conjunction either lay their burden upon the back, or set their crown upon the head of time. Yea, the very opportunities which we ascribe to time do in truth cleave to the things themselves wherewith the time is joined. As for time, it neither causeth things nor opportunities of things, although it comprise and contain both. All things whatsoever having their time, the works of God have always that time which is seasonablest and fittest for them. His works are some ordinary, some more rare; all worthy of observation, but not all of like necessity to be often remembered; they all have their times, but they all do not add the same estimation and glory to the times wherein they are. For as God by being everywhere, yet doth not give unto all places one and the same degree of holiness; so neither one and the same dignity to all times by working in all.

V lxix 1–3, 381–3

After a long discourse on feasts and fasts, adducing copious biblical and patristic support, he extols the importance of obedient fasting. This was an observance urged by the writers of the Oxford Movement in the nineteenth century. He takes a pessimistic, one might say a Calvinistic, view of human life and weakness: life was often harsh in the Tudor period.

Therefore we see how these two customs [feasts and fasts] are in divers respects equal. But of fasting the use and exercise, though less pleasant, is by so much more requisite than the other, as grief of necessity is a more familiar guest than the contrary passion of mind, albeit gladness to all men be naturally more welcome. For first, we ourselves do many more things amiss than well, and the fruit of own ill-doing is remorse, because nature is conscious to itself that it should do the contrary. Again, in as much as the world overaboundeth with malice, and few are delighted in doing good to other men, there is no man so seldom crossed as pleasured at the hands of others; whereupon it cannot be chosen but every man's woes must double in that respect the number and pleasure of his delights. Besides, concerning the very choice which oftentimes we make our corrupting inclination well considered, there is cause why our Saviour should account them the happiest that do most mourn, and why Solomon might judge it better to frequent mourning than feasting houses; not better simply in itself (for then would nature that way incline) but in regard of us and our common weakness better. Job was not ignorant that his children's banquets, though tending to amity, needed sacrifice. Neither doth any of us all need to be taught that in things which delight we easily swerve from mediocrity, and are not easily led by a right direct line. On the other side, the sores and diseases of mind which inordinate pleasure breedeth are by dolour and grief cured. For which cause as all offences use to seduce by pleasing, so all punishments endeavour by vexing to reform transgressions. We are of our accord apt enough to give entertainment to things delectable; but patiently to lack what flesh and blood doth desire, and by virtue to forbear what by nature we covet, this no man attaineth unto, but with labour and long practice. From hence, it ariseth that in former ages, abstinence and fasting more than ordinary was always a special branch of their praise in whom it could be observed and known, were they such as continually gave themselves to austere life; or men that took often occasions in private virtuous respects to lay Solomon's counsel aside, *Eat thy bread with joy*, and to be followers of David's example; which saith, *I humbled my soul with fasting* or but they who, otherwise worthy of no great commendation, have made of hunger some their gain, some their physic, some their art, that, by mastering their sensual appetites without constraint, they might grow able to endure hardness whensoever need should require: for the body accustomed to emptiness pineth not away so soon as having still used to fill itself. Many singular effects there are which should make fasting even in public consider-ations the rather to be accepted. For I presume we are not altogether without experience how great their advantage is in martial enterprises, that lead armies of men trained in a school of abstinence. It is therefore noted at this day in some, that patience of hunger and thirst hath given them many victories; in others that because if they want, there is no man able to rule them, nor they in plenty to moderate themselves, he which can either bring them to hunger or overcharge them, is sure to make them their own overthrow. What nation soever doth feel these dangerous inconveniences, may know that sloth and fullness in peace-able times at home is the cause thereof, and the remedy a strict observa-tion of that part of Christian discipline, which teacheth men in practice of ghostly warfare against themselves, those things that afterwards may help them, justly assaulting or standing in lawful defence of themselves against others. The very purpose of the Church of God both in the number and in the order of her fasts, hath been not only to preserve thereby throughout all ages the remembrance of miseries heretofore sustained, and of the causes in ourselves out of which they have risen, that men considering the one might fear the other the more, but farther also to temper the mind, lest contrary affections coming in place should make it too profuse and dissolute; in which respect it seemeth that fasts have been set as ushers of festival days, for preventing of those disor-ders as much as might be; wherein, notwithstanding, the world always will deserve as it hath done, blame; because such evils being not pos-sible to be rooted out, the most we can do, is in keeping them low, and (which is chiefly the fruit we look for) to create in the minds of men a love towards a frugal and severe life; to undermine the palaces of wantonness; to plant parsimony as nature, where riotousness hath been studied; to harden whom pleasure would melt; and to help the tumours which always fullness breedeth; that children, as it were in the wool of their infancy dyed with hardness, may never afterwards change colour; that the poor, whose perpetual fasts are of necessity, may with better contentment endure the hunger which virtue causeth others so often to choose, and by advice of religion itself so far to esteem above the contrary; that they which for the most part do lead sensual and easy lives, they which, as the prophet David describeth them, *are not plagued like other men*, may by the public spectacle of all be still put in mind what themselves are; finally, that every man may be every man's daily guide and example, as well by fasting to declare humility, as by praise to express joy in the sight of God, although it have herein befallen the Church, as sometimes David, so that the speech of the one may be truly the voice of the other, *My soul fasted, and even that was also turned to my reproof.*

V lxii 16–18, 424–6

Hooker's praise of Holy Matrimony strongly defends its sacramental dignity, although Anglican doctrine did not allow it to be truly a sacrament. He supports the ecclesiastical rule forbidding the celebration of marriage during Lent. His attitude to women, not acceptable today, was that of his time.

In this world there can be no society durable otherwise than only by propagation. Albeit therefore single life be a thing more angelical and divine, yet sith the replenishing first of earth with blessed inhabitants, and then of heaven with Saints everlastingly praising God, did depend upon conjunction of man and woman, he which made all things complete and perfect saw it could not be good to leave men without any helper unto the fore-alleged end. In things which some farther end doth cause to be desired, choice seeketh rather proportion than absolute perfection of goodness. So that woman being created for man's sake to be his helper, in regard of the end before mentioned; namely, the having and bringing up of children, whereunto it was not possible they could concur, unless there were subalternation between them, which subalternation is naturally grounded upon inequality, because things equal in every respect are never willingly directed one by another: woman therefore was even in her first estate framed by Nature, not only after in time, but inferior in excellency also unto man, howbeit in so due and sweet proportion, as being presented before our eyes, might be sooner perceived than defined. And even herein doth lie the reason why that kind of love, which is the perfectest ground of wedlock, is seldom able to yield any reason of itself. Now, that which is born of man must be nourished with far more travel, as being of greater price in Nature, and of slower pace to perfection, than the offspring of any other creature besides. Man and woman being therefore to join themselves for such a purpose, they were of necessity to be linked with some strait and insoluble knot. The bond of wedlock hath been always, more or less, esteemed of as a thing religious and sacred. The title which the very Heathens themselves do thereunto oftentimes give is *holy*. Those rites and orders which were instituted in the solemnization of marriage the Hebrews term by the name of conjugal *sanctification*. Amongst ourselves, because sundry things appertaining unto the public order of matrimony are called in question by such as know not from whence those customs did first grow, to show briefly some true and sufficient reason of them shall not be superfluous; although we do not hereby intend to yield so far unto enemies of all Church orders saving their own, as though everything were unlawful, the true cause and reason whereof at the first might hardly perhaps be now rendered. Wherefore, to begin with the times wherein the liberty of marriage is restrained; *There is*, saith Solomon, *a time for all things, a time to laugh, and a time to mourn.* That duties belonging unto marriage, and offices appertaining to penance, are things unsuitable and unfit to be matched together, the Prophets and Apostles themselves do witness. Upon which ground, as we might right well think it marvellous absurd to see in a church a wedding on the day of a public fast, so likewise in the self-same consideration our predecessors thought it not amiss to take away the common liberty of marriages during the time which was appointed for preparation unto, and for exercise of general humiliation by fasting and praying, weeping for sins.

V lxxiii 1–4, 427–9

Funeral rites were radically changed in the Reformed Churches, including the Church of England. Hooker defends the service, against Puritan objections to ceremony and customs, as giving comfort and assurance to the living.

There is a duty which the Church doth owe to the faithful departed, wherein forasmuch as the Church of England is said to do those things which are, though not unlawful, yet inconvenient, because it appointeth a prescript form of service at burials, suffereth mourning apparel to be worn; and permitteth funeral-sermons; a word or two concerning this point will be necessary, although it be needless to dwell long upon it. The end of funeral duties is, first, to show that love towards the party deceased which nature requireth; then to do him that honour which is fit both generally for man, and particularly for the quality of his person; last of all, to testify the care which the Church hath to comfort the living, and the hope which we all have concerning the resurrection of the dead . . . For signification of love towards them that are departed, mourning is not denied to be a thing convenient; as in truth the Scripture everywhere doth approve lamentation made unto this end. The Jews by our Saviour's tears therefore gathered in this case that his love towards Lazarus was great. And that as mourning at such times is fit, so likewise that there may be a kind of attire suitable to a sorrowful affection, and convenient for mourners to wear, how plainly doth David's example show, who, being in heaviness, went up the mount with his head covered, and all the people that were with him in like sort? White garments being fit to use at marriage feasts, and such other times of joy, whereunto Solomon alluding, when he requireth continual cheerfulness of mind, speaketh in this sort, *Let thy garments be always white*; what doth hinder the contrary from being now as convenient in grief, as this heretofore in gladness hath been? *If there be no sorrow*, they say, *it is hypocritical to pretend it; and if there be, to provoke it by wearing such attire is dangerous*. Nay, if there be, to show it is natural; and if there be not, yet the signs are meet to show what should be, especially sith it doth not come oftentimes to pass that men are fain to have their mourning gowns pulled off their backs for fear of killing themselves with sorrow that way nourished. The honour generally due unto all men maketh a decent interring of them to be convenient, even for very humanity's sake. And therefore, so much as is mentioned in the burial of the widow's son, the *carrying of him forth upon a bier*, and the accompanying of him to the earth, hath been used even amongst Infidels; all men accounting it a very extreme destitution not to have at the last this honour done them. Some man's estate may require a great deal more, according as the fashion of the country where he dieth doth afford. And unto this appertained the ancient use of the Jews, to embalm the corpse with sweet odours, and to adorn the sepulchres of certain. In regard of the quality of men, it hath been judged fit to commend them unto the world at their death, amongst the Heathen in funeral orations, amongst the Jews in sacred poems; and why not in funeral sermons also amongst Christians? Us it sufficeth, that the known benefit hereof doth countervail millions of such inconveniences as are therein surmised, although they were not surmised only, but found therein. The life and the death of saints is precious in God's sight. Let it not seem

odious in our eyes, if both the one and the other be spoken of then especially, when the present occasion doth make men's minds the more capable of such speech. The care, no doubt, of the living both to live and
to die well, must needs be somewhat increased, when they know that
their departure shall not be folded up in silence, but the ears of many
be made acquainted with it. Moreover, when they hear how mercifully
God hath dealt with their brethren in their last need, besides the praise
which they give to God, and the joy which they have or should have by
reason of their fellowship and communion with saints, is not their hope
also much confirmed against the day of their own dissolution?

V lxxv 1–3, 438–41

*Hooker now addresses one of the strongest and most persistent of Pu-
ritan objections, the question of holy orders. He defends the solemnity,
privilege and duties of ordination. This leads him to reflect on the vanity
of temporal pleasures unless seen in the light of the eternal. This world
places too much value on honour and reputation.*

I come now unto that function which undertaketh the public ministry
of holy things according to the Laws of Christian Religion. And because the nature of things, consisting as this doth in action, is known
by the object whereabout they are conversant, and by the end or scope
whereunto they are referred, we must know that the object of this function is both God and men; God in that he is publicly worshipped of his
Church, and men in that they are capable of happiness by means which
Christian discipline appointeth. So that the sum of our whole labour in
this kind is to honour God and to save men. For whether we severally
take and consider men one by one, or else gather them into one society
and body, as it hath been before declared, that every man's religion is in
him the well-spring of all other sound and sincere virtues, from whence
both here in some sort, and hereafter more abundantly, their full joy
and felicity ariseth; because while they live they are blessed of God,
and when they die their works follow them: so at this present we must
again call to mind how the very worldly peace and prosperity, the secular happiness, the temporal and natural good estate both of all men,
and of all dominions, hangeth chiefly upon religion, and doth evermore
give plain testimony that, as well in this as in other considerations, the
priest is a pillar of that commonwealth wherein he faithfully serveth
God. For if these assertions be true, first, that nothing can be enjoyed
in this present world against his will which hath made all things; secondly, that albeit God doth sometime permit the impious to have, yet

impiety permitteth them not to enjoy, no not temporal blessings on earth; thirdly, that God hath appointed those blessings to attend as handmaids upon religion; and fourthly, that, without the work of the ministry, religion by no means can possibly continue, the use and bene-fit of that sacred function even towards all men's worldly happiness must needs be granted. Now the first being a theorem both understood and confessed by all, to labour in proof thereof were superfluous. The second perhaps may be called in question, except it be perfectly un-derstood. By good things temporal therefore we mean length of days, health of body, store of friends and well-willers, quietness, prosperous success of those things we take in hand, riches with fit opportunities to use them during life, reputation following us both alive and dead, children, or such as instead of children we wish to leave successors and partakers of our happiness. These things are naturally every man's desire, because they are good; and on whom God bestoweth the same, them we confess he graciously blesseth. Of earthly blessings the mean-est is wealth, reputation the chiefest. For which cause we esteem the gain of honour an ample recompense for the loss of all other worldly benefits. But forasmuch as in all this there is no certain perpetuity of goodness, nature hath taught to affect these things, not for their own sake; but with reference and relation to somewhat independently good, as is the exercise of virtue and speculation of truth. None, whose de-sires are rightly ordered, would wish to live, breathe, and move without performance of those actions which are beseeming man's excellency. Wherefore having not how to employ it, we wax weary even of life itself. Health is precious, because sickness doth breed that pain which disableth action. Again, why do men delight so much in the multitude of friends, but for that the actions of life, being many, do need many helping hands to further them? Between troublesome and quiet days we should make no difference, if the one did not hinder and interrupt, the other uphold our liberty of action. Furthermore, if those things we do succeed, it rejoiceth us not so much for the benefit we thereby reap as in that it probably argueth our actions to have been orderly and well-guided. As for riches, to him which hath and doth nothing with them, they are a contumely. Honour is commonly presumed a sign of more than ordinary virtue and merit, by means whereof when ambi-tious minds thirst after it, their endeavours are testimonies how much it is in the eye of nature to possess that body, the very shadow whereof is set at so high a rate. Finally, such is the pleasure and comfort which we take in doing, that when life forsaketh us, still our desires to continue action and to work, though not by ourselves, yet by them whom we leave behind us, causeth us providently to resign into other men's hands the helps we have gathered for that purpose, devising also the best we can to make them perpetual. It appeareth, therefore, how all the parts of temporal felicity are only good in relation to that which useth them as instruments, and that they are no such good as wherein a right desire doth ever stay or rest itself.

V lxxvi 1–3, 444–6

Ordination is a divine gift which must be properly conferred by authority, is indelible, and cannot be repeated.

The ministry of things divine is a function, which as God did himself institute, so neither may men undertake the same but by authority and power given them in lawful manner. That God which is no way deficient or wanting unto man in necessaries, and hath therefore given us the light of his heavenly truth, because without that inestimable benefit we must needs have wandered in darkness to our endless perdition and woe, hath in the like abundance of mercies, ordained certain to attend upon the due execution of requisite parts and offices therein prescribed for the good of the whole world, which men thereupon assigned do hold their authority from him, whether they be such as himself immediately, or as the Church in his name investeth; it being neither possible for all, nor for every man without distinction, convenient to take upon him a charge of so great importance. They are therefore ministers of God, not only by way of subordination as princes and civil magistrates, whose execution of judgment and justice the supreme hand of Divine Providence doth uphold, but ministers of God, as from whom their authority is derived, and not from men. For in that they are Christ's ambassadors and his labourers, who should give them their commission but he whose most inward affairs they manage? Is not God alone the Father of spirits? Are not souls the purchase of Jesus Christ? What Angel in heaven could have said to man, as our Lord did unto Peter, *Feed my sheep: preach: baptize: do this in remembrance of me: whose sins ye retain, they are retained; and their offences in heaven pardoned whose faults ye shall on earth forgive?* What think we? Are these terrestrial sounds, or else are they voices uttered out of the clouds above? The power of the ministry of God translateth out of darkness into glory; it raiseth men from the earth, and bringeth God himself from heaven; by blessing visible elements it maketh them invisible grace; it giveth daily the Holy Ghost, it hath to dispose of that flesh which was given for the life of the world, and that blood which was poured out to redeem souls;

when it poureth malediction upon the heads of the wicked, they perish; when it revoketh the same, they revive. O wretched blindness, if we admire not so great power; more wretched if we consider it aright, and notwithstanding imagine that any but God can bestow it! To whom Christ hath imparted power, both over that mystical body which is the society of souls, and over that natural which is himself, for the knitting of both in one, (a work which antiquity doth call the making of Christ's body) the same power is in such not amiss both termed a kind of mark or character, and acknowledged to be indelible. Ministerial power is a mark of separation, because it severeth them that have it from other men, and maketh them a special Order consecrated unto the service of the Most High in things wherewith others may not meddle. Their difference therefore from other men is in that they are a distinct Order. So Tertullian calleth them. And St Paul himself, dividing the body of the Church of Christ into two moieties, nameth the one part *idiotas*, which is as much as to say the Order of the Laity, the opposite part whereunto we in like sort term the Order of God's Clergy, and the spiritual power which he hath given them, the power of their Order, so far forth as the same consisteth in the bare execution of holy things, called properly the affairs of God. For of the power of their jurisdiction over men's persons we are to speak in the books following. They which have once received this power may not think to put it off and on like a cloak, as the weather serveth, to take it, reject and resume it as oft as themselves list; of which profane and impious contempt these latter times have yielded, as of all other kinds of iniquity and apostasy, strange examples. But let them know, which put their hands unto this plough, that once consecrated into God, they are made his peculiar inheritance for ever. Suspensions may stop, and degradations utterly cut off the use or exercise of power before given; but voluntarily it is not in the power of man to separate and pull asunder what God by his authority coupleth. So that although there may be through misdesert degradation, as there may be cause of just separation after matrimony; yet if (as sometimes it doth) restitution to former dignity, or reconciliation after breach doth happen, neither doth the one nor the other ever iterate the first knot. Much less is it necessary, which some have urged, concerning the re-ordination of such as others in times more corrupt did consecrate heretofore.

V lxxvii 1–3, 455–7

The Puritans have objected to the words 'Receive the Holy Ghost' in ordination, as a gift which human words cannot give. They also condemn coming to the Bishop to seek ordination, as ambition rather than responding to the divine call. He defends the usage and makes a distinction between sinful ambition and allowable desire.

Forasmuch as the Holy Ghost, which our Saviour in his first ordinations gave, doth no less concur with spiritual vocations throughout all ages, than the Spirit which God derived from Moses to them that assisted him in his government did descend from them to their successors in like authority and place, we have for the least and meanest duties, performed by virtue of ministerial power, that to dignify, grace, and authorize them, which no other offices on earth can challenge. Whether we preach, pray, baptize, communicate, condemn, give absolution, or whatsoever; as disposers of God's mysteries, our words, judgments, acts, and deeds are not ours, but the Holy Ghost's. Enough, if unfeignedly and in heart we did believe it, enough to banish whatsoever may be thought corrupt either in bestowing, or in esteeming the same otherwise than is meet. For profanely to bestow, or loosely to use, or vilely to esteem of the Holy Ghost, we all in show and profession abhor. Now because the ministry is an office of dignity and honour, some are doubtful whether any man may seek for it without offence; or, to speak more properly, doubtful they are not, but rather bold to accuse our discipline in this respect, as not only permitting, but requiring also ambitious suits, or other oblique ways or means whereby to obtain it. Against this they plead, that our Saviour did stay till his Father sent him, and the Apostles till he them; that the ancient Bishops in the Church of Christ were examples and patterns of the same modesty. Whereupon in the end they infer, *Let us therefore at the length amend that custom of repairing from all parts unto the Bishop at the day of ordination, and of seeking to obtain orders; let the custom of bringing commendatory letters be removed; let men keep themselves at home, expecting there the voice of God, and the authority of such as may call them to undertake the charge.* Thus severely they censure and control ambition, if it be ambition which they take upon them to reprehend. For of that there is cause to doubt. Ambition, as we understand it, hath been accounted a vice which seeketh after honours inordinately. Ambitious minds, esteeming it their greatest happiness to be admired, reverenced, and adored above others, use all means lawful and unlawful which may bring them to high rooms. But as for the power of order considered by itself, and as in this case it must be considered, such reputation it hath in the eye of this present world, that they which affect it, rather need encouragement to bear contempt than deserve blame as men that carry aspiring minds. The work whereunto this power serveth is commended, and the desire thereof allowed by the

Apostle for good. Nevertheless, because the burden thereof is heavy, and the charge great, it cometh many times to pass, that the minds even of virtuous men are drawn into clean contrary affections, some in humility declining that by reason of hardness, which others in regard of goodness only do with fervent alacrity covet. So that there is not the least degree in this service, but it may be both in reverence shunned, and of very devotion longed for. If then the desire thereof may be holy, religious, and good, may not the profession of that desire be so likewise? We are not to think it so long good as it is dissembled, and evil if once we begin to open it. And allowing that it may be opened without ambition, what offence, I beseech you, is there in opening it there, where it may be furthered and satisfied, in case they to whom it appertaineth think meet? In vain are those desires allowed, the accomplishment whereof it is not lawful for men to seek. Power therefore of Ecclesiastical order may be desired, the desire thereof may be professed, they which profess themselves that way inclined may endeavour to bring their desires to effect, and in all this no necessity of evil. Is it the bringing of testimonial letters wherein so great obliquity consisteth? What more simple, more plain, more harmless, more agreeable with the law of common humanity, than that men, where they are not known, use for their easier access the credit of such as can best give testimony of them? Letters of any other construction our Church discipline alloweth not; and these to allow, is neither to require ambitious suings, nor to approve any indirect or unlawful act. The prophet Esay, receiving his message at the hands of God, and his charge by heavenly vision, heard the voice of the Lord, saying, *Whom shall I send? Who shall go for us?* Whereunto he recordeth his own answer, *Then I said, Here, Lord, I am; send me.* Which in effect is the rule and canon whereby touching this point the very order of the Church is framed. The appointment of times for solemn ordination is but the public demand of the Church in the name of the Lord himself, *Whom shall I send? Who shall go for us?* The confluence of men, whose inclinations are bent that way, is but the answer thereunto, whereby the labours of sundry being offered, the Church hath freedom to take whom her agents in such case think meet and requisite.

V lxxvii 8–11, 462–5

More on ordination, Hooker reminding his opponents that it is conferred into the universal Church and not to a specific congregation. He opposes the Puritans' idea of a minister being called to a particular gathered church.

There are in a minister of God these four things to be considered: his ordination which giveth him power to meddle with things sacred; the charge or portion of the Church allotted unto him for exercise of his office; the performance of his duty, according to the exigence of his charge; and lastly the maintenance which in that respect he receiveth. All Ecclesiastical Laws and Canons which either concern the bestowing or the using of the power of ministerial order have relation to these four. Of the first we have spoken before at large. Concerning the next, for more convenient discharge of ecclesiastical duties, as the body of the people must needs be severed by divers precincts, so the Clergy likewise accordingly distributed. Whereas therefore religion did first take place in cities, and in that respect was the cause why the name of Pagans, which properly signifieth a country people, came to be used in common speech for the same that Infidels and unbelievers were, it followed thereupon that all such cities had their Ecclesiastical Colleges, consisting of Deacons and of Presbyters, whom Apostles or their delegates the Evangelists did both ordain and govern. Such were the Colleges of Jerusalem, Antioch, Ephesus, Rome, Corinth, and the rest where the Apostles are known to have planted our faith and religion. Now because religion and the cure of souls was their general charge in common over all that were near about them, neither had any one Presbyter his several cure apart till Evaristus, Bishop in the See of Rome about the year 112, began to assign precincts unto every church or title which the Christians held, and to appoint unto each Presbyter a certain compass whereof himself should take charge alone, the commodiousness of this invention caused all parts of Christendom to follow it, and at the length our own churches about the year 636 became divided in like manner. But other distinction of churches there doth not appear any in the Apostles' writings, save only, according to those cities wherein they planted the Gospel of Christ, and erected Ecclesiastical Colleges. Wherefore to ordain *kata polin,* throughout every city, and *kata ecclesian,* throughout every church, do in them signify the same thing. Churches then neither were, nor could be, in so convenient sort limited as now they are; first, by the bounds of each state and then within each state by more particular precincts, till at the length we descend unto several congregations, termed parishes, with far narrower restraint than this name at the first was used. And from hence hath grown their error, who, as oft as they read of the duty which ecclesiastical persons are now to perform towards the Church, their manner is always to understand by that Church, some particular Congregation or Parish church. They suppose that there should now be no man of ecclesiastical order which is not tied to some certain parish. Because the names of all Church-officers are words of relation, because a shepherd must have his flock, a teacher his scholars, a minister his company which he ministereth unto, therefore it seemeth a thing in their eyes absurd and unreasonable that any man be ordained a minister otherwise than only to some particular congregation. Perceive they not how by this means they make it unlawful for the Church to employ men at all in converting nations? For if so be the Church may not lawfully admit to an ecclesiastical function, unless it tie the party admitted unto some particular parish, then surely a thankless labour it is whereby men seek the conversion of Infidels which know not Christ, and therefore cannot be as yet divided into their special congregations and flocks. But, to the end it may appear how much this one thing among many more hath been mistaken, there is no precept requiring that Presbyters and Deacons be made in such sort and not otherwise. Albeit therefore the Apostles did make them in that order, yet is not their example such a law, as without all exception bindeth to make them in no other order but that. Again, if we will consider: that which the Apostles themselves did, surely no man can justly say, that herein we practise any thing repugnant to their example. For by them there was ordained only in each Christian city a College of Presbyters and Deacons to administer holy things. Evaristus did a hundred years after the birth of our Saviour Christ begin the distinction of the Church into parishes. Presbyters and Deacons having been ordained before to exercise Ecclesiastical functions in the Church of Rome promiscuously, he was the first that tied them each one to his own station. So that of the two, indefinite ordination of Presbyters and Deacons did come more near the Apostles' example, and the tying of them to be made only for particular congregations may more justly ground itself upon the example of Evaristus than of any Apostle of Christ. It hath been the opinion of wise and good men heretofore, that nothing was ever devised more singularly beneficial unto God's Church than this which our honourable predecessors have to their endless praise found out by: the erecting such houses of study, as those two most famous Universities do contain, and by providing that choice wits, after reasonable time spent in contemplation, may at the length either enter into that holy vocation for which they have been so long nourished and brought up, or else give place and suffer others to succeed in their rooms, that so the Church may be always furnished with a number of men whose ability being first known by public trial in Church-labours there where men can best judge of them, their calling afterwards unto particular charge abroad may be accordingly. All this is frustrate, those worthy foundations must dissolve, their whole device and religious purpose which did erect them is made void, their orders and statutes are to be cancelled and disannulled, in case the Church be forbidden to grant any power of order unless it be with restraint to the party ordained unto some particular parish or congregation. Nay, might we not rather affirm of Presbyters and of Deacons that the very nature of their ordination is unto necessary local restraint a thing opposite and repugnant?

V lxxx 1–6, 499–502

He moves to acknowledge faults in the Church of England as at that time, censuring the acceptance of ignorant clergy, non-residence and pluralities. All these abuses, especially the last two, continued until the nineteenth-century reforms.

The truth is, that of all things hitherto mentioned, the greatest is that threefold blot or blemish of notable ignorance, unconscionable absence from the cures whereof men have taken charge, and unsatiable hunting after spiritual preferments, without either care or conscience of the public good, Whereof, to the end that we may consider, as in God's own sight and presence with all uprightness, sincerity, and truth, let us particularly mine in every of them; first, how far forth are reprovable by reasons and maxims of common right; secondly, whether that which our laws permit be repugnant to those maxims, and with what equity we ought to judge of things practised in this case, neither on the one hand defending that which must be acknowledged out of square, nor on the other side condemning rashly whom we list for whatsoever we disallow. Touching arguments therefore taken from the principles of common right to prove that ministers should be learned, that they ought to be resident upon their livings, and that more than one only benefice or spiritual living may not be granted unto one man; the first, because St Paul requireth in a minister ability to teach, to convince, to distribute the Word rightly; because also the Lord himself hath protested they shall be no priests to him which have rejected knowledge, and because if the blind lead the blind, they must both needs fall into the pit: the second, because teachers are shepherds whose flocks can be no time secure from danger; they are watchmen whom the enemy doth always besiege; their labours in the Word and Sacrament admit no intermission; their duty requireth instruction and conference with men in private; they are the living Oracles of God, to whom the people must resort for counsel; they are commanded to be patterns of holiness, leaders, feeders, supervisors amongst their own; it should be their grief, as it was the Apostles', to be absent, though necessarily, from them over whom they have taken charge: finally, the last, because plurality and residence are opposite; because the placing of one clerk in two churches is a point of merchandise and filthy gain; because no man can serve two masters; because everyone should remain in that vocation whereto he is called; what conclude they of all this? Against ignorance, against non-residence, and against plurality of livings, is there any man so raw and dull, but that the volumes which have been written both of old and of late may make him in so plentiful a cause eloquent? For by that which is generally just and requisite, we measure what knowledge there should be in a minister of the Gospel of Christ; the arguments which light of Nature offereth; the laws and statutes which Scripture hath; the canons that are taken out of ancient synods; the decrees and constitutions of sincerest times; the sentences of all antiquity; and in a word, even every man's full consent and conscience is against ignorance in them that have charge and cure of souls. Again, what availeth it if we be learned and not faithful? Or what benefit hath the Church of Christ, if there be in us sufficiency without endeavour or care to do that good which our place exacteth? Touching the pains and industry therefore, wherewith men are in conscience bound to attend the work of their heavenly calling, even as much as in them lieth bending thereunto their whole endeavour, without either fraud; sophistication, or guile; I see not what more effectual obligation or bond of duty there should be urged, than their own only vow and promise made unto God himself at the time of their ordination. The work which they have undertaken requireth both care and fear. Their sloth that negligently perform it, maketh them subject to malediction. Besides, we also know that the fruit of our pains in this function is life both to ourselves and others. And do we yet need incitements to labour? Shall we stop our ears both against those conjuring exhortations which Apostles, and against the fearful comminations which Prophets have uttered out of the mouth of God, the one for prevention, the other for reformation of our sluggishness in this behalf? [. . .] Nor let us think to excuse ourselves if haply we labour, though it be at random, and sit not altogether idle abroad. For we are bound to attend that part of the flock of Christ, whereof the Holy Ghost hath made us overseers. The residence of ministers upon their own peculiar charge is by so much the rather necessary, for that absenting themselves from the place where they ought to labour, they neither can do the good which is looked for at their hands, nor reap the comfort which sweeteneth life to them that spend it in these travels

upon their own. For it is in this, as in all things else which are through
private interest dearer than what concerneth either others wholly, or
us but in part, and according to the rate of a general regard. As for
plurality, it hath not only the same inconveniences which are observed
to grow by absence; but over and besides, at the least in common construction, a show of that worldly humour which men do think should
not reign so high.

V lxxxi 1–2, 509–12

However, it is sometimes necessary to accept less than the ideal. Men
not of sufficient learning may be ordained, but not allowed to preach.
This was one of the purposes of the Books of Homilies to be read in
churches.

Now there being general laws and rules whereby it cannot be denied
but the Church of God standeth bound to provide that the ministry
may be learned, that they which have charge may reside upon it, and
that it may not be free for them in scandalous manner to multiply ecclesiastical livings; it remaineth in the next place to be examined what the
laws of the Church of England do admit, which may be thought repugnant to any thing hitherto alleged, and in what special consideration
they seem to admit the same. Considering, therefore, that to furnish
all places of cure of this realm, it is not an army of twelve thousand
learned men that would suffice, nor two Universities that can always
furnish as many as decay in so great a number, nor a fourth part of the
livings with cure, that when they fall are able to yield sufficient maintenance for learned men, is it not plain that unless the greatest part of
the people should be left utterly without the public use and exercise of
religion, there is no remedy but to take into the Ecclesiastical Order a
number of men meanly qualified in respect of learning? For whatsoever
we may imagine in our private closets, or talk for communication sake
at our boards, yea, or write in our books through a notional conceit
of things needful for performance of each man's duty, if once we come
from the theory of learning, to take out so many learned men, let them
be diligently viewed out of whom the choice shall be made, and thereby
an estimate made what degree of skill we must either admit, or else
leave numbers utterly destitute of guides, and I doubt not but that men
endued with sense of common equity will soon discern that, beside
eminent and competent knowledge, we are to descend to a lower step,
receiving knowledge in that degree which is but tolerable. When we
commend any man for learning, our speech opporteth him to be more

than meanly qualified in that way; but when Laws do require learning as a quality, which maketh capable of any function, our measure to judge a learned man by must be some certain degree of learning, beneath which we can hold no man so qualified. And if every man that listeth may set that degree himself, shall we ever know when Laws are broken, when kept, seeing one man may think a lower degree sufficient, another may judge them unsufficient, that are not qualified in some higher degree? Wherefore of necessity either we must have some judge in whose conscience they that are thought and pronounced sufficient are to be so accepted and taken, or else the Law itself is to set down the very lowest degree of fitness that shall be allowable in this kind. So that the question doth grow to this issue. St Paul requireth learning in Presbyters, yea such learning as doth enable them to exhort in doctrine which is sound, and to disprove them that gainsay it. What measure of ability in such things shall serve to make men capable of that kind of office he doth not him precisely determine, but referreth it to the conscience of Titus and others which had to deal in ordaining Presbyters. We must therefore of necessity make this demand, whether the Church, lacking such as the Apostle would have chosen, may with good conscience take out of such as it hath in a meaner degree of fitness, them that may serve to perform the service of public prayer, to minister the sacraments unto the people, to solemnize marriage, to visit the sick, and bury the dead, to instruct by reading, although by preaching they be not as yet so able to benefit and feed Christ's flock: We constantly hold, that in this case the Apostle's law is not broken. He requireth more in Presbyters than there is found in many whom the Church of England alloweth. But no man being tied unto impossibilities, to do that we cannot we are not bound.

V lxxxi 5, 516–7

Coming towards the end of this Book, he reiterates his attack on some of the errors of his opponents. They wish to depart from early Church practice, and show excessive concern with sermons. The Church of England safeguards doctrine and discipline through its formularies and laws. The requirement of subscribing to the Articles before taking a degree at Oxford or Cambridge was imposed until well into the nineteenth century.

There is crept into the minds of men, at this day, a secret pernicious and pestilent conceit, that the greatest perfection of a Christian man doth consist in discovery of other men's faults, and in wit to discourse of our own profession. When the world most abounded with just, righteous, and perfect men, their chiefest study was the exercise of piety, wherein for their safest direction they reverently hearkened to the readings of the Law of God, they kept in mind the oracles, and aphorisms of wisdom which tended unto virtuous life; if any scruple of conscience did trouble them for matter of actions which they took in hand, nothing was attempted before counsel and advice were had, for fear lest rashly they might offend. We are now more confident, not that our knowledge and judgment is riper, but because our desires are another way. Their scope was obedience, ours is skill; their endeavour was reformation of life, our virtue nothing but to hear gladly the reproof of vice; they in the practice of their religion wearied chiefly their knees and hands, we especially our ears and tongues. We are grown, as in many things else, so in this, to a kind of intemperancy, which (only sermons excepted) hath almost brought all other duties of religion out of taste. At the least they are not in that account and reputation which they should be. Now, because men bring all religion in a manner to the only office of hearing sermons, if it chance that they who are thus conceited do embrace any special opinion different from other men, the sermons that relish not that opinion can in no wise please their appetite. Such therefore as preach unto them, but hit not the string they look for, are respected as unprofitable, the rest as unlawful; and indeed no ministers, if the faculty of sermons want. For why? A minister of the Word should, they say, be able rightly to divide the Word. Which Apostolic Canon many think they do well observe when in opening the sentences of Holy Scripture they draw all things favourably spoken unto one side; but whatsoever is reprehensive, severe, and sharp, they have others on the contrary part whom that must always concern, by which their over-partial and un-indifferent proceeding, while they thus labour amongst the people to divide the Word, they make the Word a mean to divide and distract the people. *Orthotomein*, to divide aright, doth note in the Apostles' writings soundness of doctrine only; and in meaning standeth opposite to *kainotomein, the broaching of new opinions against that which is received.* For questionless the first things delivered to the Church of Christ were pure and sincere truth; which whosoever did afterwards oppugn, could not choose but divide the Church into two moieties; in which division, such as taught what was first believed, held the truer part; the contrary side, in that they were teachers of novelty, erred. For prevention of which evil there are in this Church many singular and devised remedies; as namely, the use of subscribing to the Articles of Religion before admission to degrees of learning or to any ecclesiastical living; the custom of reading the same Articles, and of approving them in public assemblies wheresoever men have benefices with cure of soul; the order of testifying under their hands allowance of the Book of Common Prayer, and the Book of Ordaining Ministers; finally, the discipline and moderate severity which is used either in otherwise or correcting or silencing them that trouble and disturb the Church with doctrines which tend unto innovation; it being better that the Church should want altogether the benefit of such men's labours, than endure the mischief of their inconformity to good laws.

V lxxxi 10–11, 524–5

Hooker ends this long and important Book by repeating his call for reform of various abuses.

The ways to meet with disorders growing by abuse of Laws are not so intricate and secret, especially in our case, that men should need either much advertisement or long time for the search thereof. And if counsel to that purpose may seem needful, this Church (God be thanked) is not destitute of men endued with ripe judgment, whensoever any such thing shall be thought necessary. For which end, at this present, to propose any special inventions of my own might argue in a man of my place and calling more presumption perhaps than wit. I will therefore leave it entire unto graver consideration, ending now with request only and most earnest suit; first, that they which give ordination would as they tender the very honour of Jesus Christ, the safety of men, and the endless good of their own souls, take heed lest unnecessarily, and through their default, the Church be found worse or less furnished than it might be: secondly that they which by right of patronage have power to present unto spiritual livings, and may in that respect much damnify the Church of God, would, for the ease or their own account in that dreadful day, somewhat consider what it is to betray for gain the souls which Christ hath redeemed with blood, what to violate the sacred bond of fidelity and solemn promise given at the first to God and his Church by them, from whose original interest, together with the self-same title of right, the same obligation of duty likewise is descended: thirdly, that they unto whom the granting of dispensations is committed, or which otherwise have any stroke in the disposition of such preferments as appertain unto learned men, would bethink themselves what it is to respect anything either above or beside merit, considering how hardly the world taketh it when to men of commendable note and quality there is so little respect had, or so great unto them whose deserts are very mean,

that nothing doth seem more strange than the one sort because they are
not accounted of, and the other because they are; it being every man's
hope and expectation in the Church of God especially, that the only
purchase of greater rewards should be always greater deserts, and that
nothing should ever be able to plant in them a thorn where a vine ought
to grow: fourthly, that honourable personages, and they who by virtue
of any principal office in the Commonwealth are entitled to qualify a
certain number, and make them capable of favours or faculties above
others, suffer not their names to be abused, contrary to the true intent
and meaning of wholesome laws, by men in whom there is nothing
notable besides covetousness and ambition: fifthly, that the graver and
wiser sort in both Universities or whosoever they be, with whose approbation the marks and recognisances of all learning are bestowed, would
think the Apostle's caution against ill-advised ordinations not imperti-
nent or unnecessary to be borne in mind even when they grant those
degrees of schools, which degrees are not *gratia gratis datae*, kindnesses
bestowed by way of humanity, but they are *gratiae gratum facientes*,
favours which always imply a testimony given to the Church and Commonwealth concerning men's sufficiency for manners and knowledge;
a testimony upon the credit whereof sundry statutes of the realm are
built, a testimony so far available, that nothing is more respected for
the warrant of divers men's abilities to serve in the affairs of the realm,
a testimony wherein if they violate that religion wherewith it ought to
be always given, and do thereby induce into error, such as deem it a
thing uncivil to call the credit thereof in question, let them look that
God shall return back upon their heads, and cause them in the state of
their own corporations to feel either one way or other the punishment
of those harms which the Church through their negligence doth sustain
in that behalf: finally, and to conclude, that they who enjoy the benefit
of any special indulgence or favour which the laws permit, would as
well remember what in duty towards the Church and in conscience
towards God they ought to do, as what they may do by using to their
own advantage whatsoever they see tolerated; no man being ignorant
that the cause why absence in some cases hath been yielded unto and in
equity thought sufferable, is the hope of greater fruit through industry
elsewhere, the reason likewise why pluralities are allowed unto men of
note, a very sovereign and special care, that as fathers in the ancient
world did declare the pre-eminence of priority in birth by doubling
the worldly portions of their first-born, so the Church by a course not
unlike in assigning men's rewards might testify an estimation had pro-
portionably of their virtues, according to the ancient rule Apostolic,

They which excel in labour, ought to excel in honour; and therefore unless they answer faithfully the expectation of the Church herein, unless sincerely they bend their wits day and night both to sow because they reap, and to sow so much abundantly as the reap more abundantly than other men, whereunto by their very acceptance of such benignities they formally bind themselves, let them be well assured that the honey which they eat with fraud shall turn in the end into true gall, forasmuch as laws are the sacred image of his wisdom who most severely punisheth those colourable and subtle crimes that seldom are taken within the walk of human justice. I therefore conclude, that the grounds and maxims of common right whereupon ordinations of ministers unable to preach, tolerations of absence from their cures, and the multiplications of their spiritual livings are disproved, do but indefinitely enforce them unlawful, not unlawful universally and without exception; that the Laws which indefinitely are against all these things, and the privileges which make for them in certain cases are not the one repugnant to the other; that the laws of God and Nature are violated through the effects of abused privileges; that neither our ordinations of men unable to make sermons, nor our dispensations for the rest, can be justly proved frustrate by virtue of any such surmised opposition between the special Laws of this Church which have permitted, and those general which are alleged to disprove the same; that when privileges by abuse are grown incommodious, there must be redress; that for remedy of such evils, there is no necessity the Church should abrogate either in whole or in part the specialties before mentioned; and that the most to be desired were a voluntary reformation thereof on all hands which may give passage unto any abuse.

V lxxxi 15–17, 532–5

8

BOOK SIX

Matter belonging to the power of Ecclesiastical Jurisdiction

'Concerning their fifth Assertion, that our Laws are corrupt and repugnant to the Laws of God, in matter belonging to the power of Ecclesiastical Jurisdiction, in that we have not throughout all Churches certain Lay-Elders established for the exercise of that power.'

The last three Books show signs of their uncertain early movements and late publication. They are less coherently and consistently developed than the previous ones, but there is much in them which may reasonably be taken as Hooker's own ideas. He seems to have intended this Book as an argument about spiritual jurisdiction, refuting the Puritan demand for lay elders to play a major part in Church government.

Before there can be any settled determination whether truth do rest on their part or on ours, touching Lay-Elders, we are to prepare the way thereunto by explication of some things requisite and very needful to be considered; as first, how besides that spiritual power which is of order and was instituted for performance of those duties whereof there hath been speech already had, there is in the Church no less necessary a second kind, which we call the power of jurisdiction. When the Apostle doth speak of ruling the Church of God, and of receiving accusations, his words have evident reference to the power of jurisdiction. Our Saviour's words to the power of order, when he giveth his Disciples charge, saying *Preach: baptize: do this in remembrance of me.* [. . .] A Bishop (saith Ignatius) doth bear the image of God and of Christ; of God in ruling, of Christ in administering holy things. By this therefore we see a manifest difference acknowledged between the power of Ecclesiastical order, and the power of jurisdiction Ecclesiastical.

The spiritual power of the Church being such as neither can be challenged by right of nature, nor could by human authority be instituted, because the forces and effects thereof are supernatural and divine, we are to make no doubt or question but that from him which is the head it hath descended unto us that are the body now invested therewith. He gave it for the benefit and good of souls, as a mean to keep them in the path which leadeth unto endless felicity, a bridle to hold them within their convenient bounds, and, if they do go astray, a forcible help to reclaim them. Now although there be no kind of spiritual power, for which our Lord Jesus Christ did not give both commission to exercise, and direction how to use the same, although his Laws in that behalf recorded by the holy Evangelists be the only ground and foundation, whereupon the practice of the Church must sustain itself; yet, as all multitudes once grown to the form of societies are even thereby naturally warranted to enforce upon their own subjects particularly those things which public wisdom shall judge expedient for the common good; so it were absurd to imagine the Church itself, the most glorious amongst them, abridged of this liberty, or to think that no law, constitution or canon can be further made either for limitation or amplification in the practice of our Saviour's ordinances, whatsoever occasion be offered through variety of times and things, during the state of this inconstant world, which bringeth forth daily such new evils as must of necessity by new remedies be redressed, and did both of old enforce our venerable predecessors, and will always constrain others, sometime to make, sometime to abrogate, sometime augment, and again to abridge sometime; in sum, to vary, alter, and change customs incident unto the manner of exercising that power which doth itself continue always one and the same. I therefore conclude that spiritual authority is a power which Christ hath given to be used over them which are subject unto it for the eternal good of their souls, according to his own most sacred Laws and the wholesome positive institutions of his Church.

VI ii 1–2, 3–5

He soon turns from this topic to the question of repentance and pardon. He writes firmly but compassionately about repentance; it is inspired by love as well as fear.

As fear of contumely and disgrace among men, together with other civil punishments, are a bridle to restrain from heinous acts whereinto men's outrage would otherwise break; so the fear of divine revenge and punishment, where it takes place, doth make men desirous to be rid likewise from that inward guiltiness of sin whereby they would else securely continue. Howbeit when faith hath wrought a fear of the event of sin, yet repentance hereupon ensueth not, unless our belief conceive both the possibility and means to avert evil: the possibility, inasmuch as God is merciful, and most willing to have sin cured; the means, because he hath plainly taught what is requisite and shall suffice unto that purpose. The nature of all wicked men is, for fear of revenge, to hate whom they most wrong; the nature of hatred, to wish that destroyed which it cannot brook; and hence arise the furious endeavours of godless and obdurate sinners to extinguish in themselves the opinion of God, because they would not have him to be, whom execution of endless woe doth not suffer them to love.

Every sin against God abateth, and continuance in sin extinguisheth, our love towards him. It was therefore said to the Angel of Ephesus having sinned, *Thou art fallen away from thy first love*; so that, as we never decay in love till we sin, in like sort neither can we possibly forsake sin, unless we first begin again to love. What is love towards God but a desire of union with God? And shall we imagine a sinner converting himself to God, in whom there is no desire of union with God presupposed? I therefore conclude that fear worketh no man's inclination to repentance, till somewhat else have wrought in us love also: our love and desire of union with God ariseth from the strong conceit which we have of his admirable goodness; the goodness of God which particularly moveth unto repentance is his mercy towards mankind, notwithstanding sin: for let it once sink deeply into the mind of man that we have injured God, his very nature is averse from revenge, except unto sin we add obstinacy, otherwise always ready to accept our submission as a full discharge or recompense for all wrongs; and can we choose but begin to love him whom we have offended? Or can we but begin to grieve that we have offended him whom we love? Repentance considereth sin as a breach of the Law of God, an act obnoxious to that revenge, which notwithstanding may be prevented if we pacify God in time.

The root and beginning of penitency therefore is the consideration of our own sin, as a cause which hath procured the wrath, and a subject which doth need the mercy of God. For unto man's understanding there being presented, on the one side tribulation and anguish upon every soul that doth evil; on the other, eternal life unto them which by continuance in well doing seek glory, and honour, and immortality: on the one hand a curse to the children of disobedience; on the other, to lovers of righteousness all grace and benediction: yet between these extremes that eternal God, from whose unspotted justice and undeserved mercy the lot of each inheritance proceedeth, is so inclinable rather to show compassion than to take revenge, that all his speeches in Holy Scripture are almost nothing else but entreaties of men to prevent destruction by amendment of their wicked lives; all the works of his providence little other than mere allurements of the just to continue steadfast, and of the unrighteous to change their course; all his dealings and proceedings towards true converts, as have even filled the grave writings of holy men with these and the like most sweet sentences: Repentance (if I may so speak) stoppeth God in his way, when being provoked by crimes past he cometh to revenge them with most just punishments; yea, it tieth as it were the hands of the avenger, and doth not suffice for him to have his will.

Again, the merciful eye of God towards men hath no power to withstand penitency, at what time soever it comes in presence. And again, God doth not take it so in evil part, though we wound that which he hath required us to keep whole, as that after we have taken hurt there should be in us no desire to receive his help. Finally, lest I be carried too far in so large a sea, there was never any man condemned of God but for neglect; nor justified, except he had care of repentance.

From these considerations, setting before our eyes our inexcusable both unthankfulness in disobeying so merciful, foolishness in provoking so powerful a God; there ariseth necessarily a pensive and corrosive desire that we had done otherwise; a desire which suffereth us to foreslow no time, to feel no quietness within ourselves, to take neither sleep nor food with contentment, never to give over supplications, confessions, and other penitent duties, till the light of God's reconciled favour shine in our darkened soul.

VI iii 24, 8–10

After extensive and detailed discussion of the practice in various Churches and from various authorities, he considers penitence and absolution. Auricular confession is not barred but is not required; the priestly power of absolution is undoubted. This is another matter which became a major issue in the nineteenth century, when private confession was attacked by opponents of the Anglo-Catholic revival. A penitential approach is part of the discipline for Holy Communion, but excommunication is to be used sparingly and with caution.

Concerning confession in private, the Churches of Germany, as well the rest as Lutherans, agree that all men should at certain times confess their offences to God in the hearing of God's ministers, thereby to show how their sins displease them; to receive instruction for the warier

carriage of themselves hereafter; to be soundly resolved, if any scruple
or snare of conscience do entangle their minds; and, which is most material, to the end that men may at God's hand, seek every one his own
particular pardon, through the power of those Keys, which the minister
of God using according to our blessed Saviour's institution, in that case
it is their part to accept the benefit thereof, as God's most merciful ordinance for their good, and, without any distrust or doubt, to embrace
joyfully his grace so given them according to the word of our Lord,
which hath said, *Whose sins ye remit they are remitted.* So that grounding upon this assured belief, they are to rest with minds encouraged and
persuaded concerning the forgiveness of all their sins, as out of Christ's
own word and power by the ministry of the Keys.

It standeth with us in the Church of England, as touching public
confession, thus. First seeing day by day we in our Church begin our
public prayers to Almighty God with public acknowledgment of our
sins, in which confession any man, prostrate as it were before his glorious Majesty, crieth against himself, and the minister with one sentence
pronounceth universally all clear whose acknowledgment so made hath
proceeded from a true penitent mind; what reason is there every man
should not, under the general terms of confession, represent to himself
his own particulars whatsoever, and adjoining thereunto that affection
which a contrite spirit worketh, embrace to as full effect the words of
divine grace, as if the same were severally and particularly uttered with
addition of prayers, imposition of hands, or all the ceremonies and
solemnities that might be used for the strengthening of men's affiance
in God's peculiar mercy towards them? Such complements are helps to
support our weakness, and not causes that serve to procure or produce
his gifts, as David speaketh. The difference of general and particular
forms in confession and absolution is not so material that any man's
safety or ghostly good should depend upon it. And for private confession and absolution it standeth thus with us.

The minister's power to absolve is publicly taught and professed, the
Church not denied to have authority either of abridging or enlarging
the use and exercise of that power; upon the people no such necessity
imposed of opening their transgression unto men, as if remission of
sins otherwise were impossible; neither any such opinion had of the
thing itself, as though it were either unlawful or unprofitable, save only
for these inconveniences which the world hath by experience observed
in it heretofore. And in regard thereof, the Church of England hath
hitherto thought it the safer way to refer men's hidden crimes unto
God and themselves only; howbeit, not without special caution for the

admonition of such as come to the holy Sacrament, and for the comfort of such as are ready to depart the world. First, because there are but few that consider how much that part of divine service, which consists in partaking the holy Eucharist, doth import their souls; what they lose by neglect thereof, and what by devout practice they attain unto: therefore, lest carelessness of general confession should as commonly it doth, extinguish all remorse of men's particular enormous crimes, our custom (whensoever men present themselves at the Lord's table) is solemnly to give themselves fearful admonition, what woes are perpendicularly hanging over the heads of such as dare adventure to put forth their unworthy hands to those admirable mysteries of life, which have by rare examples been proved conduits of irremediable death to impenitent receivers; whom therefore, as we repel being known, so being not known we cannot but terrify. Yet, with us, the ministers of God's most holy word and sacraments, being all put in trust with the custody and dispensation of those mysteries wherein our communion is, and hath been ever, accounted the highest grace that men on earth are admitted unto, have therefore all equally the same power to withhold that sacred mystical food from notorious evil-livers, from such as have any way wronged their neighbours, and from parties between whom there doth open hatred and malice appear, till the first sort have reformed their wicked lives, the second recompensed them unto whom they were injurious, and the last condescended unto some course of Christian reconciliation, whereupon their mutual accord may ensue. In which cases, for the first branch of wicked life, and the last, which is open enmity, there can arise no great difficulty about the exercise of his power: in the second, concerning wrongs, they may, if men shall presume to define or measure injuries according to their own conceits, be depraved oftentimes as well by error as partiality, and that no less to the minister himself, than in another of the people under him.

The knowledge therefore which he taketh of wrongs must rise, as it doth in the other two, not from his own opinion or conscience, but from the evidence of the fact which is committed; yea, from such evidence as neither doth admit denial nor defence. For if the offender, having neither colour of law to uphold, or any other pretence to excuse his own uncharitable and wrongful dealings, shall wilfully stand in defence thereof, it serveth as bar to the power of the minister in this kind. Because (as it is observed by men of very good judgment in these affairs) although in this sort our separating of them be not to strike them with the mortal wound of excommunication, but to stay them rather from running desperately headlong into their own harm; yet it is not in us to sever from the holy communion but such as are either found culpable by their own confession, or have been convicted in some public secular, or ecclesiastical court. For who is he that dares take upon him to be any man's both accuser and judge? Evil persons are not rashly, and, as we list, to be thrust from communion with the Church. Insomuch that if we cannot proceed against them by any orderly course of judgment, they rather are to be suffered for the time than molested. Many there are reclaimed, as Peter; many, as Judas, known well enough, and yet tolerated; many which must remain undescribed till the day of his appearance, by whom the secret corners of darkness shall be brought into open light.

Leaving therefore unto his judgment them whom we cannot stay from casting their own souls into so great hazard, we have, in the other part of penitential jurisdiction in our power and authority to release sin, joy on all sides without trouble or molestation unto any. And, if to give be a thing more blessed than to receive, are we not infinitely happier in being authorized to bestow the treasure of God, than when necessity doth constrain to withdraw the same?

VI iv 14–15, 48–52

In a subtle and complex argument he defends Anglican sacramental doctrine against opponents; the question of signs and signifiers was prominent in Reformation disputes about the sacraments; Hooker maintains an irenical middle view. Cardinal Bellarmine (1542–1621) was one of the strongest and most intellectual Roman Catholic opponents of the Reformation Churches. William Allen (1532–94) left England and founded colleges to train priests for a Roman mission to England at Douai, Rome and Valladolid.

It passeth a man's conceit how water should be carried into the soul with any force of divine motion, or grace proceed but merely from the influence of God's Spirit. Notwithstanding, if God himself teach his Church in this case to believe that which he hath not given us capacity to comprehend, how incredible soever it may seem, yet our wits should submit themselves and reason give place unto faith therein. But they yield it to be no question of faith, because grace doth proceed from Sacraments, if in general they be acknowledged true instrumental causes, by the ministry whereof men receive divine grace. And that they which impute grace to the only operation of God himself, concurring with the external sign, do no less acknowledge the true efficacy of the Sacraments than they that ascribe the same to the quality of the sign applied, or to the motion of God applying, and so far carrying it, till grace be not created but extracted out of the natural possibility of the soul. Nevertheless, this last philosophical imagination, (if I may call it philosophical, which useth the terms but overthroweth the rules of philosophy, and hath no article of faith to support it) but whatsoever it be, they follow it in a manner all; they cast off the first opinion, wherein is most perspicuity, and strongest evidence of certain truth.

The Council of Florence and Trent defining that Sacraments contain and confer grace, the sense whereof (if it liked them) might so easily conform itself with the same opinion which they drew without any just cause quite and clean the other way, making grace the issue of bare words, in such Sacraments as they have framed destitute of any visible element, and holding it the offspring as well of elements as of words in those Sacraments where both are; but in no Sacrament acknowledging grace to be the fruit of the Holy Ghost working with the outward sign, and not by it, in such sort as Thomas himself teacheth; that the Apostles' imposition of hands caused not the coming of the Holy Ghost, which notwithstanding was bestowed together with the exercise of that ceremony; yea, by it, (saith the Evangelist) to wit, as by a mean which came between the agent and the effect, but not otherwise.

Many of the ancient Fathers presupposing that the faithful before Christ had not, till the time of his coming, that perfect life and salvation which they looked for and we possess, thought likewise their Sacraments, to be but prefigurations of that which ours in present do exhibit. For which cause the Florentine Council, comparing the one, with the other, saith, *That the old did only shadow grace, which was afterward to be given through the passion of Jesus Christ.* But the after-wit of latter days hath found out another more exquisite distinction, that evangelical Sacraments are causes to effect grace, through motions of signs legal, according to the same signification, and sense wherein evangelical sacraments are held by us to be God's instruments for that purpose. For howsoever Bellarmine hath shrunk up the Lutherans' sinews, and cut off our doctrine by the skirts; Allen, although he terms us heretics, according to the usual bitter venom of his first style, doth yet ingenuously confess, that the old Schoolmen's doctrine and ours is one concerning sacramental efficacy, derived from God himself; assisting by promise those outward signs of elements and words, out of which their Schoolmen of the newer mint are so desirous to hatch grace. Where God doth work and use these outward means, wherein he neither findeth nor planteth force and aptness towards his intended purpose, such means are but signs to bring men to the consideration of his omnipotent power, which without the use of things sensible, would not be marked.

At the time therefore when he giveth his heavenly grace, he applieth, by the hands of his ministers, that which betokeneth the same; not only betokeneth, but, being also accompanied for ever with such power as doth truly work, is in that respect termed God's instrument, a true efficient cause of grace; a cause not in itself: but only by connection of that which is in itself a cause, namely, God's own strength and power. Sacraments, that is to say, the outward signs in Sacraments, work nothing till they be blessed and sanctified by God.

But what is God's heavenly benediction and sanctification, saving only the association of his Spirit? Shall we say that Sacraments are like magical signs, if thus they have their effect? Is it magic for God to manifest by things sensible what he doth, and to do by his most glorious Spirit, really what he manifesteth in his Sacraments? The delivery and administration whereof remaineth in the hands of mortal men, by whom, as by personal instruments, God doth apply signs, and with signs inseparably join his Spirit, and through the power of his Spirit work grace. The first is by way of concomitance and consequence to deliver the rest also that either accompany or ensue.

It is not here, as in cases of mutual commerce where divers persons have divers acts to be performed in their own behalf; a creditor to show his bill, a debtor to pay his money. But God and man do here meet in one action upon a third, in whom, as it is the work of God to create grace, so it is his work by the hand of the ministry to apply a sign which should betoken, and his work to annex that Spirit which shall effect it. The action therefore is but one, God the author thereof, and man a co-partner, by him assigned to work for, with, and under him. God the giver of grace by the outward ministry of man, so far forth as he authorizeth man to apply the Sacraments of grace in the soul which he alone worketh, without either instrument or co-agent.

VI xi 11, 92–5

After a severe judgment on apostates, in terms reminiscent of the discipline of the Early Church, he affirms that all other sins if repented are covered by the redemption of Christ. Private confession is, in the Anglican way, provided for those who cannot find peace after repentance.

For all other offenders, without exception or stint, whether they be strangers that seek access, or followers that will make return unto God;

upon the tender of their repentance, the grant of his grace standeth everlastingly signed with his blood in the book of eternal life. That which in this case over-terrifieth fearful souls is a misconceit, whereby they imagine every act which they do, knowing that they do amiss, and every wilful breach or transgression of God's Law to be mere sin against the Holy Ghost, forgetting that the Law of Moses itself ordained sacrifices of expiation, as well for faults presumptuously committed, as things wherein men offend by error.

Now there are on the contrary side others who, doubting not of God's mercy towards all that perfectly repent, remain notwithstanding scrupulous and troubled with continual fear, lest defects in their own repentance be a bar against them.

These cast themselves into very great and peradventure needless agonies through misconstruction of things spoken about proportioning our griefs to our sins, for which they never think they have wept and mourned enough, yea, if they have not always a stream of tears at command, they take it for a heart congealed and hardened in sin; when to keep the wound of contrition bleeding, they unfold the circumstances of their transgressions, and endeavour to leave nothing which may be heavy against themselves.

Yet, do what they can, they are still fearful, lest herein also they do not that which they ought and might. Come to prayer, their coldness taketh all heart and courage from them; with fasting, albeit their flesh should be withered, and their blood clean dried up, would they ever the less object, what is this to David's humiliation, wherein notwithstanding there was not any thing more than necessary? In works of charity and alms-deed, it is not all the world can persuade them they did ever reach the poor bounty of the widow's two mites, by many millions of leagues come near to the mark which Cornelius touched; so far they are off from the proud surmise of any penitential supererogation in miserable wretched worms of the earth.

Notwithstanding, forasmuch as they wrong themselves with over-rigorous and extreme exactions, by means whereof they fall sometimes into such perplexities as can hardly be allayed; it hath therefore pleased Almighty God, in tender commiseration over these imbecilities of men, to ordain for their spiritual and ghostly comfort consecrated persons which, by sentence of power and authority given from above, may, as it were, out of his very mouth ascertain timorous and doubtful minds in their own particular, ease them of all their scrupulosities, leave them settled in peace and satisfied touching the mercy of God towards them. To use the benefit of this help for the better satisfaction in such cases is so natural, that it can be forbidden no man; but yet not so necessary, that all men should be in case to need it.

They are, of the two, the happier therefore that can content and satisfy themselves, by judging discreetly what they perform, and soundly what God doth require of them. For having that which is most material, the substance of penitency rightly bred; touching signs and tokens thereof, we may affirm that they do boldly, which imagine for every offence a certain proportionable degree in the passions and griefs of mind, whereunto whosoever aspireth not, repenteth in vain.

That to frustrate men's confession and considerations of sin, except every circumstance which may aggravate the same be unripped and laid in the balance, is a merciless extremity; although it be true, that as clear as we can such wounds must be searched to the very bottom. Last of all, to set down the like stint, and to shut up the doors of mercy against penitents which come short thereof in the devotion of their prayers, in the continuance of their fasts, in the largeness and bounty of their alms, or in the course of any other such like duties; is more than God himself hath thought meet, and consequently more than mortal men should presume to do.

VI vi 16–18, 104–6

9

BOOK SEVEN

Whether Ecclesiastical regiment by Bishops be lawful in the Church

'Their sixth assertion, That there ought not to be in the Church, Bishops endued with such authority and honour as ours are.'

The seventh Book is a defence of episcopacy, challenged by the Puritans who held that there were different functions of leadership and oversight in the Church, but no different degrees of holy orders. It was an argument which continued to rage in the Stuart Church, and by the late publication of this Book had not lost its force.

Whereas a question of late hath grown, whether Ecclesiastical regiment by Bishops be lawful in the Church of Christ or no, in which question they that hold the negative, being pressed with that generally received order, according whereunto the most renowned lights of the Christian world have governed the same in every age as Bishops; seeing their manner is to reply, that such Bishops as those ancient were, ours are not, there is no remedy but to show that to be a Bishop is now the self-same thing which it hath been; that one definition agreeth fully and truly as well to those elder, as to these latter Bishops. Sundry dissimilitudes we grant there are, which notwithstanding are not such that they cause any equivocation in the name, whereby we should think a Bishop in those times to have had a clean other definition that doth rightly agree unto Bishops as they are now. Many things there are in the state of Bishops, which the times have changed; many a parsonage at this day is larger than some ancient bishoprics were; many an ancient Bishop poorer than at this day; sundry under them in degree. The simple hereupon, lacking judgment and knowledge to discern between the nature of things, which changeth not, and these outward variable accidents, are made believe that a Bishop heretofore and now are things in their very nature so distinct that they cannot be judged the same. Yet to men that have any part of skill, what more evident and plain in Bishops than that augmentation or diminution in their precincts, allowances, privileges, and such like, do make a difference indeed, but no essential difference between one Bishop and another? As for those things in regard whereof we use properly to term them Bishops, those things whereby they differ from other Pastors, those things which the natural definition of a Bishop must contain what one of them is there more or less appliable unto Bishops now than of old? The name Bishop hath been borrowed from the Grecians, with whom it signifieth one which hath principal charge to guide and oversee others. The same word in ecclesiastical writings being applied unto Church governors, at the first unto all and not unto the chiefest only, grew in short time peculiar and proper to signify such episcopal authority alone, as the chiefest governors exercised over the rest; for with, all names this is usual, that inasmuch as they are not given till the things whereunto they are given have been some time first observed, therefore generally things are ancienter than the names whereby they are called.

Again, sith the first things that grow into general observation, and do thereby give men occasion to find names for them, are those which being in many subjects are thereby the easier, the oftener, and the more universally noted; it followeth that names imposed to signify common qualities of operation are ancienter than is the restraint of those names, to note an excellency of such qualities and operation in some one or few amongst others. For example, the name Disciple being invented to signify generally a learner, it cannot choose but in that signification be more ancient than when it signifies, as it were by a kind of appropriation, those learners who, being taught of Christ, were in that respect termed Disciples by an excellency. The like is to be seen in the name Apostle, the use whereof to signify a messenger must needs be more ancient than that use which restraineth it unto messengers sent concerning evangelical affairs; yea, this use more ancient than that whereby the same word is yet restrained further to signify only those whom our Saviour himself immediately did send. After the same manner the title or name of a Bishop having been used of old to signify both an ecclesiastical overseer in general, and more particularly also a principal ecclesiastical overseer; it followeth, that this latter restrained signification is not so ancient as the former, being more common. Yet because the things themselves are always ancienter than their names, therefore that thing which the restrained use of the word doth import, is likewise ancienter than the restraint of the word is, and consequently that power of chief ecclesiastical overseers, which the term of a Bishop doth import, was before the restrained use of the name which doth import it. Wherefore a lame and impotent kind of reasoning it is, when men go about to prove that in the Apostles' times there was no such thing as the restrained name of a Bishop doth now signify; because in their writings there is found no restraint of that name, but only a general use whereby it reacheth unto all spiritual governors and overseers.

But to let go the name and come to the very nature of that thing which is thereby signified. In all kind of regiment, whether ecclesiastical or civil, as there are sundry operations public, so likewise great inequality there is in the same operations, some being of principal respect, and therefore not fit to be dealt in by everyone to whom public actions, and those of good importance, are notwithstanding well and fitly enough committed. From hence have grown those different degrees of magistrates or public persons, even ecclesiastical as well as civil. Amongst ecclesiastical persons therefore Bishops being chief ones, a Bishop's function must be defined by that wherein his chiefly consisteth. A Bishop is a minister of God, unto whom, with permanent continuance, there is given not only power of ministering the Word and Sacraments, which power other Presbyters have; but also a further power to ordain ecclesiastical persons, and a power of chiefty in government over Presbyters as well as Laymen, a power to be by way of jurisdiction a Pastor even to Pastors themselves. So that this office, as he is a Presbyter or Pastor, consisteth in those things which are common unto him with other Pastors, as in ministering the Word and Sacraments; but those things incident unto his office, which do properly make him a Bishop, cannot be common unto him with other Pastors. Now even as Pastors, so likewise Bishops, being principal Pastors, are either at large or else with restraint. At large, when the subject of their regiment is indefinite and not tied to any certain place. Bishops with restraint are they whose regiment over the Church is contained within some definite local compass, beyond which compass their jurisdiction reacheth not. Such therefore we always mean when we speak of that regiment by Bishops which we hold a thing most lawful, divine, and holy in the Church of Christ.

VII ii 1–3, 145–7

He maintains, with biblical and patristic evidence, that bishops are a superior order with the sole power to ordain; he accepts the threefold ministry as catholic and traditional. Epiphanius (c.315–405), Bishop

*of Salamis, was a staunch and prolific defender of orthodoxy after the
Council of Nicaea.*

A Bishop, saith St Augustine, is a Presbyter superior: but the question
is now, wherein that superiority did consist. The Bishop's pre-eminence
we say therefore was twofold. First, he excelled in latitude of power
of order; secondly, in that kind of power which belongeth unto jurisdiction. Priests in the Law had authority and power to do greater
things than Levites, the High Priest greater than inferior Priests might
do; therefore Levites were beneath Priests, and Priests inferior to the
High Priest, by reason of the very degree of dignity, and of worthiness
in the nature of those functions which they did execute; and not only
for that the one had power to command and control the other. In like
sort, Presbyters having a weightier and worthier charge than Deacons
had, the Deacon was in this sort the Presbyter's inferior; and where we
say that a Bishop was likewise ever accounted a Presbyter's superior,
even according unto his very power of order, we must of necessity declare what principal duties belonging unto that kind of power a Bishop
might perform, and not a Presbyter. The custom of the primitive Church
in consecrating holy virgins and widows unto the service of God and
his Church, is a thing not obscure, but easy to be known both by that
which St Paul himself concerning them hath, and by the latter consonant evidence of other men's writings. Now a part of the pre-eminence
which Bishops had in their power of order was that by them only such
were consecrated. Again, the power of ordaining both Deacons and
Presbyters, the power to give the power of orders unto others, this also
hath been always peculiar unto Bishops. It hath not been heard of,
that inferior Presbyters were ever authorized to ordain. And concerning
ordination, so great force and dignity it hath, that whereas Presbyters
by such power as they have received for administration of the Sacraments are able only to beget children unto God; Bishops, having power
to ordain, do by virtue thereof create fathers to the people of God, as
Epiphanius fitly disputeth. There are which hold, that between a Bishop
and a Presbyter, touching power of order, there is no difference. The
reason of which conceit is, that they see Presbyters no less than Bishops
authorized to offer up the prayers of the Church, to preach the Gospel,
to baptize, to administer the holy Eucharist: but they considered not
withal, as they should, that the Presbyter's authority to do these things
is derived from the Bishop which doth ordain him thereunto; so that
even in those things which are common unto both, yet the power of the
one is as it were a certain light borrowed from the other's lamp. The

Apostles being Bishops at large, ordained everywhere Presbyters. Titus and Timothy having received Episcopal power, as Apostolical ambassadors or legates, the one in Greece, the other in Ephesus, both did, by virtue thereof, likewise ordain, throughout all Churches, Deacons, and Presbyters within the circuits allotted unto them. As for Bishops by restraint, their power this way incommunicable unto Presbyters, which of the ancients do not acknowledge? I make not Confirmation any part of that power, which hath always belonged only unto Bishops because in some places the custom was that Presbyters might also confirm in the absence of a Bishop, albeit, for the most part, none but only Bishops were thereof the allowed ministers.

Here it will perhaps be objected that the power of ordination itself was not everywhere peculiar and proper unto Bishops, as may be seen by a Council of Carthage, which showeth their Church's order to have been that Presbyters should together with the Bishop lay hands upon the ordained. But the answer hereunto is easy; for doth it hereupon follow that the power of ordination was not principally and originally in the Bishop? Our Saviour hath said unto his Apostles, *With me ye shall sit and judge the twelve tribes of Israel*; yet we know that to him alone it belongeth to judge the world, and that to him all judgment is given. With us even at this day Presbyters are licensed to do as much as that Council speaketh of, if any be present. Yet will not any man thereby conclude that in this Church others than Bishops are allowed to ordain. The association of Presbyters is no sufficient proof that the power of ordination is in them; but rather that it never was in them we may hereby understand, for that no man is able to show either Deacon or Presbyter ordained by Presbyters only, and his ordination accounted lawful in any ancient part of the Church; everywhere examples being found both of Deacons and Presbyters ordained by Bishops alone oftentimes, neither even in that respect thought unsufficient.

VII vi 1–5, 168–70

He uses the full force of his irony against the Puritan view of ordination and the claim to be following the example of the Apostles.

Let them cast the discipline of the Church of England into the same scales where they weigh their own, let them give us the same measure which here they take, and our strifes shall soon be brought to a quiet end. When they urge the Apostles as precedents; when they condemn us of tyranny because we do not in making ministers the same which the Apostles did; when they plead, *That with us one alone doth ordain, and that our ordinations are without the people's knowledge, contrary to that example which the blessed Apostles gave;* we do not request at their hands allowance as much as of one word we speak in our own defence, if that which we speak be of our own; but that which themselves speak they must be content to listen unto. To exempt themselves from being over-far pressed with the Apostles' example, they can answer, *That which was done by the people once upon special causes, when the Church was not yet established, is not to be made a rule for the constant and continual ordering of the Church.* In defence of their own election, although they do not therein depend on the people so much as the Apostles in the choice of Deacons, they think it very sufficient apology, that there were special considerations why Deacons at that time should be chosen by the whole Church, but not so now. In excuse of dissimilitudes between their own and the Apostles' discipline, they are contented to use this answer, *That many things were done in the Apostles' times, before the settling of the Church, which afterward the Church was not tied to observe.* For countenance of their own proceedings, wherein their governors do more than the Apostles, and their people less than under the Apostles the first Churches are found to have done, at the making of ecclesiastical officers, they deem it a marvellous reasonable kind of pleading to say, *That even as in commonweals, when the multitude have once chosen many or one to rule over them, the right which was at the first in the whole body of the people, is now derived unto those many, or that one which is so chosen; and that this being done, it is not the whole multitude, to whom the administration of such public affairs any longer appertaineth, but that which they did, their rulers may now do lawfully without them; after the self-same manner it standeth with the Church also.*

How easy and plain might we make our defence, how clear and allowable even unto them, if we could but obtain of them to admit the same things consonant unto equity in our mouths, which they require to be so taken from their own! If that which is truth, being uttered in maintenance of Scotland and Geneva, do not cease to be truth when the Church of England once allegeth it, this great crime of tyranny, wherewith we are charged, hath a plain and an easy defence. Yea, but we do not at all ask the people's approbation which they do, wherein they show themselves more indifferent and more free from taking away the people's right. Indeed, when their Lay-elders have chosen whom they think good, the people's consent thereunto is asked, and if they give their approbation, the thing standeth warranted for sound and good. But if not, is the former choice overthrown? No, but the people is to yield to reason; and if they which have made the choice do so like the people's reason, as to reverse their own deed at the hearing of it, then a new election to be made; otherwise the former to stand, notwithstanding the people's negative and dislike. What is this else but to deal with the people as those nurses do with infants, whose mouths they besmear with the backside of the spoon, as though they had fed them, when they themselves do devour the food? They cry in the ears of the people, that all men's consent should be had unto that which concerns all; they make the people believe we wrong them, and deprive them of their right in making ministers; whereas with us the people have commonly far more sway and force than with them. For inasmuch as there are but two main things observed in every ecclesiastical function: power to exercise the duty itself, and some charge of people whereon to exercise the same; the former of these is received at the hands of the whole visible Catholic Church. For it is not any one particular multitude that can give power, the force whereof may reach far and wide indefinitely, as the power of order doth, which whoso hath once received, there is no action which belongeth thereunto, but he may exercise effectually the same in any part of the world without iterated ordination. They whom the whole Church hath from the beginning used as her agents in conferring this power are not either one or more of the Laity, and therefore it hath not been heard of that ever any such were allowed to ordain ministers: only persons ecclesiastical, and they, in place of calling, superiors both unto Deacons, and unto Presbyters; only such persons ecclesiastical have been authorized to ordain both, and give them the power of order, in the name of the whole Church. Such were the Apostles, such was Timothy, such was Titus, such are Bishops. Not that there is between them no difference, but they all agree in pre-eminence of place above both Presbyters and Deacons, whom they otherwise might not ordain.

VII xiv 9–10, 227–30

Making a further defence of prelacy, particularly obnoxious to the Puritans.

Prelacy must needs be acknowledged exceedingly beneficial in the Church; and yet for more perspicuity's sake, it shall not be pains superfluously taken, if the manner how be also declared at large. For this one thing not understood by the vulgar sort causeth all contempt to be offered unto higher powers, not only ecclesiastical, but civil; whom when proud men have disgraced, and are therefore reproved by such as carry some dutiful affection of mind, the usual apologies which they make for themselves, are these: *What more virtue in these great ones, than in others? We see no such eminent good which they do above other men.* We grant indeed; that the good which higher governors do is not so immediate and near unto every of us, as many times the meaner labours of others under them and this doth make it to be less esteemed.

But we must note, that it is in this case as in a ship; he that sitteth at the stern is quiet, he moveth not, he seemeth in a manner to do little or nothing in comparison of them that sweat about other toil; yet that which he doth is in value and force more than all the labours of the residue laid together. The influence of the heavens above worketh infinitely more to our good, and yet appeareth not half so sensible as the force doth of things below. We consider not what it is which we reap by the authority of our chiefest spiritual governors, nor are likely to enter into any consideration thereof, till we want them; and that is the cause why they are at our hands so unthankfully rewarded. Authority is a constraining power; which power were needless if all were such as we should be, willing to do the things we ought to do without constraint. But because generally we are otherwise, therefore we all reap singular benefit by that authority which permitteth no men, though they would, to slack their duty. It doth not suffice, that the lord of an household appoint labourers what they should do, unless he set over them some chief workman to see they do it. Constitutions and Canons made for the ordering of Church affairs are dead taskmasters. The due execution of laws spiritual dependeth most upon the vigilant care of the chiefest spiritual governors, whose charge is to see that such laws be kept by the Clergy and people under them: with those duties which the Law of God and the Ecclesiastical Canons require in the Clergy, Lay governors are neither for the most part so well acquainted, nor so deeply and nearly touched. Requisite therefore it is that ecclesiastical persons have authority in such things; which kind of authority maketh them that have it Prelates. If then it be a thing confessed, as by all good men it needs must be, to have prayers read in all churches, to have the Sacraments of God administered, to have the mysteries of salvation painfully taught, to have God everywhere devoutly worshipped, and all this perpetually and with quietness, bringeth unto the whole Church, and unto every member thereof, inestimable good: how can that authority which hath been proved the ordinance of God for preservation of these duties in the Church, how can it choose but deserve to be held a thing publicly most beneficial? It were to be wished, and is to be laboured for as much as can be, that they who are set in such rooms may be furnished with honourable qualities and graces every way fit for their calling. But be they otherwise, howsoever, so long as they are in authority all men reap some good by them, albeit not so much good as if they were abler men. There is not any amongst us all, but is a great deal more apt to exact another man's duty, than the best of us is to discharge exactly his own; and therefore Prelates, although neglecting many ways their duty unto God and men, do notwithstanding by their authority great good, in that they keep others at the leastwise in some awe under them.

It is our duty therefore, in this consideration, to honour them that rule as Prelates, which office if they discharge well, the Apostle's own verdict is, that the honour they have they be worthy of, yea, though it were double. And if their government be otherwise, the judgment of sage men hath ever been this, that albeit the dealings of governors be culpable, yet honourable they must be, in respect of that authority by which they govern. Great caution must be used that we neither be emboldened to follow them in evil, whom for authority's sake we honour, nor induced in authority to dishonour them, whom as examples we may not follow. In a word, not to dislike sin, though it should be in the highest, were unrighteous meekness, and proud righteousness it is to contemn or dishonour highness, though it should be in the sinfullest men that live.

VII xviii 4–6, 266–8

He ends this book with an attack on the appropriation of Church property and revenue, lamenting the poverty and low state of the clergy, identifying them with the descendants of Levi, and concluding with a strong but rather uncharitable biblical quotation.

It hath fared with the wealth of the Church as with a tower, which being built at the time with the highest overthroweth itself after by its own greatness, neither doth the ruin thereof cease with the only fall of that which hath exceeded mediocrity, but one part beareth down the other, till the whole be laid prostrate. For although the state Ecclesiastical, both others and even Bishops themselves, be now fallen so low an ebb, as all the world at this day doth see; yet because there remaineth still somewhat which unsatiable minds can thirst for, therefore we seem not to have been hitherto sufficiently wronged. Touching that which hath been taken from the Church in appropriations known to amount to the value of one hundred twenty-six thousand pounds yearly, we rest contentedly and quietly without it, till it shall please God to touch the hearts

of men, of their own voluntary accord, to restore it to him again. [. . .]
What hath been taken away as dedicated unto uses superstitious, and
consequently not given unto God, or at the leastwise not so rightly
given, we repine not thereat. That which hath gone by means secret
and indirect, through corrupt compositions or compacts, we cannot
help. What the hardness of men's hearts doth make them loath to have
exacted, though being due by law, even thereof the want we do also
bear. Out of that which after all these deductions cometh clearly unto
our hands, I hope it will not be said that towards the public charge we
disburse nothing. And doth the residue seem yet excessive? The ways
whereby temporal men provide for themselves and their families are
foreclosed unto us. All that we have to sustain our miserable life with
is but a remnant of God's own treasure, so far already diminished and
clipped, that if there were any sense of common humanity left in this
hard-hearted world, the impoverished of the clergy of God would at
the length even of very commiseration be spared. The mean gentleman,
that hath but a hundred pound in land to live on, would not be hasty
to exchange his worldly estate and condition with many of these over-
abounding Prelates; a common artisan or tradesman of the city with ordinary Pastors of the Church. It is our hard and heavy lot that no other
sort of men being grudged at, how little benefit the public weal reap by
them, no state complained of for holding that which hath grown unto
them by lawful means; only the governors of our souls, they that study
day and night so to guide us, that both in this world we may have comfort, and in the world to come endless felicity and joy (for even such
is the very scope of all their endeavours; this they wish, for this they
labour, how hardly soever we use to construe of their intents): hard
that only they should be thus continually lifted at for possessing but
that whereunto they have by law both of God and man most just title.
If there should be no other remedy but that the violence of men must
in the end bereave them of all succour, further than the inclinations of
others shall vouchsafe to cast upon them as it were by way of alms for
their relief but from hour to hour; better are they not than their fathers,
who have been contented with as hard a portion at the world's hands:
let the light of the sun and moon, the common benefits of heaven and
earth, be taken away from Bishops, if the question were whether God
should lose his glory, and the safety of his Church be hazarded, or they
relinquish the right and interest which they have in the things of this
world. But sith the question in truth is whether Levi shall be deprived
of the portion of God or no, to the end that Simeon or Reuben may
devour it as their spoil, the comfort of the one in sustaining the injuries

which the other would offer, must be that prayer poured out by Moses, the prince of prophets, in most tender affection to Levi, *Bless, O Lord, his substance, accept thou the work of his hands; smite through the loins of them that rise up against him, and of them which hate him, that they rise no more.*

VII xxiv 25–26, 323–5

10

BOOK EIGHT

The Church and Commonwealth do flourish together

'Containing their seventh Assertion, That to no Civil Prince or Governor there may be given such power of Ecclesiastical dominion, as by the Laws of this land belongeth unto the supreme Regent thereof.'

This Book expounds his arguments about Church and State, which gained much approval when they were published later in the seventeenth century. The attitude of the Puritans to civil government offended him as one of the ways in which the wholeness of the divine purpose was being broken.

He defends the power of a civil ruler over the Church; after a survey of the powers of kings and priests in the Old Testament, he concludes that there is warrant for the monarch being head of the Church. He declares that all English citizens are members of the Church of England.

Had the Priests alone been possessed of all power in spiritual affairs, how should anything concerning matter of religion have been made but only by them? In them it had been, and not in the King, to change the face of religion at any time; the altering of religion, the making of ecclesiastical laws, with other the like actions belonging unto the power of dominion, are still termed *the deeds of the King*; to show that in him was placed the supremacy of power in this kind over all, and that unto their Priests the same was never committed, saving only at such times as the Priests were also Kings and Princes over them. According to the pattern of which example the like power in causes ecclesiastical is by the laws of this realm annexed unto the Crown; and there are which imagine that Kings being mere lay-persons, do by this means exceed the lawful bounds of their callings; which thing, to the end that they may persuade, they first make a necessary separation perpetual and personal between the Church and the Commonwealth. Secondly, they so tie all kind of power Ecclesiastical unto the Church, as if it were in every degree their only right, who are by proper spiritual functions termed Church governors, and might not unto Christian princes in any wise appertain. To look under shifting ambiguities and equivocations of words in matter of principal weight, is childish. A Church and the Commonwealth we grant are things in nature one distinguished from the other. A Commonwealth is one way, and a Church another way defined. In their opinions the Church and Commonwealth are corporations, not distinguished only in nature and definition, but in substance perpetually severed; so that they which are of the one can neither appoint nor execute, in whole nor in part, the duties which belong to them which are of the other, without open breach of the Law of God which hath divided them and doth require that so being divided they should distinctly or severally work, as depending both upon God, and not hanging one upon the other's approbation for that which either hath to do. We say that the care of religion being common to all societies politic, such societies as do embrace the true religion have the name of the Church given unto every one of them for distinction from the rest; so that every body politic hath some religion; but the Church that religion which is only true. Truth of religion is the proper difference whereby a Church is distinguished from other politic societies of men; we here mean true religion in gross, and not according to every particular. For they which in some particular points of religion do sever from the truth, may nevertheless truly (if we compare them to men of an heathenish religion) be said to hold and profess that religion which is true. For which cause, there being of old so many politic societies established through the world, only the Commonwealth of Israel which had the truth of religion was in that respect the Church of God: and the Church of Jesus Christ is every such politic society of men as doth in religion hold that truth which is proper to Christianity. As a politic society it doth maintain religion, as a Church that religion which God hath revealed in Jesus Christ. With us therefore the name of a Church importeth only a society of men, first united into some public form of regiment, and secondly distinguished from other societies by the exercise of religion. With them on the other side the name of the Church in this present question importeth not only a multitude of men so united and so distinguished, but also further the same divided necessarily and perpetually from the body of the Commonwealth; so that even in such a politic society as consisteth of none

but Christians, yet the Church and Commonwealth are two corporations, independently subsisting by themselves.

We hold, that seeing there is not any man of the Church of England but the same man is also a member of the Commonwealth, nor
any member of the Commonwealth which is not also of the Church of
England, therefore as in a figure triangle the base doth differ from the
sides thereof, and yet one and the self-same line is both a base and also
a side; a side simply a base if it chance to be the bottom and underlie
the rest: so albeit properties and actions of one do cause the name of
a Commonwealth, qualities and functions of another sort the name of
the Church, to be given to a multitude, yet one and the self-same multitude may in such sort be both. Nay, it is so with us, that no person
appertaining to the one can be denied also to be of the other: contrariwise, unless they against us should hold that the Church and the Commonwealth are two, both distinct and separate societies; of which two,
one comprehendeth always persons not belonging to the other (that
which they do), they could not conclude out of the difference between
the Church and the Commonwealth, namely, that the Bishops may not
meddle with the affairs of the Commonwealth, because they are governors of another corporation, which is the Church; nor kings with
making laws for the Church, because they have government, not of this
corporation, but of another divided from it, the Commonwealth; and
the walls of separation between these two must for ever be upheld: they
hold the necessity of personal separation, which clean excludeth the
power of one man's dealing with both; we of natural, but that one and
the same person may in both bear principal sway.

VIII i 1–2, 327–31

*Church and Commonwealth are not to be regarded as separate. Hooker
uses the nominalist argument which distinguishes the 'accident', or outward names and appearances, from the 'substance'.*

It will be objected, that the Fathers do oftentimes mention the Commonweal and the Church of God by way of opposition. Can the same thing
be opposed to itself? If one and the same society be both Church and
Commonweal, what sense can there be in that speech, *That they suffer
and flourish together*? What sense in that which maketh one thing to be
adjudged to the Church, and another to the Commonweal? Finally in
that which putteth a difference between the causes of the Province and
the Church, doth it not hereby appear that the Church and Commonweal are things evermore personally separate? No, it doth not hereby

appear that there is perpetually any such separation; we speak of them as two, we may sever the rights and causes of the one well enough from the other, in regard of that difference which we grant is between them, albeit we make no personal difference. For the truth is, that the Church and the Commonwealth are names which import things really different; but those things are accidents, and such accidents as may and always should lovingly dwell together in one subject. Wherefore the real difference between the accidents signified by these names doth not prove different subjects for them always to reside in. For albeit the subjects wherein they be resident be sometimes different, as when the people of God have their residence among Infidels; yet the nature of them is not such but that their subject may be one, and therefore it is but a changeable accident, in those accidents they are to be divers. There can be no error in our own conceit concerning this point, if we remember still what accident that is for which a society hath the name of a Commonwealth, and what accident that which doth cause it to be termed a Church. A Commonwealth we name it simply in regard of some regiment or policy under which men live; a Church for the truth of that religion which they profess. Now names betokening accidents inabstracted, betoken not only the accidents themselves, but also together with them subjects whereunto they cleave. As when we name a schoolmaster and a physician, those names do not only be two accidents, teaching and curing, but also some person or persons in whom those accidents are. For there is no impediment but both may be in one man, as well as they are for the most part in divers. The Commonweal and Church therefore being such names, they do not only betoken these accidents of civil government and Christian Religion which we have mentioned, but also together with them such multitudes as are the subjects of those accidents. Again, their nature being such as they may well enough dwell together in one subject, it followeth that their names, though always implying that difference of accidents that hath been set down, yet do not always imply different subjects also. When we oppose therefore the Church and Commonwealth in Christian society, we mean by the Commonwealth that society with relation to all the public affairs thereof, only the matter of true Religion excepted; by the Church, the same society with only reference unto the matter of true Religion, without any affairs besides: when that society which is both a Church and a Commonwealth doth flourish in those things which belong unto it as a Commonwealth, we then say, the Commonwealth doth flourish; when in both of them, we then say, the Church and Commonwealth do flourish together.

VIII i 5, 335–7

There is a need for order in civil society. The Sovereign is supreme in all matters, though always under God.

Without order there is no living in public society, because the want thereof is the mother of confusion, whereupon division of necessity followeth; and out of division destruction. The Apostle therefore, giving instruction to public societies, requireth that all things be orderly done. Order can have no place in things, except it be settled amongst the persons that shall by office be conversant about them; and if things and persons be ordered, this doth imply that they are distinguished by degrees: for order is a gradual disposition. The whole world consisting of parts so many so different, is by this only thing upheld; he which framed them hath set them in order. The very Deity itself both keepeth and requireth for ever this to be kept as a law, that wheresoever then is a coagmentation of many, the lowest be knit unto the highest by that which being interjacent may cause each to cleave to the other, and so all to continue one. This order of things and persons in public societies is the work of policy, and the proper instrument thereof in every degree is power; power being that ability which we have of ourselves, or receive from others for performance of any action. If the action which we have to perform be conversant about matters of mere religion, the power of performing of it is then spiritual; and if that power be such as hath not any other to overrule it, we term it dominion, or power supreme, so far as the bounds thereof extend. When therefore Christian kings are said to have spiritual dominion or supreme power in ecclesiastical affairs and causes, the meaning is, that within their own precincts and territories they have an authority and power to command, even in matters of Christian Religion, and that there is no higher nor greater that can in those cases over-command them, where they are placed to reign as kings. But withal we must likewise note that their power is termed supremacy, as being the highest, not simply without the exception of anything. For what man is so brainsick, as not to except in such speeches God himself, the King of all dominion? Who doubteth but that the king who receiveth it must hold it of and under the law?

VIII ii 23, 341–2

The extent and limitations of sovereign power. Questions which Hooker raises in the sixteenth century would become acute in the next.

In power of dominion all kings have not an equal latitude. Kings by conquest make their own charter; so that how large their power either civil or spiritual is, we cannot with any certainty define further, than only to set them in the line of the Law of God and Nature for bounds. Kings by God's own special appointment have also that largeness of power which he doth assign or permit with approbation. Touching kings which were first instituted by agreement and composition made with them, how far their power may extend, the articles of compact between them are to show; not only the articles of compact at the first beginning, which for the most part are either clean worn out of knowledge, or else known to very few, but whatsoever hath been after in free and voluntary manner condescended unto, whether by express consent (whereof positive laws are witnesses) or else by silent allowance famously notified through custom, reaching beyond the memory of man. By which means of after-agreement, it cometh many times to pass in kingdoms, that they whose ancient predecessors were by violence and force made subject, do by little and little grow into that sweet form of kingly government which philosophers define, *Regency willingly sustained, and endued with chiefty of power in the greatest things*. Many of the ancients in their writings do speak of kings with such high and ample terms, as if universality of power, even in regard of things and not of persons, did appertain to the very being of a king. The reason is, because their speech concerning kings they frame according to the state of those monarchs to whom unlimited authority was given; which some not observing, imagine that all kings, even in that they are kings, ought to have whatsoever power they judge any sovereign ruler lawfully to have enjoyed. But the most judicious philosopher, whose eye scarce anything did escape which was to be found in the bosom of nature, he considering how far the power of one sovereign ruler may be different from another regal authority, noteth in Spartan kings: *That of all others they were most tied to law, and so the most restrained in power.* A king which hath not supreme power in the greatest things is rather entitled a king than invested with authority. We cannot properly term him a king, of whom it may not be said, at the leastwise as touching certain the chiefest affairs of the state, his right in them is to have rule, not subject to any other predominancy. I am not of opinion that simply in kings the most, but the best limited power is best both for them and the people: the most limited is that which may deal in fewest things, the best that which in dealing is tied unto the soundest, perfectest, and most indifferent rule, which rule is the Law; I mean not only the Law of Nature and of God, but the national or municipal Law consonant thereunto.

VIII ii 11–12, 350–2

In further defending the title of Head of the Church given to the Sovereign, he makes a subtle and somewhat casuistical argument about the use of the word 'the'. Theodore Beza (1519–1605) was a French Protestant theologian who became the leader of the Genevan Church after the death of Calvin.

As for the force of the article where our Lord and Saviour is called the *Head*, it serveth to tie that title to him by way of excellency, which in meaner degrees is common to others; it doth not exclude any other utterly from being termed *Head*, but from being entitled, as Christ is, *the Head*, by way of the very highest degree of excellency. Not in the communication of names, but in the confusion of things, there is error. Howbeit, if *Head* were a name that could not well be, nor never had been used to signify that which a magistrate may be in relation to some Church, but were by continual use of speech appropriated unto the only thing it signifieth; being applied unto Jesus Christ then, although we must carry in ourselves a right understanding, yet ought we otherwise rather to speak, unless we interpret our own meaning by some clause of plain speech, because we are all else in manifest danger to be understood according to that construction and sense, wherein such words are personally spoken. But here the rarest construction, and most removed from common sense, is that which the word doth import being applied unto Christ; that which we signify by it in giving it to the magistrate, it is a great deal more familiar in the common conceit of men.

The word is so fit to signify all kinds of superiority, pre-eminence and chiefty, that nothing is more ordinary than to use it in vulgar speech, and in common understanding so to take it. If therefore Christian Kings may have any pre-eminence or chiefty above all others, although it be less than that which Theodore Beza giveth, who placeth Kings amongst the principal members whereunto public function in the Church belongeth; and denieth not, but that of them which have public function, the civil magistrate's power hath all the rest at command in regard of that part of his office which is to procure that peace and good order be especially kept in things concerning the first Table; if even hereupon they term him *the Head of the Church*, which is *his kingdom*, it should not seem so unfit a thing; which title surely we could not communicate to any other, no not although it should at our hands be exacted with torments, but that our meaning herein is made known to the world, so that no man which will understand can easily be ignorant that we do not give to kings, when we term them *Heads*, the honour which is properly given to our Lord and Saviour Christ, when the blessed Apostle in Scripture doth term him the *Head of the Church*.

VIII iv 3–4, 371–3

Further discussion about Headship; human power can have spiritual jurisdiction.

They argue, *If there be no Head but Christ, in respect of spiritual government, there is no Head but he in respect of Word, Sacraments, and Discipline administered by those whom he hath appointed, forasmuch also as it is his spiritual government.* Their meaning is, that whereas we make two kinds of power, of which two, the one being spiritual is proper unto Christ; the other, men are capable of because it is visible and external; we do amiss altogether in distinguishing, they think, forasmuch as the visible and external power of regiment over the Church is only in relation unto the Word and Sacraments, and Discipline, administered by such as Christ hath appointed thereunto, and the exercise of this power is also his spiritual government: therefore we do but vainly imagine a visible and external power in the Church differing from his spiritual power. Such disputes as this do somewhat resemble the practising of well-willers upon their friends in the pangs of death; whose manner is, even then, to put smoke in their nostrils, and so to fetch them again, although they know it a matter impossible to keep them living. The kind of affection which the favourers of this labouring cause bear towards it will not suffer them to see it die, although by what means they should make it live, they do not see. But they may see that these wrestlings will not help. Can they be ignorant how little it booteth to overcast so clear a light with some mist of ambiguity in the name of spiritual regiment? To make things therefore so plain, that henceforward a child's capacity may serve rightly to conceive our meaning, we make the spiritual regiment of Christ to be generally that whereby his Church is ruled and governed in things spiritual. Of this general we make two distinct kinds; the one invisible, exercised by Christ himself in his own person; the other outwardly administered by them whom Christ doth allow to be rulers and guiders of his Church. Touching the former of these two kinds, we teach that Christ, in regard thereof, is particularly termed the Head of the Church of God; neither can any other creature, in that sense and meaning, be termed Head besides him, because it importeth the conduct and government of our souls by the hand of that blessed Spirit wherewith we are sealed and marked as being peculiarly his. Him only therefore do we acknowledge to be the Lord, which dwelleth, liveth, and reigneth in our hearts; him only to be that Head which giveth salvation and life unto his body; him to be that fountain from whence the influence of heavenly graces distilleth, and is derived into all parts, whether the Word, or the Sacraments, or Discipline, be the means whereby it floweth. As for the power of administering these things in the Church of Christ, which power we call the power of Order, it is indeed both spiritual and his; spiritual, because such properly concerns the Spirit; his, because by him it was instituted. Howbeit, neither spiritual, as that which is inwardly and invisibly exercised; nor his as that which he himself in person doth exercise. Again, that power of dominion, which is indeed the point of this controversy, and doth also belong to this second kind of spiritual government, namely, unto that regiment which is external and visible; this likewise being spiritual in regard of the matter about which it dealeth, and being his, inasmuch as he approveth whatsoever is done by it, must notwithstanding be distinguished also from that power whereby he himself in person administereth the former kind of his own spiritual regiment, because he himself in person doth not administer this; we do not therefore vainly imagine, but truly and rightly discern a power external and visible in the Church exercised by men, and severed in nature from that spiritual power of Christ's own regiment; which power is termed spiritual, because it worketh secretly, inwardly, and invisibly; his, because none doth, nor can it personally exercise, either besides or together with him; seeing that him only we may name our Head, in regard of his power, and yet, in regard of that other power from this, term others also besides him Heads, without any contradiction at all.

VIII iv 10, 388–91

Further defence of the right of the civil power to make laws for the Church. A return to discussion of natural and divine law.

If they with whom we dispute were uniform, strong, and constant in that which they say, we should not need to trouble ourselves about their persons, to whom the power of making laws for the Church belongs. For they are sometime very vehement in contention, that from the greatest thing unto the least about the Church, all must needs be immediately from God. And to this they apply the pattern of the ancient tabernacle which God delivered unto Moses, and was therein so exact, that there was not left as much as the least pin for the wit of man to devise in the framing of it. To this they also apply that strait and severe charge which God so often gave concerning his own

Law; *Whatsoever I command you, take heed ye do it; thou shalt put nothing thereto, thou shalt take nothing from it* whether it be great of small. Yet sometimes bethinking themselves better, they speak as acknowledging that it doth suffice to have received in such sort the principal things from God, and that for other matters the Church had sufficient authority to make laws. Whereupon they now have made it a question, what persons they are whose right it is to take order for the Church's affairs, when the institution of any new thing therein is requisite? Law may be requisite to made either concerning things that are to be known and believed in, or else touching that which is to be done by the Church of God. The Law of Nature and the Law of God are sufficient for declaration in both what belongeth unto each man separately, as his soul is the spouse of Christ; yea, so sufficient that they plainly and fully show whatsoever God doth require by way of necessary introduction unto the state of everlasting bliss. But as a man liveth joined with others in common society, and belongeth to the outward politic body of the Church, albeit the same Law of Nature and Scripture hath in this respect also made manifest the things that are of greatest necessity; nevertheless, by reason of new occasions still arising which the Church, having care of souls, must take order for as need requireth, hereby it cometh to pass that there is, and ever will be, so great use even of human laws and ordinances, deducted by way of discourse as a conclusion from the former divine and natural, serving as principle thereunto. No man doubteth but that for matters of action and practice in the affairs of God, for manner in divine service, for order in Ecclesiastical proceedings about the regiment of the Church, there may be oftentimes cause very urgent to have laws made: but the reason is not so plain, wherefore human laws should appoint men what to believe. Wherefore in this we must note two things. 1 That in matter of opinion, the law doth not make that to be truth which before was not, as in matter of action it causeth that to be a duty which was not before; but manifesteth only and giveth men notice of that to be truth, the contrary whereunto they ought not before to have believed. 2 That opinions do cleave to the understanding and are in heart assented to, it is not in the power of any human law to command them, because to prescribe what men shall think belongeth only unto God. [. . .] As opinions are either fit or inconvenient to be professed, so man's laws have to determine of them. It may for public unity's sake require men's professed assent, or prohibit their contradiction to special articles, wherein, as there haply hath been controversy what is true, so the same were like to continue still, not without grievous detriment unto a number of souls, except Law, to remedy that evil, should set down a certainty which no man afterwards is to gainsay. Wherefore, as in regard of divine laws which the Church receiveth from God, we may unto every man apply those words of wisdom, *My son, keep thou thy father's precepts*; even so concerning the statutes and ordinances which the Church itself makes, we may add thereunto the words that follow, *And forsake thou not thy mother's law.*

It is a thing even undoubtedly natural, that all free and independent societies should themselves make their own laws, and that this power first should belong to the whole, not to any certain part of a politic body, though haply some one part may have greater sway in that action than the rest; which thing being generally fit and expedient in the making of all laws, we see no cause why to think otherwise in laws concerning the service of God, which in all well-ordered states and commonwealths is the first thing that Law hath care to provide for. When we speak of the right which belongeth to a commonwealth, we speak of which must needs belong to the Church of God. For if the commonwealth be Christian if the people which are of it do publicly embrace the true religion, this very thing doth make it the Church, as hath been showed.

VIII vi 5–6, 399–402

Monarchs have always had power to make laws of religion, even in pagan days, so much more in a Christian country. Hooker then looks at the question of wicked ministers, one of the oldest ecclesiological problems. The 'family of Brown' refers to Robert Browne (c.1550–1633), a separatist who founded independent congregations but later was ordained in the Church of England. The 'Brownists' were the beginning of the Congregational movement. Bernard Knipperdolling was one of the leading Anabaptists in Munster, executed after the sack of the city in 1535.

In devising and discussing of laws, wisdom especially is required; but that which establisheth them and maketh them, is power, even power of dominion; the chiefty whereof (amongst us) resteth in the person of the king. Is there any law of Christ's which forbiddeth kings and rulers of the earth to have such sovereign and supreme power in the making of laws either Civil or Ecclesiastical? If there be, our controversy hath an end. Christ, in his Church, hath not appointed any such Law concerning temporal power as God did of old unto the commonwealth of Israel; but leaving that to be at the world's free choice, his chiefest care is that the spiritual Law of the Gospel might be published far and wide. They that received the Law of Christ were, for a long time, people scattered in sundry kingdoms, Christianity not exempting them from the laws which they had been subject unto, saving only in such cases as those laws did enjoin that which the religion of Christ did forbid. Hereupon grew their manifold persecutions throughout all places where they lived; as oft as it thus came to pass, there was no possibility that the emperors and kings under whom they lived, should meddle any whit at all with making laws for the Church. From Christ, therefore, having received power, who doubteth but as they did, so they might, bind them to such orders as seemed fittest for the maintenance of their religion, without the leave of high or low in the commonwealth; forasmuch as in religion it was divided utterly from them; and they from it? But when the mightiest began to like of the Christian faith, by their means whole free states and kingdoms became obedient to Christ. Now the question is whether kings, by embracing Christianity do thereby receive any such law as taketh from them the weightiest part of that sovereignty which they had even when they were heathens? Whether being Infidels, they might do more in causes of religion, than now they can by the Laws of God, being true believers? For, whereas in regal states the King or supreme Head of the commonwealth had, before Christianity, a supreme stroke in making of laws for religion; he must by embracing Christian religion utterly deprive himself thereof, and in such causes he become subject unto his subjects, having even within his own dominions them whose commandment he must obey; unless his power be placed in the hand of some foreign spiritual potentate: so that either a foreign or domestic commander upon earth, he must admit more now than before he had, and that in the chiefest things whereupon commonwealths do stand. But apparent it is unto all men which are not strangers unto the doctrine of Jesus Christ, that no state of the world receiving Christianity is by any law therein contained bound to resign the power which they lawfully held before: but over what persons, and in what causes soever the same hath been in force, it may so remain and continue still. That which as kings they might do in matters of religion, and did in matter of false religion being idolatrous and superstitious kings, the same they are now even in every respect fully authorized to do in all affairs pertinent to the state of true Christian religion. And concerning the supreme power of making laws for all persons in all causes to be guided by, it is not to be let pass that the head enemies of this Headship are constrained to acknowledge the King endued even with this very power, so that he may and ought to exercise the same, taking order for the Church and her affairs, of what nature or kind soever, in case of necessity: as when there is no lawful ministry, which they interpret then to be (and surely this is a point very remarkable) wheresoever the ministry is wicked. A wicked ministry is no lawful ministry; and in such sort no lawful ministry, that what doth belong unto them as ministers by right of their calling, the same is annihilated in respect of their bad qualities; their wickedness is itself a deprivation of right to deal in the affairs of the Church, and a warrant for others to deal in them which are held to be of a clean other society the members whereof have been before so peremptorily for ever excluded from power of dealing with affairs of the Church. They which once have learned thoroughly this lesson will quickly be capable perhaps of another equivalent unto it. For if the wickedness of the ministry transfers their right unto the King, in case the King be as wicked as they, to whom then shall the right descend? There is no remedy, all must come by devolution at length, even as the family of Brown will have it, unto the godly among the people, for confusion unto the wise and the great by the poor and the simple; some Kniperdolling, with his retinue, must take this work of the Lord in hand, and the making of Church laws and orders must prove to be their right in the end. If not for love of the truth, yet for shame of gross absurdities, let these objections and trifling fancies be abandoned.

VIII xii 12–14, 413–6

Glossary

abroach	disseminate
abscission	severing
accompt	account
apology	defence
behoofull	necessary
board	table
brook	tolerate
cavillations	quibbling
coaction	coercion
coagmentation	joining together
collection	inference (from wide reading)
conceit	error
conduct	control
conversation	behaviour
empiric	unqualified physician
Esay	Isaiah
Esdras	Ezra
expedite	indisputable
foreslow	lose by neglect
frustrate	futile
glozing	specious
hability	ability
handsel	pledge
Heli	Eli
imbecility	weakness
impertinent	irrelevant
impugning	accusing
ingenuously	candidly
indited	dictated

interjacent	lying between
inure	accustom
iterate	repeat
let	prevent (also allow)
list	desire
mere	absolute
misdesert	misconduct
moieties	halves; small parts
Nebuchodonosor	Nebuchadnezzar
Nehemias	Nehemiah
oppugn	oppose
palpable	obvious
painfully	carefully
paraphrastically	by free interpretation
paraphrasts	private interpreters
perfited	perfected
physick	medicine
prevent	anticipate, go before (also stop)
promiscuous	without limitation
puissance	power
regiment	rule
respective	discriminating
Salomon	Solomon
scholy	comment on a text
secure	confident
sedulity	diligence
sensible	capable of understanding
silly	simple
sith	since, because
sithence	since, because
stint	limitation
subalternation	subordination
surcease	refrain
travel	work, labour
trencher-mates	comrades (eating-companions)
unmeet	unfitting
ure	use
want	lack

Further reading

Nigel Atkinson, *Richard Hooker and the Authority of Scripture, Tradition and Reason*, Carlisle: Paternoster Press, 1997

P. Avis, 'Richard Hooker and John Calvin', *Journal of Ecclesiastical History* 32, 1981

R. Bauckham, 'Hooker, Travers and the Church of Rome in the 1580s', *Journal of Ecclesiastical History* 29, 1978

J. E. Booty, 'Richard Hooker' in *The Spirit of Anglicanism*, Edinburgh: T. & T. Clark, 1979

Michael Brydon, *The Evolving Reputation of Richard Hooker: an Examination of Responses 1600–1714*, Oxford: OUP, 2006

E. T. Davies, *The Political Ideas of Richard Hooker*, London: SPCK, 1946

E. Grislis, 'Commentary' in *The Folger Library Edition of the Works of Richard Hooker*, Cambridge Mass: The Bellknap Press of Harvard University Press, 1990

'The Anglican Spirituality of Richard Hooker', *Toronto Journal of Theology* 12, 1996

H. F. Kearney, 'Richard Hooker: a Reconstruction', *Cambridge Journal* 5, 1952

Peter Lake, *Anglicans and Puritans? Presbyterian and English Conformist Thought from Whitgift to Hooker*, London: Allen & Unwin, 1988

J. S. Marshall, *Hooker and the Anglican Tradition*, London: A. & C. Black, 1963

Arthur Middleton, 'Richard Hooker and the Puritans' in *Fathers and Anglicans*, Leominster: Gracewing, 2001

P. Munz, *The Place of Hooker in the History of Thought*, London: Routledge, Kegan Paul, 1952

J. F. H. New, *Anglican and Puritan*, London: A. & C. Black, 1964

M. E. C. Perrott, 'Richard Hooker and the Problem of Authority in the Elizabethan Church', *Journal of Ecclesiastical History* 49, 1998

P. B. Secor, *Richard Hooker: Prophet of Anglicanism*, Tunbridge Wells: Burns & Oates, 1999

C. J. Sisson, *The Judicious Marriage of Mr Hooker and the Birth of the Laws of Ecclesiastical Polity*, Cambridge: Cambridge University Press, 1940

L. Thornton, *Richard Hooker*, London: SPCK, 1924

W. J. Torrance Kirby, *Richard Hooker's Doctrine of the Royal Supremacy*, Leiden: E. J. Brill, 1940

Nigel Voak, *Richard Hooker and Reformed Theology: a Study of Reason, Will and Grace*, Oxford: OUP, 2003